IT'S MY COUNTRY TOO

IT'S MY COUNTRY TOO

Women's Military Stories

from the American

Revolution to Afghanistan

Edited by JERRI BELL *&* TRACY CROW

Foreword by KAYLA WILLIAMS

Potomac Books
An imprint of the University of Nebraska Press

Acknowledgments for the use of copyrighted material appear on pages 319–21, which constitute an extension of the copyright page.

Library of Congress Cataloging-in-Publication Data
Names: Bell, Jerri, editor. | Crow, Tracy, editor.
Title: It's my country too: women's military stories from the American Revolution to Afghanistan / edited by Jerri Bell and Tracy Crow; foreword by Kayla Williams.
Other titles: Women's military stories from the American Revolution to Afghanistan
Description: Lincoln NE: Potomac Books, an imprint of the University of Nebraska Press, [2017] | Includes bibliographical references.
Identifiers: LCCN 2016054040 (print)
LCCN 2016057132 (ebook)
ISBN 9781612348315 (cloth: alk. paper)
ISBN 9781612349343 (epub)
ISBN 9781612349350 (mobi)
ISBN 9781612349367 (pdf)
Subjects: LCSH: United States—Armed Forces—Women—Biography. | Women and the military—United States. | Women soldiers—United States—Biography.
Classification: LCC UB418.W65 B448 2017 (print) | LCC UB418.W65 (ebook) | DDC 355.0092/520973—dc23
LC record available at https://lccn.loc.gov/2016054040

Set in Sabon LT Next Pro by Rachel Gould.

It isn't just my brother's country, or my husband's country, it's my country as well. And so the war wasn't just their war, it was my war, and I needed to serve in it.

—Maj. Beatrice Stroup, Women's Army Corps, World War II

CONTENTS

ILLUSTRATIONS

21. Lt. Col. Victoria Hudson, USA
22. Capt. Linda Bray, USA
23. M.Sgt. Linda Cox, USAF
24. Sgt. Lauren Nowak, USMC
25. Sgt. Leigh Ann Hester, USA

FOREWORD

KAYLA WILLIAMS

When I came home from Iraq and began the longer and more complicated journey back into civilian life, feelings of isolation and alienation often dominated during my interactions with people outside the military.[1] I could pick out military men from across the room: the haircut, posture, set of jaw. Civilians often could, too, and the common phrase would come: *Thank you for your service.* Out of uniform, this didn't often happen to me or the other women I served with. Even sporting obvious markers of military affiliation like bumper stickers or unit shirts was more likely to inspire questions about our husbands' service, rather than our own.

Seeking to understand my new identity after the fundamentally life-altering experience of going to war, it only belatedly dawned on me that I was a veteran and shared something profound with other veterans stretching back through untold generations. Yet even in books, movies, and gatherings of fellow veterans, I still often felt invisible. Erased. My experiences questioned or subtly discounted.

My first book, *Love My Rifle More Than You: Young and Female in the U.S. Army*, was partly a response to this marginalization. By telling my story, I wanted to give a richer and more nuanced window into the experiences of women serving in the global war on terror. Women who served in prior eras came up to me after talks to thank me for giving voice to experiences similar to their own:

---

[1]. This foreword was prepared in Kayla Williams's personal capacity; the opinions expressed are her own and do not reflect the view of the Department of Veterans Affairs or the United States government.

"I started to think I was just crazy. No one understood what I was talking about—but you went through the same thing!" It was humbling and gratifying, but also disconcerting: surely I wasn't the first to share these tales.

Of course I wasn't. But stories by and of women at war were not deeply embedded into the literary canon, enacted on stage and screen, commemorated in memorials across the land. They were scattered, hidden, erased, and hard to uncover.

Until this volume.

Jerri and Tracy have assembled an incredible trove of stories dating back to the Revolutionary War that ground the service and sacrifice of women serving today and tomorrow in the broader sweep of history. Each war in which we served was also another battle to prove our worth and the legitimacy of our contributions. Roughly a quarter millennium after we fought for freedom in the Revolutionary War, that struggle was victorious: women can now serve in any job and unit for which they are qualified.

While women today may not face the same legal and policy barriers to service that those who came before them did, they will still find much to recognize in these stories, from the astute observation from a woman who fought in the Civil War that "the biggest talkers are not always the best fighters" to a World War I nurse's marveling at how easily humans get accustomed to sounds of "terrific explosions." Many recount missing, years later, the sense of purpose and close relationships that developed while serving, despite the challenges and threats.

These essential stories illustrate the tremendous, ongoing effort toward full freedom and equality in which generations of women, people of color, and other minorities have been engaged since this country was founded. They are essential reading not only for military and veteran women, but for all who want a fuller accounting of how we became the nation we are becoming today.

PREFACE

"Too Often Women Were Viewed as Incidental"

One spring afternoon, a sailor and a Marine walked into a bar in the nation's capital ...

Stories with this beginning sometimes end with a bar fight. Our meeting, however, led to a yearlong collaboration and a new understanding of our combined thirty years of military service.

We began with the observation that contemporary books *about* military women are available and even commercially successful. But the voices *of* America's women veterans rarely make it into print, and never with the same level of publicity or critical acclaim as those of their male counterparts. We felt that the public was missing something important about military women, though we weren't sure exactly what it was. We were also frustrated that the women veterans' stories told by others didn't reflect our experience of service in the armed forces, or the service of other women veterans we knew. We wondered what we might discover if we told the story of women's military service in America from the point of view of—and *through the voices of*—the women who had actually been there and done that.

The authors of the anthology *In the Words of Women: The Revolutionary War and the Birth of the Nation, 1765–1799* note that "too often women were viewed as incidental to the men who dominated the course of momentous occurrences and affected their lives." This has also been true of America's view of the role of women in the nation's defense.

When *we* raised our right hands and took our oaths of enlistment and commissioning during the height of the Cold War, accession training did not include information about women's contributions to national defense. Trainers intimated or said outright that our contributions were less significant because women only served in support roles. Women didn't command divisions, battleships, or air wings; we made only administrative policy. Men often informed us that women's integration into the armed forces was a social experiment imposed on the military by so-called feminazis who sought equal rights for women at the expense of military readiness and the national defense. We quickly learned to explain that we never took on tough jobs to prove a point about women, or to advance women's causes. We saw for ourselves that the services used women to fill manpower gaps, but when a critical need no longer existed, military leaders—usually men—once again restricted our roles and opportunities; but having also worked with men who supported us, mentored us, and pushed us to exceed expectations, we knew that the story that women were pawns of men who used our labor in times of crisis and cast us aside afterward was also only a partial truth at best.

In the process of writing this book, we discovered to our chagrin that we had served our country without knowing our own history. We didn't know whose shoulders we were standing on, whose shoes we should be trying to fill, who had set the example for women's service and leadership and what they had done, or what we might achieve if we ignored or chipped away at externally imposed limits. We certainly didn't know how women had come to serve in the armed forces, or what our predecessors had done and endured so that we might have opportunities they did not, and so that we might contribute fully to the defense of the Constitution. Nor had we known what it cost many of them to step outside the conventional roles society prescribed for women.

After reading hundreds of military women's memoirs, personal essays, diaries, letters, pension depositions, oral histories, interviews, and scholarly histories of women's participation in the armed forces, we realized that the excerpts we've chosen can only be properly understood in historical, literary, and historiographical context. The service of our predecessors—and the ways in which they told their stories—can't be judged by modern standards. Women veterans of previous wars, some of whose narratives sound absurdly conventional and whose perspectives seem narrow to a modern reader, were operating in a different social and political environment than the one in which we served—a world radically different from the one in which women went off to fight in Iraq and Afghanistan.

We learned that women veterans had voices. They published book-length memoirs and professional articles. Their stories had been overlooked, ignored, or dismissed as unimportant. Some even had long, distinguished literary careers (though they seldom wrote about their military experiences).

Their stories are not the stories we were told during our time on active duty. Nor are they the stories frequently told in the news media and other contemporary accounts in which women veterans are seen in limited, binary terms as either "she-roes" or "victims of the patriarchy." Journalists, politicians, and others have appropriated women veterans' stories for a variety of reasons. Especially in early narratives, military women's stories were shaped and sometimes even changed to serve a political, social, or commercial agenda.

We have a different story to tell about the women who have chosen to take up the profession of arms. We believe that we have uncovered a unique historical and narrative arc—a new story about the military service of women in America.

Choosing from the stories we found wasn't easy. We decided to include stories from women who served unofficially, before women were "allowed" to enlist or to be commissioned into the armed forces, because from the earliest days of our nation women have fought alongside men and worked to ensure that the armed forces were competently supported and equipped. We selected narratives of cooks, laundresses, spies, and medical professionals along with those of women who fired rifles, launched missiles, and dropped bombs. If a woman filled a role now performed by trained and uniformed military professionals before women were legally allowed to enlist, we felt that she deserved a place in the ranks of "veterans." To separate fact from fiction in memoirs of women soldiers written before the twentieth century, we relied on the work of professional historians.

We looked for the stories of both officers and enlisted women to avoid creating a contribution history, which limits its focus to a handful of successful, decorated women who are acknowledged trailblazers. We wanted women currently serving and those who will follow them to see themselves and their experiences reflected in these pages. We looked beyond the writing of educated, literate women to ways that others told their stories. Illiteracy or a lack of formal education and social stigma prevented many women who served in the eighteenth and nineteenth centuries from writing and publishing their stories; narratives of women of color who served in those times were most often passed down orally but never committed to paper. Too many have been lost forever. To capture some part of their stories, we used transcribed pension depositions in which clerks captured women's authentic voices, and lengthy quotes recorded by journalists.

We did not anticipate discovery of such a rich, diverse first-person record of women's military service. However, most of the stories could only be found in out-of-print books that had been self-published or had enjoyed limited print runs; in professional journals; in unpublished manuscripts carefully preserved in libraries, universities, and archives; and in personal papers. We could include only a fraction of the good stories we found. We cut thousands of words of excellent prose, retaining only the stories that best amplified the themes we found in reading scholarly histories.

Frustrating gaps remain. Too many trailblazers' stories were told only by others, often men. We ran into dead ends in our research: for example, the family of African American Civil War spy Mary Bowser discarded her diary in the 1950s, unaware of its significance. Women who served in the Korean War era—like their male counterparts, veterans of the "Forgotten War"—reintegrated into civilian society, and most chose not to talk about their experiences. We were unable to do justice to the record of women veterans of color—some of whom left excellent and candid memoirs—or to the complex intersection of race and sex that shaped their stories. We wished that more of our Coast Guard colleagues had committed their stories to paper.

We edited narratives for content and length. We removed or summarized passages that we felt were not essential to the stories. We summarized interviewers' questions, important in oral histories and even part of the story, if done well: we preferred to focus on the voices of the women veterans they interviewed.

We restored the correct spelling to Harriet Tubman's telling of her story to journalist Emma Telford of New York. Telford deliberately misspelled words to re-create Tubman's "picturesque Southern dialect"—a stereotyped "Negro" accent rather than the dialect of Maryland's Eastern Shore, where Tubman was raised. Restoration of correct spelling reveals Tubman as a storyteller with a sharp wit, a keen eye for description, an ear for the rhythm and music of language, and an understanding of the power of biblical allusion and metaphor in storytelling. We hope that we have accorded her words the dignity that her contribution deserves. We edited unpublished contemporary manuscripts for spelling, for punctuation, and occasionally for word use.

Finally, we copyedited for conformity with the rules of the *Chicago Manual of Style*, with a few exceptions for standard practice in military writing: "Marine" is always capitalized!

Had our first meeting ended in a bar fight, we know who would have won.

ACKNOWLEDGMENTS

"Kam sia!" cried the beggars of the bustling Chinese treaty port of Amoy (now Xiamen). The Hokkien words for "Grateful thanks!" took root in the nautical lexicon as "cumshaw," meaning something procured outside official channels or without official payment, usually obtained through barter. In writing this book we became "cumshaw artists," adept at getting the help and information we needed in exchange for nothing more than our gratitude.

Dozens of curators, librarians, and historians came to our aid. We could not have written this book without the assistance, advice, time, and patience of curator Britta Granrud and oral historian Robbie Fee of the Women in Military Service for America Memorial Foundation. If you're a woman veteran reading this book and you haven't yet registered there or donated to the Memorial, please do so without delay.

Beth Ann Koelsch at the University of North Carolina in Greensboro helped us navigate through the Martha Blakeney Hodges Special Collections and University Archives and resources of the Betty H. Carter Women Veterans Historical Project. Chris Ellis and Kara Newcomer at the Archives and Special Collections Branch of the U.S. Marine Corps Library; Nancy Wilt, Women Marines Association Curator of the Women of the Corps Collection; and Coast Guard Historian Scott Price steered us to valuable sources of information that we would never have found on our own.

Angie Stockwell, Collection Specialist at the Margaret Chase Smith Library in Skowhegan, Maine; Kate Clifford Larson, author of *Bound for the Promised Land: Harriet Tubman, Portrait of an American Hero*; Sharon M. Harris, author of *Dr. Mary Walker: An American Radical, 1832–1919*; Eileen McHugh at the Cayuga Museum of History and Art; Michael Golden of the OSS Society; Anna Chovanec, Reference Assistant at the Syracuse University Libraries Special Collections Research Center; Amanda Vasquez, archivist for the Daughters of the American Revolution; and Marian Moser-Jones at the University of Maryland found no detail of our questions too insignificant, trivial, or unworthy of their attention and professional expertise.

Joel Thomas Webster in the Special Collections Branch of the James Madison University Library wrote a biographical summary for us, literally overnight, from a collection of one veteran's personal papers that had not yet been sorted and cataloged. Stephen Rice at the Connecticut State Library in Hartford found a historical newspaper article that we needed and sent it to us in a matter of hours.

We were awed at the expertise and bloodhound-quality detective skills of the librarians at the Library of Congress; the archivists at the National Archives and Records Administration in Washington DC; College Park, Maryland; and St. Louis, Missouri; and the reference librarians at the Southern Maryland Public Library in Prince Frederick, Maryland—especially Carrie Raines and Molly Crumbley.

The Service Women's Action Network (SWAN) steered us to Captain Lory Manning, USN (Ret.), whose behind-the-scenes knowledge about equal protection lawsuits and the efforts to repeal combat exclusion laws made our later chapters immeasurably better.

Our research assistant, Noah Beall, saved us hours of work on the bibliography.

Kayla Williams agreed to write the foreword even before we'd finished the proposal. She made time to read the manuscript while she was moving her family back to Washington DC and starting her new job as the director of the Center for Women Veterans. Kayla, we love you.

To our team at the University of Nebraska Press and Potomac Books—Bridget Barry, Kristin Elias Rowley, Thomas Swanson, Emily Wendell, Elizabeth Zaleski, and Colleen Romick Clark—we thank you for your earliest belief in this project and for your unwavering support as this project changed and expanded from the original proposal.

We are grateful to the women veterans who shared their original essays with us, and to the women who graciously contributed oral histories and personal papers to the Women's Memorial; the Betty H. Carter Women Veterans Historical Project at UNC Greensboro; the Veterans History Project at the Library of Congress; and university libraries. We salute their courage and candor.

Finally, Jerri would like to thank the staff of the Veterans Writing Project and the contributors to *O-Dark-Thirty* for tolerating her distraction in the final months of writing; her husband, David Bury, for taking on more than his fair share of the household chores; her sons, Will and Jon Bury, for eating far too many soup-and-sandwich dinners; her sister, Joan Bell, for "holding space"; the "Desperate Housewives of Calvert County" for dragging her away from the keyboard and down to the gym; and her mother, her first female role model. Mom, you don't realize how strong and brave you have always been.

And Tracy would like to thank her husband, Mark Weidemaier, who always has the misfortune, it seems, to return home from his life in Major League Baseball during the final weeks leading up to a book deadline, yet treads softly and offers all means of support. Tracy would also like to thank her daughter, Morgan, and son-in-law, Brian; her parents; her brother; Jeffery Hess; Libby Oberg; CJ Scarlet; Sam and Novella Kennedy; and the immensely supportive friends in her town of Liberty.

Last, but never least, we would like to dedicate this book to the women who are now serving America on active duty, in the reserve, and in the Guard—and to the generations of women who follow. This is your *her*-story. We wrote this book for you.

IT'S MY COUNTRY TOO

The American Revolution

"A Natural Priviledge"

In April 1775, Prudence Cummings Wright, a thirty-five-year-old mother of six from Pepperell, Massachusetts, recruited a group of thirty to forty local women to guard a bridge over the Nashua River. The women elected Wright unit captain. She chose Sarah Shattuck of Groton as her lieutenant. One night the women dressed in men's clothing, armed themselves, mustered at the bridge, and captured a suspected British courier mounted on horseback. They ordered him to dismount. Searched him. Found potentially incriminating papers. Placed him under guard overnight. In the morning, they delivered him and his documents to the nearest Committee of Safety.

Prudence Wright's Guard—an all-women's militia unit—exemplifies one of the many ways American women engaged in military activity during the American Revolution. Militia muster rolls and contemporary accounts show that women fought as irregulars in local militias and defended their homes on the frontier. They also served in the Continental Army—most in support and medical positions, some as regular uniformed troops.

Historians do not know exactly how many women—or men—fought in the American Revolution. One estimates that as many as twenty thousand women served in support roles in the Continental Army between 1775 and 1783. A few hundred may have fought in uniform. The largest number fought sporadically in local defensive combat operations.

In his general orders, George Washington called women attached to the Continental Army in support roles "Women of the Army." These women were not camp followers or prostitutes. Most soldiers in the Continental Army, whose pay was frequently in arrears and who often lacked adequate food and clothing, could not afford to hire prostitutes. Some of the women were officers' and soldiers' wives; others were refugees who sought food and safety with the Continental Army. These women—usually limited to no more than five per company—competed for available positions. They drew rations and pay for cooking, sewing, and laundry; they could also charge officers and soldiers for personal laundry at rates regulated by the Army. Male sergeants directed the women, expecting them to accompany the baggage train, keep off the wagons, do their assigned jobs, and refrain from unsavory conduct. The women were subject to military discipline. Some were court-martialed for desertion; others were punished or dismissed for disorderly conduct.

The Army also recruited women nurses. In 1777 the Army medical staff was authorized one matron (supervisor) and ten female nurses for every hundred wounded soldiers. Matrons received double the salary of a sergeant and drew a daily food ration. The Army never found enough women nurses to fill the available positions.

Some women disguised themselves and enlisted as regular soldiers. Commanders recorded the (usually nonpunitive) discharge of women who had entered the ranks dressed as men.

Women also carried water to cool artillery pieces so they did not explode. Sally St. Clare, a woman of color who served in men's attire as a gunner, became the first woman killed in action during the Battle of Savannah on December 29, 1778. Margaret Corbin replaced her husband at his gun when he was killed at the Battle of Fort Washington on November 16, 1776. She continued to fire her cannon with accuracy until British troops overran her position, captured her, and detained her as a prisoner of war. Three musket balls and grapeshot had damaged her jaw and nearly detached her arm. Because of her permanent and severe disability, sustained in the line of fire, Congress awarded her a military disability pension in 1779 and the Army assigned her to the Invalid Regiment at West Point. In 1926 her remains were reinterred with full military honors at West Point.

Contemporary civilian women such as African American poetess Phyllis Wheatley and playwright Mercy Otis Warren published literary work addressing the war and patriotic themes. Others, mostly elite white women whose husbands fought in the Revolution or helped create the new government, kept journals and wrote letters containing intimate details of their lives and their views of current events. But the stories of women who fought in or supported the Continental Army survived mainly in journal accounts written by men, brief entries in military records, pension depositions and awards, and oral histories collected early in the nineteenth century. Historians did not consider the experiences of common soldiers and women in support jobs important enough to preserve for the historical record. The military experiences of women of color, many of whom were illiterate, appear only as brief references in others' writing.

Writers and historians romanticized and distorted some stories of women's service. They combined accounts of women who served with gun crews into the legend of "Molly Pitcher," reshaping the story to conform to a socially acceptable women's role—carrying water to the gun crews to drink. Other stories may have been fabricated altogether. No documentation supports the existence of Lucy Brewer, who supposedly dressed as a man to enlist with the Marines on USS *Constitution* as "George Baker" to fight during the War of 1812.

To date, only two accounts written by women who served in or with the Continental Army have surfaced. Susanna Osborn, widow of a veteran, describes in a pension deposition how she followed her husband into the Continental Army in a support role (she received the pension). Deborah Sampson Gannett, who enlisted in the Continental Army dressed as a man, left a memoir, the text of a public address she delivered twenty years after her service, and a few pages of a diary she kept on the lecture circuit.

Sarah Osborn

(1745–1854)

CONTINENTAL ARMY

Sarah Matthews Osborn married blacksmith Aaron Osborn in Albany, New York, in January 1780. He re-enlisted as a commissary guard in the Continental Army, and she agreed to accompany him to war only after his commanding officer assured her that her husband would be "first on the Commissary Guard" and that she could ride in a wagon and on horseback—a privilege usually denied to women who accompanied the soldiers. In 1837 she applied for Osborn's widow's pension even though he had abandoned her and she had remarried. She dictated the deposition to a clerk, describing her experiences with the Continental Army at West Point and Yorktown. She noted that the wives of a lieutenant and a sergeant also accompanied their husbands, and that an African American woman named Letta also supported the unit. The excerpt below is taken from her deposition.

West Point (1780–1781)

While at West Point, deponent lived at Lieutenant Foot's, who kept a boarding house. Deponent was employed in washing and serving for the soldiers. Her said husband was employed about the camp. She well recollects the uproar occasioned when word came that a British officer had been taken as a spy. She understood at the time that Maj. André was bro't up on the opposite side of the river and kept there till he was executed. On the returning of the bargemen who assisted Arnold to escape deponent recollects seeing two of them, one by the name of Montecu, the other by the name of Clarke. That they said Arnold told them to hang up their dinners for he had to be at Stoney Point in so many minutes, and when he got there he hoisted his pocket handkerchief and his sword and said "Row on, boys," and that they soon arrived in Haverstraw Bay and found the British ship. That Arnold jumped on board and they were all invited and they went aboard and had their choice to go or stay. And some chose to stay and some to go and did accordingly.

When the army were about to leave West Point and go south they crossed over the river to Robinsons Farms and remained there for a length of time to induce the belief . . . that they were going to take up quarters there, whereas they recrossed the river in the night time into the Jerseys and travelled all night in a direct course for Philadelphia. Deponent was part of the time on horse back and part of the time in a wagon. In their march for Philadelphia they were under command of Generals Washington and [James] Clinton. . . . They continued their march to Philadelphia, deponent on horse back through the streets, and arrived at a place towards the Schuylkill where the British had burnt some houses, where they encamped for the afternoon and night. Being out of bread deponent was employed in baking the afternoon and evening. Deponent recollects no females but Sergeant Lamberson's and Lt. Forman's wives, and a colored woman by the name of Letta. The ladies, who came round, urged deponent to stay, but her said husband said "No, he could not leave her behind." Accordingly next day they continued their march from day to day till they arrived at Baltimore where deponent and her said husband and the forces under command of Gen. Clinton, Capt. Gregg and several other officers . . . embarked on board a vessel and sailed down the Chesapeake. There were several vessels along and deponent was in the foremost. Gen. Washington was not in the vessel with deponent and she does not know where he was till he arrived at Yorktown where she again saw him. He might have embarked at another place, but deponent is confident she embarked at Baltimore and that Gen. Clinton was in the same vessel with her. Some of the troops went down by land. They continued sail until they had got up the St. James River as far as the tide would carry them, about twelve miles from the mouth, and then landed, and the tide being spent, they had a fine time catching sea lobsters which they ate. They however marched immediately for a place called Williamsburg . . . deponent alternately on horse back and on foot. There arrived, they remained two days till the army all came in by land and then marched for Yorktown, or Little York as it was then called.

The Battle of Yorktown (1781)

The York troops were posted at the right. The Connecticut troops next and the French to the left. In about one day or less than a day they reached the place of encampments about one mile from Yorktown. Deponent was on foot, and the other females above named....[Her] attention was arrested by the appearance of a large plain between them and Yorktown and an entrenchment thrown up. She also saw a number of dead Negroes lying round their encampment whom she understood the British had driven out of the town and left to starve or were first starved and then thrown out. Deponent took her stand just back of the American tents ... about a mile from the town and busied herself washing, mending and cooking for the soldiers, in which she was assisted by the other females; some men washed their own clothing. She heard the roar of the artillery for a number of days, and the last night the Americans threw up entrenchments. It was a misty, foggy night, rather wet but not rainy.... Deponent's said husband was there throwing up entrenchments and deponent cooked and carried in beef and bread, and coffee (in a gallon pot) to the soldiers in the entrenchment.

On one occasion when deponent was thus employed carrying in provisions she met Gen. Washington, who asked her if she "was not afraid of the cannonballs."

She replied, "No, the bullets would not cheat the gallows—that it would not do for the men to fight and starve too."

They dug entrenchments nearer and nearer to Yorktown every night or two till the last. While digging, the enemy fired very heavy till about nine o clock next morning, then stopped, and the drums from the enemy beat excessively....

The drums continued beating, and all at once the officers hurra'd and swung their hats, and deponent asked them, "What is the matter now?"

One of them replied, "Are not you soldier enough to know what it means?"

Deponent replied, "No."

They then replied, "The British have surrendered."

Deponent, having provisions ready, carried the same down to the entrenchments that morning and four of the soldiers whom she was in the habit of cooking for ate their breakfasts. Deponent stood on one side of the room and the American officers upon the other side, when the British officers came out of the town and rode up to the American officers.... And the British officers rode right on before the army who marched out beating and playing a melancholy tune, their drums covered with black handkerchiefs and their fifes with black ribbands tied around them, into an old field, and there grounded their arms and then returned into town again to await their destiny.

Deponent recollects seeing a great many American officers some on horse back and some on foot but can not call them all by name—Washington, LaFayette, and Clinton were among the number. The British general at the head of the army was a large portly man, full face, and the tears rolled down his cheeks as he passed along. She does not recollect his name. But it was not Cornwallis. She saw the latter afterwards and noticed his being a man of diminutive appearance and having cross eyes....

Deponent and her husband spent certainly more than three years in the service.

Deborah Sampson Gannett
(1760–1827)
CONTINENTAL ARMY

Deborah Sampson Gannett, the first American woman to tell the story of her military service to a public audience, disguised herself in men's clothing in 1782 to enlist in the Continental Army under the name Robert Shurtlieff. She was wounded in combat later that year. In 1783 doctors discovered her sex when she caught a fever. She was discharged from the Army but successfully petitioned Congress for a military pension.

The vocabulary Gannett used in her diary suggests that she was literate and well-read. Aspiring to make her story appeal to wealthy, educated readers, she chose an ambitious but inexperienced male journalist, Herman Mann, to co-write her memoir in 1797. Mann included a number of factual inaccuracies, and he seems to have taken entire sections from a popular contemporary memoir of British soldier Hannah Snell. Gannett was said not to have been entirely pleased with it.

In 1802, again working with Mann, she revised her memoir into a lecture and became the first American woman to appear on the public lecture circuit. In uniform, she recited the speech from memory. Afterward, when someone was available to call the commands, she demonstrated her skill at rifle drill.

Gannett's lecture, from which the excerpt below is taken, avoids most of the outright falsifications in the memoir. Laden with high diction, sophisticated vocabulary, and exaggerated sentiment, it would have appealed to wealthy, educated men of the time. In alluding to Greek and Roman classics when describing her experiences, Gannett claims that her military service was as noble and valuable as a man's. She apologizes profusely for violating social conventions governing women's behavior; she wanted to reintegrate into postwar society. But a close read of the lecture suggests that she did not regret having fought for her country. She even compares men's control over women to the tyranny of the Crown over the Colonies.

The solicitations of a number of worthy characters and friends, too persuasive and congenial with my own disposition to be answered with indifference, or to be rejected, have induced me thus to advance and bow submissive to an audience, simply and concisely to rehearse a tale of truth . . . a tale—the truth of which I was ready to say, but which, perhaps, others have already said for me, ought to expel me from the enjoyment of society, from the acknowledgement of my own sex, and from the endearing friendship of the other. But this, I venture to pronounce, would be saying too much: For as I should thus not respect myself, should be entitled to none from others.

I indeed recollect it as a foible, an error and presumption, into which, perhaps, I have too inadvertently and precipitately run; but which I now retrospect with anguish and amazement. . . . And yet I must frankly confess, I recollect it with a kind of satisfaction, which no one can better conceive and enjoy than him, who, recollecting the good intentions of a bad deed, lives to see and to correct any indecorum of his life. . . .

But most of all, my mind became agitated with the enquiry—why a nation, separated from us by an ocean more than three thousand miles in extent, should endeavor to enforce on us plans of subjugation, the most unnatural in themselves, unjust, inhuman, in their operations, and unpractised even by the uncivilized savages of the wilderness? Perhaps nothing but the critical juncture of the times could have excused such a philosophical disquisition of politics in woman. . . .

Confirmed by this time in the justness of a defensive war on the one side, from the most aggravated one on the other—my mind ripened with my strength; and while our beds and our roses were sprinkled with the blood of indiscriminate youth, beauty, innocence, and decrepit old age, I only seemed to want the license to become one of the severest avengers of the wrong. . . .

Wrought upon at length, you may say, by an enthusiasm and frenzy, that could book no control—I burst the tyrant bonds, which held my sex in awe, and clandestinely, or by stealth, grasped an opportunity, which custom and the world seemed to deny, as a natural priviledge. And whilst poverty, hunger, nakedness, cold, and disease had dwindled the American Armies to a handful—while universal terror and dismay ran through our camps, ran through our country—while even WASHINGTON himself, at their head, though like a god, stood, as it were, on a pinacle tottering over the abyss of destruction, the last prelude to our falling a wretched prey to the yawning jaws of the monster aiming to devour—not merely for the safe of gratifying a fecetious curiosity, like that of my reputed Predecessor, in her romantic excursions through the garden of bliss—did I throw off the soft habiliments of my sex, and assume those of the warrior, already prepared for battle.

Thus I became an actor in that important drama, with an inflexible resolution to persevere through the last scene; when we might be permitted and acknowledged to enjoy what we had so nobly declared we would possess, or lose with our lives—FREEDOM and INDEPENDENCE! . . .

What shall I say further? Shall I not stop short, and leave to your imaginations to pourtray the tragic deeds of war? Is it not enough, that I here leave it even to inexperience to fancy the hardships, the anxieties, the dangers, even of the best life of a soldier? And were it not improper, were it not unsafe, were it not indelicate, and were I certain I should be intitled to a pardon, I would appeal to the soft bosom of my own sex to draw a parallel between the perils and sexual inconveniences of a girl in her teens, and not only in the armour, but in the capacity, at any rate, obliged to perform the duties in the field—and those who go to the camp without a masquerade, and consequently subject only to what toils and sacrifices they please: Or, will a conclusion be more natural from those who sometimes take occasion to complain by their own domestic fire-sides; but who, indeed, are at the same time in affluence, cherished in the arms of their companions, and sheltered from the storms of war by the rougher sex in arms?

Many have seen, and many can contemplate, in the field of imagination, battles, and victories amidst garments rolled in blood: but it is only one of my own sex, exposed to the storm, who can conceive of my situation. . . .

But the question again returns—What particular inducement could she have thus to elope from the soft sphere of her own sex, to perform a deed of valor by way of sacrilege on unhallowed ground—voluntarily to face the storms both of elements, and war, in the character of him, who is more fitly made to brave and endure all danger? . . .

> And dost thou ask what fairy hand inspired
> A Nymph to be with martial glory fired?
> Or, what from art, or yet from nature's laws,
> Has join'd a Female to her country's cause?
> Why on great Mars's theatre she drew
> Her female pourtrait, though in soldier's hue?
> Then ask—why *Cincinnatus* left his farm?
> Why science did old PLATO's bosom warm?
> Why HECTOR in the Trojan war should dare?
> Or why should HOMER trace his actions there?
> Why NEWTON in philosophy has shown?

Or CHARLES, for solitude, has left his throne?
Why LOCKE in metaphysics should delight—
Precisian sage, to set false reason right?
Why ALBION'S SONS should kindle up a war?
Why JOVE or VULCAN hurried on the car?
Perhaps the same propensity you use,
Has prompted her a martial course to choose.
Perhaps to gain refinements where she could,
This rare achievement for her country's good....

I would not purposely evade a pertinent answer; and yet I know not, at present, how to give a more particular one than has already been suggested.

I am indeed willing to acknowledge what I have done, an error and presumption. I will call it an error and presumption, because I swerved from the accustomed flowery paths of female delicacy, to walk upon the heroic precipice of feminine perdition!—I indeed left my morning pillow of roses, to prepare a couch of brambles for the night; and yet I awoke from this refreshed, to gather nought but the thorns of anguish for the next night's repose—and in the precipitancy of passion, to prepare a moment for repentance at leisure!

Had all this been achieved by the rougher hand, more properly assigned to wield the sword in duty and danger in a defensive war, the most cruel in its measures, though important in its consequences; these thorns might have been converted into wreaths of immortal glory and fame. I therefore yield every claim of honor and distinction to the hero and patriot, who met the foe in his own name; though not with more heartfelt satisfaction, with the trophies, which were most to redound to the future grandeur and importance of the country in which he lives.

2

The Civil War

"I Gave My Services Willingly"

"I long to be a man; but as I can't fight, I will content myself with working for those who can," the New England spinster wrote in her diary in April 1861.

On her birthday in November 1862, she decided to go to Washington as a nurse. She loved nursing, wanted an outlet for her energy, dreaded the boredom of winter, and hoped not to burden her family with her upkeep.

And she wanted new experiences.

She had been at Georgetown Hospital only three days when cartloads of men wounded at the Battle of Fredericksburg began to arrive. She wished for a moment that she was safe at home again, with a quiet day ahead. From behind a pile of clothing, bandages, and supplies, she watched orderlies carry stretchers of wounded men into her ward, the former ballroom of a hotel. She realized then that her homesickness and distaste for the vile odor of the wounded men must wait: she was "there to work, not to wonder or weep."

Another nurse handed her a basin, a sponge, towels, and a block of brown soap. "Come, my dear," she said. "Begin to wash as fast as you can. Tell them to take off socks, coats, and shirts, scrub them well, put on clean shirts." The order shocked the modest thirty-year-old. But there was no time for nonsense.

Her first patient was an older Irishman with a head wound. He was horrified that a lady would deign to wash him, and he rolled up his eyes and blessed her in an effusive style that made them both laugh. When she knelt to remove his shoes, he refused to let her touch his "dirty craters."

"May your bed above be aisy darlin', for the day's work ye ar doon!—Whoosh! there ye are, and bedad, it's hard tellin' which is the dirtiest, the fut or the shoe."

This made everyone laugh. The nurse thought that if the soldier had said nothing she might have continued pulling on his foot, mistaking it for his boot. Amused and reassured, Louisa May Alcott—Army contract nurse—went to work with a will.

Not all women contented themselves with support roles. Sanitary Commission worker and memoirist Mary Livermore wrote in 1888 that nearly four hundred women fought on both sides of the Civil War disguised as men. She estimated that there were many more. Historians Deanne Blanton and Lauren Cook Wise documented the existence of almost two hundred and fifty such "distaff soldiers." They believe that more fought disguised as men but were never discovered.

Women took advantage of lax Army physicals; doctors often checked only for a trigger finger and enough teeth to tear open a cartridge. Both the field environment and social expectations helped women maintain their disguises. Working-class and frontier women were used to manual labor; many knew how to fire a weapon. Underage male enlistees had higher voices and lacked facial hair. Loose clothing hid feminine curves, and few men knew how women looked in pants. Healthy women easily carried an infantryman's equipment: rifles weighed ten or fifteen pounds, and soldiers on march carried about thirty pounds of gear. Soldiers slept in their clothes and used nearby woods or bushes as latrines. Some women adopted "masculine vices": they drank, swore, smoked and chewed tobacco, gambled, fought, and even courted civilian women to enhance their disguise.

According to Blanton and Wise, "distaff soldiers" served in every rank from private to major, and in infantry, artillery, and cavalry units. They worked as guards, scouts, clerks, dragoons, teamsters, musicians, provost marshals, orderlies, nurses, couriers, and spies. The youngest discovered was a girl of twelve.

Women fought and died at Manassas, Antietam, Shiloh, and Gettysburg; in the sieges of Vicksburg and Richmond; on the Peninsula, Shenandoah, and Red River campaigns; at many minor battles; and at Appomattox. They were promoted more frequently than their male counterparts—possibly because misbehavior attracted attention and threatened their disguises. The Army court-martialed no women for dereliction of duty, military crimes, or disgracing the uniform. Only three are known to have deserted; two of them later reenlisted. Two changed sides from the Confederacy to the Union.

About 15 percent were wounded, often multiple times. They sustained gunshot wounds in the head, neck, and torso; saber cuts; and arm and leg wounds resulting in amputation. More than 10 percent died of wounds sustained in battle or diseases endemic in crowded, unsanitary camp conditions. Soldiers discovered some distaff soldiers' sex only after their deaths; others, like Rosetta Wakeman, remained undiscovered and were buried as men.

Six served while pregnant. A Union soldier fought at Antietam in her second trimester and at Fredericksburg in her third; two Confederate soldiers gave birth while prisoners of war. All kept their pregnancies secret until they gave birth.

Only one distaff soldier reported a sexual assault. The intended rape victim, a Union soldier, shot her assailant in the face.

Some women who were taken prisoner were released when their sex was discovered. Both armies incarcerated others as prisoners of war. Austere and unsanitary conditions at all prisons had serious health consequences for men and women alike, discipline was harsh, and guards treated prisoners brutally. The death rate during incarceration was high.

The disguises of three-quarters of the women whose service Blanton and Wise documented were revealed when they became casualties or were taken prisoner, or in rare cases when feminine gestures or behaviors gave them away. A few disclosed their sex to obtain a discharge. The Army usually discharged women caught serving as men—often honorably. Approximately 10 percent of those discovered completed their enlistment as men; almost twice that many eventually served openly as women. Some women reenlisted in other units. Others remained with the Army as nurses, laundresses, or spies.

Women spied for both sides, in uniform and as civilians. Attitudes about women often kept them above suspicion, but the work was dangerous: both armies imprisoned, shot, or hanged captured spies.

After the Wars of Independence, the Army Medical Corps used men as nurses. Aside from a handful of corpsmen and orderlies, most soldiers assigned to nursing duty had proven themselves incompetent soldiers on the battlefield. Predictably, this policy drained manpower from the fight, and invalid soldiers received poor care. In August of 1861, Congress authorized the Union Army to contract women as untrained civilian nurses.

Over the course of the war some 3,200 women nurses, contracted to the Army under the leadership of mental health advocate Dorothea Dix, worked long hours and exposed themselves to deadly contagious diseases. Others volunteered with the U.S. Sanitary Commission, Western Sanitary Commission, and U.S. Christian Commission—forerunners of the American Red Cross. Catholic, Lutheran, and Episcopalian nuns trained in nursing skills also volunteered. The Confederate army did not organize or train a corps of nurses, but relied instead on volunteers.

African American women served as soldiers, spies, and nurses, though their stories were rarely recorded. Some disguised themselves as men to fight. Others filled support roles in racially segregated units. The Union Army conscripted freedwomen as "contraband" cooks and laundresses. African American women volunteered in nursing and relief organizations.

Union spy Elizabeth Van Lew convinced Confederate First Lady Varina Davis to accept the service of Mary Elizabeth Bowser, a former slave freed by the family. Bowser, educated in a Philadelphia school, read Confederate president Jefferson Davis's correspondence when she cleaned his study and eavesdropped on his conversations with Confederate leaders. She reported the information to Ulysses S. Grant through Van Lew's espionage network. Because of racial prejudice and assumptions about the literacy and intelligence of African Americans, Davis did not suspect her of being the leak until late in the war. In 1865 she fled. After the war, the War Department destroyed records of her work; in 1952 her family discarded her diary, unaware of its significance.

Civil War soldiers, most of whom were literate, left a rich heritage of diaries, uncensored letters, and memoirs. Women left far fewer written records of their wartime experiences. Those who enlisted, like the men they served alongside, often came from working-class or immigrant families who placed less value on women's education. Researchers have discovered the letters of only three women who served as men, and only two published memoirs. (Men documented the existence of hundreds of others.) Some letters, diaries, and memoirs of contract and volunteer nurses have survived.

Sarah Emma Edmonds's memoir of her service as Pvt. Frank Thompson immediately became a bestseller upon its publication in 1864. After being twice reissued, it sold 175,000 copies. Actress Pauline Cushman published a memoir of her espionage activities in 1875. Loreta Janeta Velazquez published her controversial memoir of service as a Confederate soldier a year later. The wide audience for these stories led to publication of fictional accounts: women in uniform appeared in short stories on the pages of magazines like *Harper's* and in a slew of novels published during and just after the war—most seemingly aimed at a literate but lower-class audience, and all conforming to socially acceptable images of women warriors.

After the war Louisa May Alcott wrote commercially successful fiction. Dr. Mary Edwards Walker wrote progressive essays and two books on women's issues and dress reform. Contract and volunteer nurses continued in the profession as civilians and contributed to a revolution of the nursing profession. Sarah Emma Edmonds and Harriet Tubman engaged in relief work for soldiers and freedmen. A few, like Albert Cashier (Jenny Hodgers), continued to live as men. Some, widowed by the war or married to fellow soldiers, lived in poverty or in poor health from diseases contracted during the war. Few women attempted to claim a pension or other benefits; many contract nurses probably did not realize that they were eligible.

Newspapers continued to publish stories about women who served as men, spied, or nursed. Male veterans passed down their stories, assisted some of the impoverished or supported their pension applications, and even buried others with full military honors. But public interest waned with the onset of World War I and the passing of the generation that fought in the Civil War. Historians of the early twentieth century, mostly white men, discounted or dismissed the stories of women who served in the Civil War.

The women who served in the Civil War exceeded the expectations of Victorian society and left a legacy of dedication, courage, patriotism, and sacrifice. Louisa May Alcott wrote, "The height of my ambition was to go to the front after a battle." Mary Edwards Walker believed that women had the ability to fight. And Sarah Edmonds spoke for many: "I could only thank God that I was free and could go forward and work, and I was not obliged to stay at home and weep."

Sarah Emma Edmonds
(1841–1898)
U.S. ARMY

Sarah Emma Edmonds dressed as a man and enlisted for three years as "Franklin Thompson" in the Second Michigan Infantry in 1861. She served as a mail carrier and a spy. In the spring of 1863, having suffered internal injuries in battle and contracted malaria, she deserted to avoid discovery. She continued to serve as a nurse under her real name from June 1863 until the end of the war. In 1864 she published her memoir, *Memoirs of a Soldier, Nurse and Spy: A Woman's Adventures in the Union Army*, from which the following excerpt is taken.

> I took the cars the next day and went to Lebanon—dressed in one of the rebel prisoner's clothes—and thus disguised, made another trip to rebeldom. My business purported to be buying up butter and eggs, at

the farmhouses, for the rebel army. I passed through the lines some-where, without knowing it; for on coming to a little village toward evening, I found it occupied by a strong force of rebel cavalry. The first house I went to was filled with officers and citizens. I had stum-bled upon a wedding party, unawares. Captain Logan, a recruiting officer, had been married that afternoon to a brilliant young widow whose husband had been killed in the rebel army a few months before. She had discovered that widow's weeds were not becoming to her style of beauty, so had decided to appear once more in bridal costume, for a change.

I was questioned pretty sharply by the handsome captain in regard to the nature of my business in that locality, but finding me an inno-cent, straightforward Kentuckian, he came to the conclusion that I was all right. But he also arrived at the conclusion that I was old enough to be in the army, and bantered me considerably upon my want of patriotism. . . .

I tried to make my escape from the village as soon as possible, but who should confront me but Captain Logan. Said he: "See, here, my lad; I think the best thing you can do is enlist, and join a company which is just forming here in the village, and will leave in the morn-ing. We are giving a bounty to all who freely enlist, and are conscript-ing those who refuse. Which do you propose to do, enlist and get the bounty, or refuse, and be obliged to go without anything?" I replied, "I think I shall wait a few days before I decide." "But we can't wait for you to decide," said the captain; "the Yankees may be upon us any moment, for we are not far from their lines, and we will leave here either tonight or in the morning early. I will give you two hours to decide this ques-tion, and in the meantime you must be put under guard." So saying, he marched me back with him, and gave me in charge of the guards. In two or three hours he came for my decision, and I told him that I had concluded to wait until I was conscripted. "Well," said he, "you will not have long to wait for that, so you may consider yourself a soldier of the Confederacy from this hour, and subject to military discipline."

This seemed to me like pretty serious business, especially as I would be required to take the oath of allegiance to the Confederate Govern-ment. . . . I was determined to be among the missing ere it became necessary for me to make any professions of loyalty to the rebel cause. I knew that if I should refuse to be sworn into the service after I was conscripted, that in all probability my true character would be suspected, and I would have to suffer the penalty of death—and that, too, in the most barbarous manner.

I was glad to find that it was a company of cavalry that was being organized, for if I could once get on a good horse there would be some hope of my escape. . . . Music and dancing was kept up all night, and it was some time after daylight when the captain made his appearance. A few moments more and we were trotting briskly over the country, the captain complimenting me upon my horsemanship, and telling me how grateful I would be to him when the war was over and the South had gained her independence, and that I would be proud that I had been one of the soldiers of the Southern Confederacy, who had steeped my saber in Yankee blood, and driven the vandals from our soil. "Then," said he, "you will thank me for the interest which I have taken in you, and for the *gentle persuasives* which I made use of to stir up your patriotism and remind you of your duty to your country."

In this manner we had traveled about half an hour, when we suddenly encountered a reconnoitering party of the Federals, cavalry in advance, and infantry in the rear. A contest soon commenced; we were ordered to advance in line, which we did, until we came within a few yards of the Yankees.

The company advanced, but my horse suddenly became unmanageable, and it required a second or two to bring him right again; and before I could overtake the company and get in line the contending parties had met in a hand-to-hand fight.

All were engaged, so that when I, by accident, got on the Federal side of the line, none observed me for several minutes, except the Federal officer, who had recognized me and signed to me to fall in next to him. That brought me face to face with my rebel captain, to whom I owed such a debt of gratitude. Thinking this would be a good time to cancel all obligations in that direction, I discharged the contents of my pistol in his face.

This act made me the center of attraction. Every rebel seemed determined to have the pleasure of killing me first, and a simultaneous dash was made toward me and numerous saber strokes aimed at my head. Our men with one accord rushed between me and the enemy, and warded off the blows with their sabers, and attacked them with such fury that they were driven back several rods.

The infantry now came up and deployed as skirmishers, and succeeded in getting a position where they had a complete cross fire on the rebels, and poured in volley after volley until nearly half their number lay upon the ground. Finding it useless to fight longer at such a disadvantage they turned and fled, leaving behind them eleven killed, twenty-nine wounded, and seventeen prisoners.

The Confederate captain was wounded badly but not mortally; his handsome face was very much disfigured, a part of his nose and nearly half of his upper lip being shot away. I was sorry, for the graceful curve of his mustache was sadly spoiled, and the happy bride of the previous morning would no longer rejoice in the beauty of that manly face and exquisite mustache of which she seemed so proud, and which had captivated her heart ere she had been three months a widow.

Loreta Janeta Velazquez
(1842–1897)
CONFEDERATE STATES ARMY

Loreta Janeta Velazquez's memoir has been controversial since its publication in 1876. Velazquez claimed to be born of a Spanish father and French American mother in Cuba in 1842. When the Civil War began, she persuaded her husband to join the Confederate Army. She cross-dressed and masqueraded as Lt. Harry T. Buford; participated in several major battles; and then left the Army to work for the Confederacy as a double agent.

Upon reading the memoir in 1876, Gen. Jubal Early, incensed at the memoir's anachronisms, factual errors, and portrayal of Southern men, publicly attacked its authenticity. Velazquez wrote Early in protest in May of 1878, asking him to stop discrediting her story and claiming that she needed the income from the book to support herself and her young son.

She embellished her account, which a former Union naval officer edited for publication. Historians have found only tantalizing possibilities rather than conclusive documentary evidence for her actual identity and her exploits. However, a number of contemporary accounts mention her existence, including those of Gen. James Longstreet and Maj. John Newman of the Twenty-First Louisiana Volunteers, who claimed to have known her well for thirteen years. Her descriptions of battles, mostly accurate, contain only minor errors of detail. Even modern veterans will recognize the authenticity of her comments on the nature of fighting, battle, and the character and activities of military men.

Velazquez's narrative defied established conventions for literature about women soldiers. She enlisted as a man from a desire for adventure, rather than from patriotic idealism or love of a man. She married and remarried four times. She claimed a number of additional romantic encounters—including some with other women while she was disguised as a man. Her unwillingness to shape her narrative to conform to Victorian romantic ideals probably contributed to the memoir's controversial critical reception.

The excerpts below are taken from her 1876 memoir, *The Woman in Battle: A Narrative of the Exploits, Adventures, and Travels of Madame Loreta Janeta Velazquez, Otherwise Known As Lieutenant Harry T. Buford, Confederate States Army.*

[Velazquez tells her husband that she wants to accompany him to war. He tries to persuade her not to go by saying that "the hordes of rude, coarse men collected together in a camp in an emergency like this, would have but little resemblance to the regular troops in garrison with whom (she) had been familiar."]

First Assumption of Male Attire

Finally, my husband, finding that his words made no impression, thought that he would be able to cure me of my erratic fancies by giving me an insight into some of the least pleasing features of masculine life. The night before his departure, therefore, he permitted me to dress myself in one of his suits, and said he would take me to the bar-rooms and other places of male resort, and show me something of what I would be compelled to go through if I persisted in unsexing myself. Braiding my hair very close, I put on a man's wig, and a false mustache, and by tucking my pantaloons in my boots, as I had seen men do frequently, and otherwise arranging the garments, which were somewhat large for me, I managed to transform myself into a very presentable man. As I surveyed myself in the mirror I was immensely pleased with the figure I cut, and fancied that I made quite as good looking a man as my husband. My toilet once completed, it was not long before we were in the street, I doing my best to walk with a masculine gait, and to behave as if I had been accustomed to wear pantaloons all my life. I confess, that when it actually came to the point of appearing in public in this sort of attire, my heart began to fail me a little; but I was bent on going through with the thing, and so, plucking up courage, I strode along by the side of my husband with as unconcerned an air as it was possible for me to put on.

Presently we crossed over to a bar-room, which we found nearly filled with men smoking and drinking, and doing some pretty tall talking about the war, and the style in which the Yankees were going to be wiped out. To judge by the conversation, every man present was full of fight, and was burning with a furious desire to meet the enemy. I was too frightened and bewildered by the novelty of my situation to pay very close attention to all I saw and heard, but it flashed upon me that some of these loud-talking, hard-drinking, and blaspheming patriots were not so valiant, after all, as they professed to be. My after experiences fully confirmed my first impressions, that the biggest talkers are not always the best fighters, and that a good many men will say things over a glass of whiskey in a bar-room, who won't do a tenth part of what they say if they are once placed within smelling distance of gunpowder.

Camp Life

The style of conversation that was common in camp, and the kind of stories told around our fires at night, I will leave to the reader's imagination, hoping, however, that he or she has not imagination enough to compass anything so utterly vile. My favorite amusement was a game of cards, and I preferred this way of entertaining myself, and of beguiling the weary hours, to listening to anecdotes which could only debase my mind. Anything relating to military affairs, to social science, to the deeds of great men or women, or whatever else I could improve myself by listening to, I took great delight in. From my earliest recollection, however, I have had a thorough disgust for vulgarity of language and profanity, and my camp experiences only tended to increase my disgust at the blackguardism which many men are so fond of indulging in. The manner in which too many men are in the habit of referring to the other sex in conversation among themselves is, in my opinion, thoroughly despicable; and I really think that it would be morally and intellectually beneficial to many of my sex, especially those who are the victims of masculine viciousness, if they could only listen to some such conversations as I have been compelled to listen to, and learn how little respect or real regard of any kind men have for them. . . .

Many and many a time has the subject of women serving in the army as soldiers been discussed at the mess-tables and around the camp-fires; and officers, who have been in my company for days, and weeks, and months, have boasted, with very masculine positiveness, that no woman could deceive them, little suspecting that one was even then listening to them. I have sometimes been asked my opinion on the subject; but have generally answered evasively, without expressing, in very decided terms, my ideas one way or the other. Some of the men with whom I have been associated have spoken in respectful and even commendatory terms concerning women serving as soldiers; but too many have had nothing but vileness to utter on the subject. I can never forget, although I may forgive, the disgraceful language which some of these individuals have used with regard to this matter; and my experiences in the army will not have been in vain, even if they have taught me nothing more than the utter contemptibleness of some individuals, whom it would be a stretch of courtesy to call gentlemen.

The Pleasures of Fighting

The sensations of a soldier in the thick of a fight baffle description; and, as his hopes rise or sink with the ebb and flow of the battle, as he sees comrades falling about him dead and wounded, hears the sharp hiss of the bullets, the shrieking of the shells, the yells of the soldiers on each side as they smite each other, there is a positive enjoyment in the deadly perils of the occasion that nothing can equal. . . .

The second battle in which I participated—that at Ball's Bluff— was accompanied by every circumstance of horror; and although in the excitement of the moment, when every faculty of mind and body was at extreme tension, and I was only inspired with an intense eagerness to do my whole duty for my cause, I did not fully realize the enormities of such a slaughter as was involved in the defeat of the Federals at that place, [and] I have never been able to think of it without a shudder, notwithstanding that I have fought on more than one bloody field since. Such scenes, however, are inseparable from warfare, and those who take up arms must steel themselves against them.

[She describes the battle at some length.]

Shortly after the fight commenced, I took charge of a company which had lost all its officers, and I do not think that either my men or myself failed to do our full duty. Perhaps, if I had been compelled to manoeuvre my command in the open field, I might not have done it as skilfully as some others would, although I believe that I could have played the part of a captain quite as well as a good many of them who held regular commissions as commanders of companies, and a good deal better than some others who aspired to be officers before learning the first rudiments of their business, and without having the pluck to conduct themselves before the enemy in a manner at all correspondent to their braggart style of behavior when not smelling gunpowder under compulsion. In this battle, however, fighting as we were for the most part in the woods, there was little or no manoeuvring to be done, and my main duties were to keep the men together, and to set them an example. This latter I certainly did.

After the battle was over, the first lieutenant of the company which I was commanding came in and relieved me, stating that he had been taken prisoner, but had succeeded in making his escape in the confusion incident to the Federal defeat. I did not say anything, but had my very serious doubts as to the story which he told being the exact truth. He had a very sheepish look, as if he was ashamed of himself for playing a sneaking, cowardly trick; and I shall always believe that when the firing commenced, he found an opportunity to slink away to the rear for the purpose of getting out of the reach of danger.

I have seen a good many officers like this one, who were brave enough when strutting about in the streets of cities and villages, showing themselves off in their uniforms to the women, or when airing their authority in camp, by bullying the soldiers under them, but who were the most arrant cowards under fire, and who ought to have been court-marshalled and shot, instead of being permitted to disgrace their uniforms, and to demoralize their men, by their dastardly behavior when in the face of the enemy. My colored boy Bob was a better soldier than some of the white men who thought themselves immensely his superiors; and having possessed himself of a gun, he fought as well as he knew how, like the rest of us. When the enemy gave way, I could hear Bob yelling vociferously; and I confess that I was proud of [his] pluck and enthusiasm.

Harriet Tubman
(ca. 1820–1913)
U.S. ARMY

Harriet Tubman, best known for guiding escaping slaves north along the Underground Railroad and for her selfless charitable work with freedmen, served with the Union Army as a nurse, scout, spy, and soldier in South Carolina. She helped to plan and lead an Army raid into enemy territory on the Combahee River.

In January 1862, Massachusetts governor John Andrew arranged for Tubman to travel to Beaufort, South Carolina, to assist in the Union war effort—probably in the capacity of relief worker dealing with the hundreds of escaped slaves, or "contrabands," arriving at the Union camps. Voluntarily refusing soldiers' rations to avoid creating a perception among the freedmen that she received preferential treatment, and drawing no Union pay, she supported herself through purchase and resale of supplies, baking "gingerbread pies," and brewing root beer to sell to soldiers. Through her relief work, she developed a human intelligence network of "contra-bands" (freed slaves) and freedmen who knew the local area. She passed information on Confederate locations and troop movements to Generals Stevens, Sherman, and Hunter; in January 1863 she received $100 for scouting, which she and her scouts used to support themselves and to bribe informants.

In February 1863, Col. James Montgomery—a veteran of John Brown's guerrilla campaign in Kansas—took command of the Second South Carolina Volunteer Infantry, a regiment of freedmen. He and Tubman developed a close working relationship. In June he used intelligence about Confederate troop locations and naval mines that Tubman and her network of scouts provided to develop plans for a raid up the Combahee River.

On the night of June 1, 1863, Montgomery, Tubman, and three hundred men of the Second South Carolina penetrated twenty-five miles upriver into Confederate-held territory on two steam-powered gunboats. On June 2, encountering little opposition, they burned plantations and barns; destroyed rice mills and equipment; flooded fields to ruin summer crops; confiscated rice, corn, cotton, horses, and livestock worth thousands of dollars; destroyed the pontoon bridge at Combahee Ferry; and freed around seven hundred and fifty slaves.

In four years of service, Tubman received only twenty days' rations from the government, as well as small sums of money that she used primarily to pay scouts.

After the war Tubman spoke frequently about the inequity in black and white soldiers' pay. She also made numerous unsuccessful attempts to claim back pay and a pension. To support her family and to continue her resettlement and relief work on behalf of freedmen, she raised hundreds of dollars, borrowed funds, and told her story to journalists. The most famous set of interviews, published in 1869 by Sarah Bradford as *Scenes in the Life of Harriet Tubman*, is flawed by Bradford's sentimental style, hasty authorship, factual inaccuracies, exclusion of large parts of Tubman's story, imposition of her own cultural prejudices on the narrative, and use of stereotyped dialect to convey her subject's speech patterns. However, the book's commercial success enabled Tubman to pay down debts.

Despite her illiteracy, Tubman left a permanent record of her life—an important contribution to America's historical record. She is said to have had a remarkable memory; her description of the Combahee River Raid in an interview with journalist Emma P. Telford of Auburn, New York, nearly matches verbatim the description she gave to Bradford thirty-four years earlier. The excerpt below is taken from Telford's 1905 manuscript, now housed at the Cayuga Museum of Art and History.

They gave us Colonel Montgomery, one of John Brown's men, to command the expedition. And three gunboats and all colored soldiers and we found where the torpedoes was and saw that we could find another channel. When we went up the river in the morning, 'twas just about light, the fog was rising over the rice fields and the people was just doing their breakfast and was going out to the field.

I was in the forward boat where the Colonel and Captain and the colored man that was to tell us where the torpedoes was. The boats was a quarter of a mile apart, one after the other, and just about light, the Colonel blowed the whistle and stopped the boat and the Captain and a company of soldiers went ashore. About a quarter of an hour after he done blowed the whistle, and when the sun got clear, so that the people could see the boats, you could look over the rice fields, and see them coming to the boat from every direction. I never seen such a sight.

[Harriet "becomes convulsed with laughter" at the recollection.]

Some was getting their breakfasts, just taking their pots of rice right off the fire, and they'd put a cloth on top their head and set that on, rice a-smoking, young one hanging on behind, one hand around the mother's forehead to hold on, t'other hand digging into the rice pot, eating with all its might. Some had white blankets on their heads with their things done up in 'em and them that hadn't a pot of rice would have a child in their arms, sometimes one or two holding onto the mother's dress; some carrying two children one astride of the mother's neck, holding onto her forehead, and in her arms; appears like I never seen so many twins in my life. Some had bags on their backs with pigs in them; some had chickens tied by the legs; and so child squalling, chickens squawking, and pigs squealing, they all come running to the gun boats through the rice fields just like a procession.

Thinks I: these here puts me in mind of the children of Israel, coming out of Egypt. When they got to the shore, they'd get in the rowboat, and they'd start for the gunboat; but others would run and hold on so they couldn't leave the shore. They wasn't coming and they [ain't] nobody else come. The soldiers beat 'em on the hands but they wouldn't let go. They was afraid the gunboats [would] go off and leave them. At last the Captain looked at 'em and he called me. They called me "Moses Garrison" down there. Said he: "Moses, come here and speak to your people."

Well they wasn't my people any more than they was his'n,—only we was all negroes—'cause I didn't know any more about 'em than he did. So I went when he called me on the gunboat, and they the shore. They didn't know anything about me and I didn't know what to say. I looked at 'em for about two minutes, and then I sung to 'em.

Come from the East;
Come from the West;
Among all the glorious nations
This glorious one's the best;
Come along! Come along! Don't be alarmed,
For Uncle Sam is rich enough
To give you all a farm.

Then they throwed up their hands and began to rejoice and shout "Glory!" and the rowboats would push off.

I kept on a-singin' until all were brought on board. We got eight hundred people that day, and we tore up the railroad and fired the bridge. And we went up to a big house and catched two pigs and named the white pig Beauregard and the black pig Jeff Davis.

When we got back to Hilton Head in the morning, and landed there nine hundred contrabands, I took a hundred of the men to the recruiting officer and they enlisted in the army. Colonel Whittle said I ought to be paid for every soldier as much as a recruiting officer; but laws! I never got nothing.

Elizabeth Van Lew
(1818–1900)
UNION SPY

Elizabeth Van Lew, from Richmond, Virginia, led a network of white and African men and women who relayed messages regarding Confederate operations to Union generals and helped Union soldiers escape from Richmond prisons. Her spy network relied on invisible ink and coded messages. She placed literate freedwoman Mary Bowser in the household of Confederacy president Jefferson Davis. After the war, President Ulysses S. Grant, for whom Van Lew and her network had supplied vital intelligence during the war, appointed her postmaster of Richmond. She employed African Americans, and she has been credited with modernizing the Richmond postal system. She was dismissed from the position in 1877, possibly because of her gender and partisan politics. In her later years she continued to support women's rights and African American rights. According to David D. Ryan, editor of Van Lew's published diary, Van Lew buried her "Occasional Journal" for safekeeping. Just over half of the seven hundred pages survived. After the war, the War Department destroyed many records of her activities for her safety. The excerpts that follow are from the journal, published in 1996 as *A Yankee Spy in Richmond: The Civil War Diary of "Crazy Bet" Van Lew*.

Sept. 27, 1864

This lady was afterward taken from her home, and made to answer such questions as they pleased to propose, but, true to friendship, they learned nothing from her. Doswell had also other friends of the same family brought before him and forced to testify. One of them a clergyman of this city, the Rev. Philip B. Price, a man of superior excellence of character, was told when he could say and think of nothing to betray the mistress of this house, "to refresh his memory." The whole and sole object was to obtain by persecution the possession of their property, and imprison and badger a lady upwards of sixty years of age whose standing and character were impeachable, and who, without some sworn lie, they dared not molest. One who never did aught against their "dear young government," and was ever kind to their people, in whose home, for humanity's sake, the Confederate private ever found a friend. I shall ever remember the pale face of this dear lady, her feeble health and occasional illness from anxiety; her dread of Castle Thunder and Salisbury, for her arrest was constantly spoken of and frequently reported on the street. . . .

Our true hearts grew brave. Love of our country in its trials absorbed our being; enthusiasm lightened gloom. Fine patriotism principles and strengthens character. I have known the best of men feel their lives in danger from their partners in business & from their sons-in-law, who felt differently from them. Some aged parents endured much from their children who were disloyal. Ministers lived ever under a siege of terror. I was afraid to even pass the prison. I have had occasion to stop near it, when I dared not look up at the windows. Have turned to speak to a friend and found a detective at my elbow. Strange faces could sometimes be seen peeping around the columns and pillars of the back portico, & I can name gentlemen, some of our oldest and best citizens, who trembled when their door bell rang, fearing arrest.

Towards the close of the war Jeff Davis was earnest to have a writ of Habeas Corpus again suspended and to be clothed with fullest power. Visitors were watched. When the cold wind would blow on the darkest & stormiest night, Union people would visit one another. With shutters closed & curtains pinned together, how have we been startled at the barking of a dog and drawn nearer together, the pallor coming over our faces & the blood rushing to our hearts, as we would perhaps be tracing on a map [General William Tecumseh] Sherman's progress and Sherman's brilliant raids, or glorying in our Federal leaders. Then to follow the innocent visitor to the door, to lower the gas as, with muffled face, they said good night & the last words were often, "Do you think I am watched?" Such was our life.

Belle Boyd

(1844–1900)

CONFEDERATE SPY

Maria Isabella "Belle" Boyd, from Martinsburg, Virginia (now West Virginia), began her work as a Confederate spy at the age of seventeen. Following a skirmish at nearby Falling Waters on July 2, 1861, Federal troops occupied Martinsburg. On July 4, Belle Boyd shot and killed a drunken Union soldier who had insulted her mother. Boyd frequented the Union camps, gathering information and acting as a courier. Eavesdropping through a peephole, she discovered the military plans for units under the command of Union Maj. Gen. Nathaniel Banks and rode fifteen miles on horseback during the night to inform Confederate Maj. Gen. Thomas J. "Stonewall" Jackson, quartered nearby in the Shenandoah Valley. Several weeks later, when she realized Jackson was about to attack Front Royal, she ran onto the battlefield to provide the general with last-minute information about the Union troop dispositions. Jackson captured the town and acknowledged her contribution and her bravery in a personal note. Boyd was arrested at least six times, but managed to avoid incarceration until July 29, 1862, when she was finally imprisoned in Old Capitol Prison in Washington DC. In 1864 she sailed for England, where she began writing her memoir and performed on stage. She returned to America in 1866, a widow and mother, and lectured on her war experiences, billing her show as "The Perils of a Spy" and herself as "Cleopatra of the Secession." The following are excerpts from her 1865 memoir *Belle Boyd: In Camp and Prison*.

> The village was at their mercy, and consequently entitled to their forebearance; and it would at least have been more dignified in them had they been content to enjoy their almost bloodless conquest with moderation; but, whatever might have been the intentions of their officers, they had not the inclination, or they lacked the authority, to control the turbulence of their men. . . .

Those hateful strains of "Yankee Doodle" resounded in every street, with an accompaniment of cheers, shouts, and imprecations.

Whiskey now began to flow freely.... The doors of our houses were dashed in; our rooms were forcibly entered by soldiers who might literally be termed "mad drunk."

[Boyd describes the ransacking of homes, the shots fired through windows, "chairs and tables hurled into the street." When the soldiers reach Boyd's house, they begin a mad search for rebel flags; however, Boyd's maid has already beat them by tearing down the flag from upstairs and burning it.]

They had brought with them a large Federal flag, which they were now preparing to hoist over our roof in token of our submission to their authority; but to this my mother would not consent. Stepping forward with a firm step, she said, very quietly, but resolutely, "Men, every member of my household will die before the flag shall be raised over us."

Upon this, one of the soldiers, thrusting himself forward, addressed my mother and myself in language as offensive as it is possible to conceive. I could stand it no longer; my indignation was roused beyond control; my blood was literally boiling in my veins; I drew out my pistol and shot him. He was carried away mortally wounded, and soon after expired.

Our persecutors now left the house, and we were in hopes we had got rid of them, when one of the servants, rushing in, cried out— "Oh, missus, missus, dere gwine to burn de house down; dere pilin' de stuff ag'in it! Oh, if massa were back!"

The prospect of being burned alive naturally terrified us, and, as a last resource, I contrived to get a message conveyed to a Federal officer in command. He exerted himself with effect, and had the incendiaries arrested before they could execute their horrible purpose.

In the mean time it had been reported at head-quarters that I had shot a Yankee soldier, and great was the indignation at first felt and expressed against me.

[Boyd explains that a commanding officer arrived to investigate, questioned all the witnesses, and finally declared that Boyd had "done perfectly right."]

Sentries were now placed around the house, and Federal officers called every day to inquire if we had any complaint to make of their behavior. It was in this way that I became acquainted with so many of them[—]an acquaintance "the rebel spy" did not fail to turn to account on more than one occasion.

• • •

General Shields [Union Army] introduced me to the officers of his staff, two of whom were young Irishmen; and to one of these, Captain K., I am indebted for some very remarkable effusions, some withered flowers, and last, not least, for a great deal of very important information, which was carefully transmitted to my countrymen. I must avow the flowers and the poetry were comparatively valueless in my eyes; but let Captain K. be consoled: these were days of war, not of love, and there are still other ladies in the world besides the "rebel spy."

The night before the departure of General Shields, who was about, as he informed us, to "whip" Jackson, a council of war was held in what had formerly been my aunt's drawing room. Immediately above this was a bed-chamber, containing a closet, through the floor of which I observed a hole had been bored, whether with a view to espionage or not I have never been able to ascertain. It occurred to me, however, that I might turn the discovery to account; and as soon as the council of war had assembled, I stole softly up stairs, and lying down on the floor of the closet, applied my ear to the hole, and found, to my great joy, I could distinctly hear the conversation that was passing below.

The council prolonged their discussion for some hours; but I remained motionless and silent until the proceedings were brought to a conclusion, at one o'clock in the morning. As soon as the coast was clear I crossed the court-yard, and made the best of my way to my own room, and took down in cipher everything I had heard which seemed to me of any importance.

I felt convinced that to rouse a servant, or make any disturbance at that hour, would excite the suspicions of the Federals by whom I was surrounded; accordingly I went straight to the stables myself, saddled my horse, and galloped away in the direction of the mountains.

Fortunately I had about me some passes which I had from time to time procured for Confederate soldiers returning south, and which, owing to various circumstances, had never been put in requisition. They now, however, proved invaluable; for I was twice brought to a stand-still by the challenge of the Federal sentries, and who would inevitably have put a period to my adventurous career had they not been beguiled by my false passport. Once clear of the chain of sentries, I dashed on unquestioned across fields and along roads, through fens and marshes, until, after a scamper of about fifteen miles, I found myself at the door of Mr. M.'s house. All was still and quiet: not a light was to be seen. I did not lose a moment in springing from my horse; and, running up the steps, I knocked at the door with such vehemence that the house re-echoed with the sound.

It was not until I had repeated my summons, at intervals of a few seconds, for some time, that I heard the response, "Who is there?" given in a sharp voice from the window above.

"It is I."

"But who are you? What is your name?"

"Belle Boyd. I have important intelligence to communicate to Colonel Ashby: is he here?"

"No; but wait a minute: I will come down."

The door was opened, and Mrs. M. drew me in, and exclaimed in a tone of astonishment—"My dear, where did you come from? and how on earth did you get here?"

"Oh, I forced the sentries," I replied, "and here I am; but I have no time to tell you the how, and the why, and the wherefore. I must see Colonel Ashby without the loss of a minute: tell me where he is to be found."

Upon hearing that his party was a quarter of a mile farther up the wood, I turned to depart in search of them, and was in the very act of remounting when a door on my right was thrown open, and revealed Colonel Ashby himself, who could not conceal his surprise at seeing me standing before him.

"Good God! Miss Belle, is this you? Where did you come from? Have you dropped from the clouds? or am I dreaming?"

I first convinced him he was wide awake, and that my presence was substantial and of the earth—not a visionary emanation from the world of spirits—then, without further circumlocution, I proceeded to narrate all I had overheard in the closet, of which I have before made mention. I gave him the cipher, and started on my return.

I arrived safely at my aunt's house, after a two hours' ride, in the course of which I "ran the blockade" of a sleeping sentry, who awoke to the sound of my horse's hoofs just in time to see me disappear round an abrupt turning, which shielded me from the bullet he was about to send after me. Upon getting home, I unsaddled my horse and "turned in." ...

A few days afterwards General Shields marched south, laying a trap, as he supposed, to catch "poor old Jackson and his demoralized army," leaving behind him, to occupy Front Royal, one squadron of cavalry, one field battery, and the 1st Maryland Regiment of Infantry, under command of Colonel Kenly; Major Tyndale, of Philadelphia, being appointed Provost-Marshal.

Dr. Mary Edwards Walker
(1832–1919)
U.S. ARMY

Mary Edwards Walker grew up in a progressive household in Oswego, New York. Her parents valued women's education, and the family home was a stop on the Underground Railroad. She earned a medical degree at Syracuse Medical College in 1855 and continued there for advanced study. She wrote prolifically and contributed to the reform journal *The Sibyl: A Review of the Tastes, Errors and Fashions of Society*, where in 1859 she advocated for women to serve as soldiers in wartime. In 1861, after the Second Battle of Bull Run overwhelmed Washington hospitals with wounded, she filed for divorce from an unfaithful husband and went to the capital to request an appointment as an assistant surgeon for the Union Army. Secretary of War Simon Cameron denied her initial request. Undaunted, she made the rounds of Washington relief hospitals and convinced Dr. J. N. Green of the Indiana Hospital to allow her to serve as his assistant. She wrote about her war experiences in an unpublished series of sketches, "Incidents Connected with the Army," from which the following excerpts are taken.

As I desired to act in the capacity of an assistant surgeon in the army, I visited hospitals on my arrival in Washington for the purpose of finding a vacancy. Dr. Green was at that time the only medical officer in that hospital. He stated that his predecessor had died from over work, there being not a sufficient number of surgeons in the army so that he could have an assistant. He stated that he had himself applied to Surgeon General Finley for an assistant in the hospital, but had been answered that there was none that he could give him. I asked him to write to the surgeon general requesting him to appoint me as his assistant. This he did and I took the paper to the office.

[Walker delivers the letter in person and presents her credentials; Finley returns them and says he cannot appoint a woman.]

As I had heard Dr. Green speak of Assistant Surgeon General Wood, I inquired for him, showed him my credentials, and stated to him that I had brought a letter from Dr. Green, and asked to be appointed. After Dr. Wood had read my credentials he said to me that if the surgeon general had been out and he had been acting that day he would have appointed me, and he expressed his regrets that the surgeon general had not been delayed beyond that hour.

I returned to the Patent Office Hospital and reported what had been said, and then told Dr. Green that I would act as his assistant without any appointment. . . .

I urged [Dr. Green to go out for a short break] now, saying that I would attend to all the patients in his absence; and it sometimes occurred that the hospital steward accompanied me with the book to write down the condition of the cases every day as explained by the surgeon, and the prescription that was given to each individual case, as must be done in a large hospital, as it is impossible for a physician to remember every individual case where there are a hundred to be seen every day. There were times when I examined and prescribed and continued the treatment of these hundred patients. . . .

[Dr. Green] told me that he would give me a part of his salary. I replied that he needed all that he had for his wife and children, and that I should not accept of any, but I would be his assistant surgeon just the same as though I had been appointed.

[During her tenure at Indiana Hospital, Walker encounters Superintendent of Army Nurses Dorothea Dix.]

I was somewhat amused when Dorothy [*sic*] Dix visited the hospital. . . . I did not understand at that time why she seemed in such a troubled mood about something when she first saw me but afterwards learned that a part of her mission was to try to keep young and good looking women out of the hospital.

She had stated that no woman less than thirty years old ought to be allowed to go into a hospital where there were soldier patients but as she could not possibly have any control over myself she walked through the hospital in a manner that it is hard to describe. When she saw a patient who was too ill to arrange the clothing on his cot if it became disarranged and a foot was exposed she turned her head the other way seeming not to see the condition while I was so disgusted with such sham modesty that I hastened to arrange the soldier's bed clothing if I chanced to be near when no nurses were to do this duty. I was not able to understand and am not to the present day of what use any one can be who professes to work for a cause and then allows sham modesty to prevent them from doing little services that chance to come in their way.

[She goes on to call Dix "a good hearted woman" and notes that the country should be grateful to her for her work in improving conditions in "lunatic asylums." Dix is not the only member of the military medical establishment with whose ideas of treatment Walker disagrees.]

There were cases where [soldiers] had been wounded in the arm or leg, and in the most pitiful manner that made it very difficult for me to suppress my emotions, they would ask me if that leg would have to come off, if that arm would have to come off, telling me that the ward surgeon said it would have to come off, and that they would rather die than lose a leg or lose an arm, whichever the case happened to be. I did not wish to be unprofessional and say anything to any other medical officer's patients that would seem like giving advice outside of a council; but as I had a little experience and observation regarding the inability of some of the ward surgeons to diagnose properly, and truthfully I considered that I had a higher duty than came under the head of medical etiquette.

I had assisted in an operation where there was amputation of an arm where it was no more necessary than to amputate anybody's arm that had never been injured. The two surgeons in the ward who had decided to have that arm amputated when there had been only a slight flesh wound, seemed to me to take this opportunity to amputate for the purpose of their own practice, which was utterly cruel: but knowing that if I gave my opinion against amputating that I would be debarred from entering one of the largest hospitals in Washington, I gave antiseptics and the arm was removed.

I then made up my mind that it was the last case that would ever occur if it was in my power to prevent such cruel loss of limbs, therefore I made it my business, when visiting hospitals, whenever I found that there were contemplated operations, and a complaint from a soldier that a decision had been made to remove a limb, I casually asked to see it, and in almost every instance I saw amputation was not only unnecessary, but to me it seemed wickedly cruel. I would then swear the soldier not to repeat anything that I told him, and then I would tell him that no one was obliged to submit to an amputation unless he chose to do so, that his limbs belonged to himself. I then instructed him to protest against amputation, and that if the physicians insisted upon it that if he had never used swearing words to swear and declare that if they forced him to have an operation that he would never rest after his recovery until he had shot them dead. I need not say that secrecy regarding what I had told to the soldier was kept and that my advice was followed and that many a man today has for it the perfect and good use of his limbs who would not have had but for my advice, to say nothing about the millions of dollars in pensions that would have been paid without all the suffering, had I not decided it my solemn duty to the soldiers instead of carrying out etiquette towards my medical and surgical brothers.

[This is confirmed after the war by written testimony of several soldiers whose arms and legs were saved as a result of Walker's advice. Because the mortality rate after amputation was so high—up to 60 percent in amputations below the knee and 80 percent in cases of amputation at the hip— Walker probably also saved lives as well as limbs.

Through 1862, Walker continues to assist in surgeries and wound dressings at Washington DC hospitals. She also engages in relief work with soldiers and their families, developing a nationwide reputation for her compassion and devotion. In March she completes a course in new treatments at the Hygeio-Therapeutic College in New York City. That fall, she returns to Washington. Casualties from the Battle of Antietam and actions in northern Virginia have overwhelmed hospitals in the town of Warrenton, near the front lines and occupied at this time by Union forces. Walker acquires a pass to serve there, where she finds appalling conditions and such a severe shortage of supplies that she is forced to rent a single two-quart basin from a local woman for a dollar and to tear up her own nightgown for towels. Later she goes to headquarters to request permission to move a number of the patients to Washington, where they can be treated more effectively. They set out on November 15, 1862.]

General Burnside gave me written authority to go with them, and that all persons should afford me all facilities that I required.

The condition of the army at this time was such that raids from the opposing forces were expected at any time between there and Alexandria. Seven car-loads, but one of which was a passenger car, were loaded up. Some of the not very sick were placed upon the tops of the cars, as there was not room enough in the freight cars for them all. In the passenger cars were some brave persons who had been down to the army . . . and others whose business in running to Washington I was not informed concerning all were specially anxious to get out of danger. Among these was Henry Wilson, then a member of the House of Representatives at Washington.

When we had proceeded but a short distance the train stopped at a barren place. . . . While we were waiting I went to the cars, that were so high that it was difficult to get into, to see how my patients were, all of whom were as comfortable as they could expect, as they expressed themselves, with the exception of two. As I approached one I saw that he was near the other shore, and asked him his name, which I wrote down, but before I could get anything more except his regiment, he had passed to the beyond. Another was so far gone that he could not speak plainly, and when I asked his name he could barely speak the same and I guessed at the rest and told him to press my hand if I got it right. He did so.

[Walker then figures out before the soldier dies that he came from Ohio. She documents the soldiers' deaths with the War Department, which will enable the family of the second soldier to learn of his death and to successfully file a pension claim nearly two decades later.]

After quite a long stop I inquired what they were staying there for, then I found that there was not an officer on board, or any body who had any authority whatever on the train that was left except myself, and I directed the engineer to proceed to Washington, which he did as soon as the directions were given. I could not help suppressing a smile at the thought of his stating that he was waiting for orders, and that in reality I was then military conductor of the train that bore one of the law-makers of the nation not only, but its citizens and its helpless defenders. Since then it has been with some pride that I have recalled the fact that I have been the conductor of a train that had conveyed the future Vice President of the United States.

After the Battle of Fredericksburg, surgeons whom Walker had assisted tried, again unsuccessfully, to secure an appointment and commission for her. She made her own uniform and continued providing medical care in hospitals and evacuation points in and around Washington DC, often at her own expense.

In the fall of 1863 she traveled to the battlefield hospitals near Chickamauga, where Union forces had suffered a defeat and 16,000 casualties. Her work there earned the admiration of General George H. Thomas. In 1864 she persuaded Congressman (and former brigadier general) John Franklin Farnsworth to recommend her appointment to Assistant Surgeon General Wood, long one of her supporters. Wood ordered Walker to Chattanooga for a medical board evaluation of her skills. The evaluating officers, hostile to contract surgeons and women physicians, dismissed her qualifications. They questioned her only on women's health issues, derided her answers to their questions, and ignored her previous wartime service.

General Thomas overruled the board's recommendation to

deny her appointment. He commissioned her as an assistant surgeon at the lieutenant grade and assigned her to the 52nd Ohio Volunteers at Fort Gordon, Georgia, under the supervision of Col. Daniel McCook Jr. McCook sent Walker on humanitarian and espionage missions across Confederate lines.

On April 10, 1864, Confederate soldiers captured Walker on one of her missions behind Confederate lines. Suspecting her of espionage, they transferred her to Richmond's infamous Castle Thunder prison. She slept on an infested mattress in a poorly ventilated room, where gas lighting damaged her eyes so that she would never again perform surgery. She nearly starved on limited rations of cornbread, bacon, and pea or rice soup. She was allowed only thirty minutes of exercise in the prison yard each day. Guards treated her poorly, and Richmond newspapers ridiculed her. She was exchanged for a Confederate surgeon on August 12, 1864.

After her release, Walker returned south to treat wounded from the Battle of Atlanta. Afterward she served as surgeon in charge of the Female Prison in Louisville, Kentucky, and as director of the Refugee House in Clarksville, Tennessee. Her military service officially ended on June 15, 1865.

President Andrew Johnson awarded Walker the Medal of Honor for "valuable service to the government" and devotion with "patriotic zeal to the sick and wounded soldiers, both in the field and hospitals, to the detriment of her own health," and for enduring "hardships as a prisoner of war four months in a Southern prison while acting as a Contract-Surgeon."

After the war Walker wrote and lectured on women's rights, petitioned Congress to secure military pensions for Civil War nurses, and ran a tuberculosis sanitarium. She received a pension half that of her male peers. In 1917 the War Department changed the criteria for the Medal of Honor and rescinded her award, along with those awarded to William "Buffalo Bill" Cody and 909 other men. She refused to return the medal, and wore it until her death two years later.

In 1977 President Jimmy Carter restored Walker's award, citing her "distinguished gallantry, self-sacrifice, patriotism, dedication and unflinching loyalty to her country, despite the apparent discrimination because of her sex." To date, she remains the only woman so recognized.

Cornelia Hancock
(1840–1927)
U.S. Army

Cornelia Hancock, a Quaker, served as a nurse with the Union Army. After the Battle of Gettysburg, her brother-in-law, Dr. Henry T. Child, requested her service as a volunteer nurse to help with those wounded in the fighting. Dorothea Dix turned her offer of service down because she was young and attractive, but Hancock went anyway. She spent the rest of the war in nursing, except for a short period working with escaped African American slaves in Washington DC. The excerpts below are from her letters home, first published posthumously in 1937 as *South after Gettysburg: Letters of Cornelia Hancock*.

> Gettysburg, Pa. July 7th, 1863.
>
> My dear cousin
>
> I am very tired tonight; have been on the field all day.... There are no words in the English language to express the sufferings I witnessed today. The men lie on the ground; their clothes have been cut off them to dress their wounds; they are half naked, have nothing but hard-tack to eat.... I was the first woman who reached the Second Corps after the three days fight at Gettysburg. I was in that Corps all day, not another woman within a half mile.... [I] received nothing but the greatest politeness from even the lowest private. You can tell Aunt that there is every opportunity for "secesh" sympathizers to do a good work among the butternuts; we have lots of them here suffering fearfully. To give you some idea of the extent and numbers of the wounds, four surgeons, none of whom were idle fifteen minutes at a time, were busy all day amputating legs and arms. I gave to every man that had a leg or arm off a gill of wine, to every

wounded in Third Division, one glass of lemonade, some bread and preserves and tobacco—as much as I am opposed to the latter, for they need it very much, they are so exhausted.

I feel very thankful that this was a successful battle; the spirit of the men is so high that many of the poor fellows said today, "What is an arm or leg to whipping Lee out of Penn." I would get on first rate if they would not ask me to write to their wives; *that* I cannot do without crying, which is not pleasant to either party. I do not mind the sight of blood, have seen limbs taken off and was not sick at all.

Gettysburg—July 8th, 1863

My dear sister

We have been two days on the field; go out about eight and come in about six—go in ambulances or army buggies.... I feel assured I shall never feel horrified at anything that may happen to me hereafter. There is a great want of surgeons here; there are hundreds of brave fellows, who have not had their wounds dressed since the battle.... Get the Penn Relief to send clothing here; there are many men without anything but a shirt lying in poor shelter tents, calling on God to take them from this world of suffering; in fact the air is rent with petitions to deliver them from their sufferings.

[She discusses here specifics of supplies needed and provisions that they have been able to feed the wounded.]

It took nearly five days for some three hundred surgeons to perform the amputations that occurred here, during which time the rebels lay in a dying condition without their wounds being dressed or scarcely any food. If the rebels did not get severely punished for this battle, then I am no judge. We have but one rebel in our camp now; he says he never fired his gun if he could help it, and, therefore, we treat him first rate....

I could stand by and see a man's head taken off I believe— you get so used to it here.... William says I am very popular here as I am such a contrast to some of the office-seeking women who swarm around hospitals. I am black as an Indian and dirty as a pig and as well as I ever was in my life—have a nice bunk and about twelve feet square. I have a bed that is made of four crotch sticks and some sticks laid across and pine boughs laid on that with blankets on top. It is equal to any mattress ever made.

• • •

I received, a few days ago, a Silver Medal worth twenty dollars. The inscription on one side is "Miss Cornelia Hancock, presented by the wounded soldiers 3rd Division 2nd Army Corps." On the other side is "Testimonial of regard for ministrations of mercy to the wounded soldiers at Gettysburg, Pa.—July 1863."

There have been in the Corps Hospital I suppose some thirty women, and it seems I am the favored one in the lot. Several, since they have seen mine, have started a subscription for two other ladies. Most of the ladies are dead heads completely.

City Point, 1st Div. 2nd Corps Hospital

July 18th, 1864.

To Joanna Dickerson, Pres. Of Ladies Aid, Hancock's Bridge, Salem Co., N.J.

My dear friends:

At Fredericksburg we received the wounded from the [Battle of the] Wilderness. There was more suffering there for want of food than I ever witnessed anywhere. From Fredericksburg we went to Port Royal. Had the base of operations there for a short time only when all moved to White House. There the wounded were brought from the fight upon the North Anna River and it was another dreadful scene. I joined the train which had been three days coming from the field having had no attention except what could be given to them lying in the ambulances. . . .

I was with the San[itary] Com[mission] train and in the wagon were stores plenty. Mrs. Lee in company with me cooked them a bountiful meal and I took water from the river and washed the face and hands of all in our Div[ision] train. To wash one's face and hands when on duty is considered a luxury at any time, but no one can know the relief one feels in using water after a three days' march, especially when wounded. Some men you could hardly recognize if you knew them intimately.

There has been no day's work that I have done since this campaign that gave such extreme relief as cleansing those poor fellows' faces. All were cases of severe wounds. At dark night while it was raining the long train moved over a newly constructed bridge and loaded the men in transports. In the second Corps hospital the wounded continued rapidly to arrive until they laid out in the open field without any shelter. Here I dressed more wounds than in all my experience before. There were not surgeons near enough who were willing to stay in the sun and attend to the men and it was too awful to leave them uncared for. Just for one moment consider a slivered arm having been left three days, without dressing and the person having ridden in an army wagon for two days with very little food. They mostly arrived at night when all the ladies would fill their stores and feed them as they came in. They would then remain in the ambulance until morning when probably no shelter could be procured for them and here they lay in the scorching sun during 1/2 the day. It was at this time there was such crying need to dress their wounds, some of which had not been opened for thirty-six hours. Such tired, agonized expressions no pen can describe. By the time one set of men were got in and got comfortable another set would arrive, and so it continued night and day for about two weeks. At that time there was a very good opportunity to make a visit to the hospital up at the extreme front. There I stayed for a week, the men were then in the rifle-pits and if they moved out to get a drink of water were shot in the action. I saw them as soon as they were wounded but the custom is here to operate upon the wound and immediately send them to the rear.

[The Sanitary Commission train then attempts to relocate, but it is delayed a week waiting for a cavalry escort.]

The monotony was broken upon the 20th of June by the Rebels planting a battery upon a hill and shelling our train for six hours, in which time it behooved all to make the best of the situation and keep out of the shells as best we could. One shell struck in the rear of the carriage I was in and one rifled cannon came between Mrs. Husbands and myself while we were walking along the beach. However, suffice it to say no lives were lost in our train except three horses.

Susie King Taylor
(1848–1912)
U.S. Army

In April 1862, fourteen-year-old slave Susie King and an uncle went aboard a Federal gunboat near Savannah and gained their freedom, becoming "contraband of war." Her uncle joined the First South Carolina Volunteers, a black regiment led by a white colonel. Educated in two secret schools taught by black women in Savannah, King found herself serving not only as unit laundress but also as a valued literacy teacher for off-duty troops. She nursed wounded when the First South Carolina Volunteers and the Fifty-Fourth Massachusetts Volunteers, one of the Union Army's first official African American regiments, engaged in guerrilla actions along the swampy southern Atlantic coast. In 1862 she married Edward [King], a sergeant in the First South Carolina Volunteers. After the war, King settled in Savannah and opened a private school, where she taught children during the day and adult freedmen at night. Edward died unexpectedly in 1866, leaving King pregnant with their first child; through 1869 she supported her family on her teaching salary, receiving no freedmen's relief funds. In the 1870s she moved to Boston, remarried, and served in the Women's Relief Corps. In 1902 she privately published her memoir, *A Black Woman's Civil War Memoirs: Reminiscences of My Life in Camp with the 33rd U.S. Colored Troops, Late 1st South Carolina Volunteers*, from which the excerpt below is taken.

The first colored troops did not receive any pay for eighteen months, and the men had to depend wholly on what they received from the commissary, established by General Saxton. A great many of these men had large families, and as they had no money to give them, their wives were obliged to support themselves and [their] children by washing for the officers of the gunboats and the soldiers, and making cakes and pies which they sold to the boys in camp. Finally, in 1863, the government decided to give them half pay, but the men would not accept this. They wanted "full pay" or nothing. They preferred rather to give their services to the state, which they did until 1864, when the government granted them full pay, with all the back pay due.I remember hearing Captain Heasley telling his company, one day, "Boys, stand up for your full pay! I am with you, and so are all the officers." This captain was from Pennsylvania, and was a very good man, all the men liked him. . . .

I taught a great many of the comrades in Company F to read and write, when they were off duty. Nearly all were anxious to learn. My husband taught some also when it was convenient for him. I was very happy to know my efforts were successful in camp, and also felt grateful for the appreciation of my services. I gave my services willingly for four years and three months without receiving a dollar. I was glad, however, to be allowed to go with the regiment, to care for the sick and afflicted comrades. . . . . .

Outside of the fort [Fort Wagner, the site of a significant engagement in which the First South Carolina and 54th Massachusetts Volunteers sustained heavy casualties] were many skulls lying about; I have often moved them one side out of the path. The comrades and I would have quite a debate as to which side the men fought on. Some thought that they were the skulls of our boys; others thought they were the enemy's; but as there was no definite way to know, it was never decided which could lay claim to them. They were a gruesome sight, those fleshless heads and grinning jaws, but by this time I had become accustomed to worse things and did not feel as I might have earlier in my camp life.

It seems strange how our aversion to seeing suffering is overcome in war,—how we are able to see the most sickening sights, such as men with their limbs blown off and mangled by the deadly shells, without a shudder; and instead of turning away, how we hurry to assist in alleviating their pain, bind up their wounds, and press the cool water to their parched lips, with feelings only of sympathy and pity.

Cathy Williams
(ca. 1844–n.d.)
U.S. ARMY

The Eighth Indiana Volunteer Infantry Regiment impressed seventeen-year-old freedwoman Cathy Williams into service as a cook and laundress during the 1861 Union occupation of Jefferson City, Missouri. Williams accompanied the regiment in the Battle of Pea Ridge and the Red River Campaign. She dressed as a man and joined the segregated Thirty-Eighth Infantry Regiment— later known as the "Buffalo Soldiers"—on November 15, 1866, for a three-year enlistment. She contracted smallpox soon after her enlistment, recovered, and was ordered to New Mexico. As a result of the smallpox, the heat, or the effects of years of marching, she began to require frequent hospitalization. The post surgeon discovered that she was a woman. Her commanding officer, Capt. Charles E. Clarke, discharged her from the Army on October 14, 1868. Although she is presumed to have been illiterate, she told her story to a reporter who published it in the January 2, 1876, issue of the *St. Louis Daily Times*.

> My father was a free man, but my mother a slave, belonging to William Johnson, a wealthy farmer who lived at the time I was born near Independence, Jackson County, Missouri. While I was a small girl my master and family moved to Jefferson City. My master died there and when the war broke out and the United States soldiers came to Jefferson City they took me and other colored folks with them to Little Rock. Col. Benton of the 13th army corps was the officer that carried us off. I did not want to go. He wanted me to cook for the officers, but I had always been a house girl and did not know how to cook. I learned to cook after going to Little Rock and was with the army at the battle of Pea Ridge. Afterwards the command moved over various portions of Arkansas and Louisiana. I saw the soldiers burn lots of cotton and was at Shreveport when the rebel gunboats were captured and burned on Red River. We afterwards went to New Orleans, then by way of the Gulf to Savannah, Georgia, then to Macon and other places in the South. Finally I was sent to Washington City,

and at the time Gen. Sheridan made his raids in the Shenandoah Valley I was cook and washwoman for his staff. I was sent from Virginia to some place in Iowa and afterwards to Jefferson Barracks, where I remained some time. You will see by this paper that on the 15th day of November 1866, I enlisted in the United States army at St. Louis, in the Thirty-eighth United States Infantry, company A, Capt. Charles E. Clarke commanding.

I ENLISTED TO SERVE THREE YEARS!

The regiment I joined wore the Zouave uniform and only two persons, a cousin and a particular friend, members of the regiment, knew that I was a woman. They never "blowed" on me. They were partly the cause of my joining the army. Another reason was I wanted to make my own living and not be dependent on relations or friends. Soon after I joined the army, I was taken with the small-pox and was sick at a hospital across the river from St. Louis, but as soon as I got well I joined my company in New Mexico. I was

A GOOD SOLDIER.

As that paper says, I was never put in the guard house, no bayonet was ever put to my back. I carried my musket and did guard and other duties while in the army, but finally I got tired and wanted to get off. I played sick, complained of pains in my side, and rheumatism in my knees. The post surgeon found out I was a woman and I got my discharge. The men all wanted to get rid of me after they found out I was a woman. Some of them acted real bad to me. After leaving the army I went to Pueblo, Colorado, where I made money by cooking and washing. I got married while there, but my husband was no account. He stole my watch and chain, a hundred dollars in money and my team of horses and wagon. I had him arrested and put in jail, and then I came here. I like this town. I know all the good people here, and I expect to get rich yet. . . . I shall never live in the states again. You see I've got a good sewing machine and I get washing to do and clothes to make. I want to get along and not be a burden to my friends or relatives.

Mary Reynolds
(n.d.–n.d.)
U.S. LIGHTHOUSE SERVICE

Mississippi governor Albert Gallatin Brown appointed Mary Reynolds, a woman with a "large family of orphan children," keeper of the Biloxi Light on April 11, 1854, at an annual salary of four hundred dollars. Reynolds shifted her allegiance to the Confederacy after the war began. She remained at her post even though the citizens of Biloxi extinguished the light to prevent Union ships from using it for navigation. She continued to serve as lighthouse keeper until 1866. The following excerpt is from a letter she wrote to Governor Pettus, held in the Mississippi Department of Archives and History; his reply, if any, has not been preserved.

Biloxi, Nov. 26th, 1861

To His Excellency Gov. Pettus

Dear Sir,

With the request that you will pardon my informality in my letter, I beg to inform you that I am a woman entirely unprotected. I have for several years past been the Keeper of the Light House at Biloxi, the small salary accruing from which has helped me to support a large family of orphaned children.

[She explains that the children, orphans of her deceased relatives, are heirs to property in Maryland, but that due to the war the executor of their estate is unlikely to send the yearly stipend for their support.]

I do not know if my salary as the Keeper of the Light House will be continued.

On the 18th of June last, the citizens of Biloxi ordered the light to be extinguished which was immediately done and shortly after others came and demanded the key of the Light Tower which has ever since remained in the hands of a Company calling themselves "Home Guards."

At the time they took possession of the Tower it contained valuable Oil, the quantity being marked on my books. I have on several occasions seen disreputable characters taking out the oil in bottles. Today they carried away a large stone jug capable of containing several gallons. They may take also in the night as no one here appeared to have any authority over them.

Their Captain, J. Fewell, is also Mayor of the City of Biloxi, and if you would have the kindness to write him orders to have the oil measured and placed under my charge at the dwelling of the Light House I would be very grateful to you for so doing.

I write to you merely as a Light Keeper believing that injustice has been and is still [being done] here. . . .

I have ever faithfully performed the duties of Light Keeper in storm and sunshine attending it. I ascended the Tower at and after the last destructive storm [in 1860] when men stood appalled at the danger I encountered.

After the Light was extinguished, I wrote to New Orleans and offered my services to make Volunteer Clothing [for Confederate soldiers]. Received a large bale of heavy winter clothing which I made during the hottest season of the year working day and night to have them done in time.

I do not speak thus of myself through vanity or idle boasting but to assure you that I have tried to do my share in our great and holy cause of freedom.

3

The Spanish-American War

"Upon Our Shoulders Rests a Great Responsibility"

The Cuban mosquito that bit Rose Heavren transferred an incurable virus into her bloodstream. The virus traveled to her lymph nodes and began to replicate. Overwork and the limited Army diet might have caused the fatigue and malaise she felt later in the week. But when the chills, high fever, and severe muscular pain began, the chief nurse at the Army yellow fever hospital in Havana must have suspected that she had contracted the very disease she had been fighting.

Heavren hated to watch the young soldiers in her care die. Through a short week of severe illness, they remained conscious and free of delirium. Their livers released bile that yellowed their skin and the whites of their eyes. In a matter of days, some began to recover. But others developed hemorrhagic fever, marked by internal bleeding and black vomit. If the patient lost enough blood and fluid to cause convulsions, then shock, organ failure, and death followed in a matter of hours.

Heavren survived. She returned to her duties.

One day after she had recovered, an officer came to visit a critically ill patient. She had expected two officers, the patient's friend and a friend of his father's. Unfamiliar with rank insignia, she asked, "Are you Lieutenant Curry, or Captain Cary?"

The soldier looked her in the eye. "Neither, I'm afraid," he replied. "I am Colonel Theodore Roosevelt."

She apologized and explained that she had been expecting two other officers.

"He's as much my boy as he is theirs," Roosevelt said.

Heavren led the future president to the soldier's bedside and left him alone.

Well aware of the historical significance of the contract nurses' service and their contribution, Dr. Anita Newcom McGee suggested to the members of the Spanish-American War Nurses' organization in 1903 that they compile a book. "I propose that we combine to 'write a picture' of 'Nursing in the Spanish War,' such as will give a vivid account of all sides of your lives with the army," she said. "Each hospital should have a committee to see that . . . all sides—work, pathos, humor—are shown." The book never materialized. Little writing from Spanish-American War contract nurses has survived. Some nurses published brief accounts for limited audiences such as the members of the Daughters of the American Revolution (DAR), or in professional journals and newspaper interviews.

The implementation of military entrance physicals late in the nineteenth century ended women's ability to disguise themselves as men to fight. However, in the decades immediately following the Civil War, a growing recognition of the value of trained nurses led to the professionalization of nursing in America. In the 1870s large hospitals established nursing schools that attracted ambitious middle-class and working-class women, and nursing was one of the few occupations in which women could earn professional respect and a wage.

Having forgotten or dismissed the contributions of contract nurses in the Civil War, and discounting the importance of professional certification, Army surgeons were reluctant to hire women nurses when the United States declared war on Spain in February 1898. But Army Surgeon General Sternberg soon realized that the military hospital corps of 520 men, 100 stewards, and 100 acting stewards would be unable to meet the needs of 25,000 soldiers—or to keep up with the epidemics of typhoid and yellow fever that were killing more soldiers than the fighting.

In April, Congress authorized Sternberg to hire female contract nurses. Dr. Anita Newcomb McGee, a socially prominent anthropologist and physician in Washington DC, offered to screen prospective nurses under the auspices of the DAR. McGee required applicants to be between thirty and fifty years old, graduates of a professional nursing school, with supervisors' endorsements of their moral character and good health. However, the large demand undermined her standards: she eventually accepted younger nurses and some untrained volunteers.

Sternberg appointed McGee acting assistant surgeon general of the Army on August 29, 1898. Her office assumed the responsibility of screening applicants. Between May 1898 and July 1899, McGee and DAR volunteers screened nearly six thousand applications and sent 1,563 female nurses to Army hospitals in the United States. In July 1898 the Army began sending nurses to Cuba. A small group served with the Navy on the hospital ship *Relief* off the Cuban coast. Contract nurses worked to exhaustion in primitive, unsanitary conditions; many contracted dysentery and chronic intestinal conditions that remained with them for life.

At that time, many doctors believed erroneously that women of color had "natural immunity" to tropical diseases. In July 1898, when Dr. McGee's staff could not recruit enough nurses with immunity to yellow fever, Sternberg sent Mrs. Namahyoke Curtis, wife of the surgeon in chief of the Freedmen's Hospital (later the Howard University Medical School), to New Orleans to recruit "immune" women of color. Thirty-two African American women signed contracts; over the course of the war, eighty served. Two African American nurses died of typhoid. Four Lakota Sioux women, nuns of the American Order of the Sisters, joined the First Division hospital of the Seventh Army Corps at Pinar del Río. In addition to Dr. McGee, six women physicians served with the Army during the Spanish-American War—as contract nurses, not physicians or surgeons.

Hostilities in the Spanish-American War ended August 12, 1898;

a formal peace treaty was signed in December. At least fourteen contract nurses had died of tropical diseases during the war.

Contract nurses continued to serve with the Army after the war in hospitals in new U.S. territories ceded by Spain: Puerto Rico, Guam, and the Philippine Islands, where they treated casualties of the Philippine Insurrection (1899–1902). One, Clara Maass, volunteered as a subject in the Yellow Fever Commission experiments on transmission of the disease at Las Animas Hospital in Havana, Cuba. Her death on August 24, 1901, led to the end of human experimentation and a change in public health policy from disinfection to mosquito eradication.

The Dodge Commission, appointed by President William McKinley to investigate the conduct of the Spanish-American War, found significant problems in the Army Medical Department but lauded the effectiveness of contract nurses in saving lives. The Commission recommended replacing contract nurses with a trained reserve nursing force.

Over the objections of Army physicians opposed to creating a corps of trained Army nurses, Sternberg assigned Dr. McGee to draft the section of the Army Reorganization Act that established the Army Nurse Corps on February 2, 1901. It took another twenty years for the Army to approve pensions for contract nurses who served in the Spanish-American War. Army nurses did not hold military rank at that time, but they had opened the door for women's military service. It would never be closed again.

Dr. Anita Newcom McGee
(1864–1940)
U.S. ARMY

Dr. Anita Newcomb McGee of Washington DC studied in private schools and trained in anthropology at Cambridge University and the University of Geneva (Switzerland). In 1892 she received her medical degree from Columbian University (now George Washington University). She served with the Red Cross Society of Japan during the Russo-Japanese War in 1904; as an attaché to the American Legation in Tokyo in 1905, she visited battlefields in north-eastern China. After her death in 1940, she was buried with full military honors in Arlington National Cemetery. McGee drafted the legislation establishing the Army Nurse Corps and published articles in DAR and nursing periodicals. The excerpts below come from two of McGee's reports to the DAR.

Report to the Daughters of the American Revolution

JUNE 28, 1898

At the April meeting of the National Board of the Daughters the question of what the Daughters should do in the war was naturally prominent. I had the honor at that time of presenting the plan for a hospital corps, which as originally conceived was in the form of a body of trained nurses who should be ready to answer a call from The Surgeon General for service in the army or navy and which should be thoroughly endorsed by the DAR. That plan was, on consultation with the officials, afterward enlarged by the proposal that we should undertake the examination of all applications which were received from women for hospital positions. At that time the Surgeon General had been overwhelmed with applications, which had been responded to in a formal way and placed on file, without any means of examining into the qualifications of the applicants or making use of their offers of service. They therefore welcomed heartily the extended proposal made by the Daughters, and turned over to our society every application, no matter to whom originally addressed.

At the outbreak of the war The Surgeon General of the Army had at his command a corps of hospital stewards numbering nearly 800 men and assistants; the Surgeon General of the Navy had no such corps. It will be seen that the need of assistants in the field seems to be met by the army corps of men now enlarged to a war basis. In hospitals, however, the skilled assistance of trained women nurses is needed.

This responsibility in the hands of the Daughters is, I think, quite a unique matter. This recognition by the Government is something of which we had every reason to be very proud indeed. I have received up to the present time (June 28) applications to the number of 2,500. The majority are from untrained women who offer from patriotic motives. They have been sent to the President of the United States, Secretaries of War and Navy, Surgeons General, Senators, members of Congress, officials of the Treasury, all reaching ultimately the office of the Daughters. The work of examining these, as you can imagine, has been no easy one, especially as we began when there were 1,100 received, which we had to take in bulk. I am happy to say the work for the last two or three weeks has been quite up to date. I counted my mail the other day, and one envelope contained thirty applications from the War Department—in addition to that there were forty-six letters, either with applications or returned blanks or indorsements. This was simply one mail.

When an application is received which gives some promise of being from a person who knows something about nursing we send her a small blank [a questionnaire to help the DAR with screening candidates]. The requirements printed at the head of some of our letters are those suggested by The Surgeon General of the Army. He specified in a general way what he wanted. The age requirement he does not insist upon absolutely. The matter of keeping up the standard depends entirely upon the number of applicants and the number appointed. As long as applicants who are suitable number by the hundreds and the appointments number by the ones, of course I feel obliged to keep rather closely to the highest requirements. The Surgeon General has given me strict injunctions that all parts of the country are to be represented, and naturally those who have had yellow fever are preferred for Southern hospitals. In selecting applicants my rule has been to take those who have in the first place come well indorsed, and whose hospital records are good. Then I prefer those who have the indorsement from Daughters who know them. Then those recommended by the schools from which they graduated, and I have established a regular method of writing to the superintendents of every school to get all possible information.

Of course it is impossible at the present time to make any statement as to how many will be called or where they will go, and I am therefore unable to state whether any particular applicant is accepted or not. I cannot decide until the call comes; then I look over all and select according to the fullest knowledge I have at the time.

Report to the DAR

The DAR hospital corps has the honor to report that its work has grown
and multiplied to an extent far beyond what was considered proba-
ble. The first nurses sent were viewed in the light of an experiment,
and much depended on the record which they should make. To the
lasting gratification, not only to the DAR, but of womenkind in general, we are proud to record that the nurses whom we first selected
proved themselves fully worthy of the trust imposed on them, and fit
co-workers with the brave men whose names are entered on the roll
of honor of the army. The inevitable results of their noble work was
the ever increasing demand from army hospitals for trained women
nurses, and the decision which has now been reached on every hand,
that satisfactory hospital work, without such nurses, is almost impossible. Some fifty times has The Surgeon General of the Army called
on the DAR hospital corps to designate suitable nurses for some specified duty, and these calls, originally for about half a dozen persons
each time, increased to as many as 150 nurses in a single order. The
total number thus appointed is in the neighborhood of 1,000 nurses—a regiment of women. As is already known to you, all applications
from women addressed to the War Department were forwarded to us
for examination, and all but the earliest received at the Navy Department were also forwarded. In addition to these, hosts of applicants
wrote or applied in person to us until the total number we examined
rose to about 4,600. Realizing, as we fully did, that there was a great
principle at stake, we exercised the greatest care in the preparation
of our list of eligible women. First of all, the candidate must be of
irreproachable character and suitable age. Second, she must possess
good health. Third, she must have the training which is all essential to
the successful prosecution of her work. This last requisite is one that
recent progress has made not only possible, but an absolute necessity, to secure the best results, and we feel that the one safe policy—
safe above all to the sick soldiers—was to demand actual graduation
from training school.

Kittie (Whiting) Eastman Doxsee
(1899–1943)
U.S. ARMY

Kittie Whiting of Cicero, New York, served as an Army contract nurse from August 1898 to July 1899. The following is excerpted from her "Memoirs of a Spanish-American War Nurse," a lecture that she read at the annual meeting of nurses in Ogdensburg, New York, July 1899.

Received order to report for duty as a nurse in Spanish American War on August 21, 1898.... I arrived in New York City August 22, was entertained with other nurses at Steward House, Lexington Avenue, a home for nurses. Orders to leave for Montauk, Long Island, Camp Wickoff, August 23 at seven a.m. Reached Montauk about noon. There were many soldiers waiting for the hospital train to convey them to their homes and friends. Some who were not strong enough to sit up but were lying on rough benches as the station was temporary and made of rough lumber. Here is where our first work began in trying to make them more comfortable by using our wraps for pillows and carrying milk and water from a nearby canteen. These soldier boys (as all the soldiers were called boys, regardless of age) were direct from [the] battlefield and were suffering from exposure and malaria fever. They were very grateful for any little kindness shown them and most of the nurses were given souvenirs such as shells, Mauser bullets, cross guns and buttons which had been in the fight at San Juan Hill. We were conveyed to camp in Army ambulances drawn by four good mules. The camp was one and a half miles from station and it was a continuous string of Army wagon ambulances. Troops of cavalry and regiments marching to and from. Camp had been staked about eight days when we arrived on the scene. There were twenty nurses in our party from New York which had centered through from different parts of the USA. I was assigned night duty on Ward F where there were sixty patients with malaria, some pneumonia, and typhoid, but more cases of dysentery.

The hospital was on [an] extreme point of Montauk and not a tree to be seen, just sand dunes. We were all quartered in tents, no buildings had been erected. It was my great pleasure to shake hands with President McKinley, Secretary Alger and some of the cabinet officers as they passed through the hospital. There were about fifteen nurses in this camp and many sisters [Catholic Sisters of Charity] in this camp hospital. I remained here about four weeks when the call came for more nurses for duty in Lexington, Kentucky. This being an inland town very few nurses cared to go as many were anxious to see foreign service—go to Cuba, Puerto Rico or Philippines. . . . I had no desire to go to Cuba or any place away from USA. So I offered to go.

[Whiting is then transferred to the John Blair Gibbs Hospital in Lexington, which she notes has a very good record for typhoid fever recovery. She describes patients' baths and meals, and a dance suggested by one of the nuns. The hospital is then moved to Camp Conrad, near Columbus, Georgia. Whiting is there six weeks, then is ordered to Cuba after the Spanish surrender. Eleven nurses and ten nursing Sisters are sent to Matanzas; fifteen nurses, including Whiting, are sent to Cienfuegos.]

We steamed out of Charleston December 30 at 7:30 a.m., past Old Fort Sumter and were at sea and out of sight of land in about two hours. The sea was fairly calm and we enjoyed the voyage. We went around the eastern end of Cuba to Cienfuegos which is on the southern coast. . . . We passed by Moro Castle at entrance to Santiago Harbor. American troops were there and Old Glory waved from the highest point on the Castle and Uncle Sam's boys waved their hats as we passed by. The scenery was very picturesque. We sat on deck of the largest transport and watched the flying fish and porpoise. Every now and then a sail in sight when every neck was craned to catch a glimpse of the tiny speck in the distance. As we entered the harbor at Cienfuegos thousands of Spanish soldiers and natives swarmed on the docks and shore while the Sixth Ohio Band played the National Air [anthem], "Star Spangled Banner," and immediately afterwards, "A Hot Time in the Old Town" which later on the people always connected with the National Air. We dropped anchor in harbor about two miles from shore as the harbor was not dredged and large vessels could not go nearer with safety. We had on board General Bates and Headquarters Staff Colonel McMaken and Sixth Ohio Regiment, fifteen nurses, Hospital Corps, officers, horses, Army mules, wagons, tentage, lumber for flooring and supplies for thirty days. It took some time to unload as all was done by lighters and the natives are very slow workers. There were thirty-five thousand Spanish soldiers centered at Cienfuegos when we landed and all were armed. But our boys were such large muscular men and handled guns so rapid and accurately that when giving a drill at the Plaza the natives looked amazed. They marched to camp which was about four miles and in the center of a royal palm grove. The nurses were to remain on board ship until accommodations could be made in camp.

Captain Gibbons, the ship's captain, invited all the nurses to visit the Mayflower gunboat which was lying in the harbor. We were taken in steam yacht and met by the captain of the Mayflower, who showed us all around, then we went ashore. We were as much of a curiosity to the people as they were to us, as we rode by. There were five Cuban carriages of volantes [two-wheeled pleasure carriages in which the body is in front of the axle and the driver rides on the horse], each drawn by one little Cuban pony. . . . We drove about town and the curtains were thrown back from nearly every Cuban house and many faces peeking out at us, as we passed by. The houses were built mostly of concrete and tile roofs. Nearly all are one-story houses, no windows, but iron bars about an inch through, running length[wise] about six inches apart up and down the windows with shutters or blinds inside like doors. [In] most of the villages the huts are made of the palm tree and look very much like old straw stacks.

There was a family near our camp that I took quite an interest in. There were five children, two boys, three girls. One of the children was playing with a bundle of rags and a newspaper, which some called a doll. I had a little time to myself one day and I found one of my old uniform aprons and a few ribbons in my trunk so made each little girl a doll. I am no artist in making rag dolls as I never made one before but the three little girls were delighted and would run and get dolls as soon as I was near their home. The one about four years old was sick one day and the mother wanted me to go and see her. She was lying on what was intended for a bed but was not fit for a good American dog to sleep on. The room had no windows and was dark.

The child had quite a temperature. I could speak enough Spanish to make the mother understand I wanted water to bathe the child. She brought some water in an old tomato can. I found it was the best the shanty afforded so the mother held the can and I gave the child a bath as best I could under circumstances. I went back to the hospital and brought some medicine and next day the little one ran out to meet me and kissed my hand. The woman spit on the wall and I observed that she was chewing tobacco. Many of the women of the poorer class chew and smoke. . . .

The hospital averaged about sixty patients. We found the natives good beggars and they seem to think the Americans loaded with money, especially so when we wanted to purchase an article. Easter Sunday I attended services at the Cathedral, the only church in Cien fuegos, there [were] many altars, one main altar and many on each side of the church less elaborate. The Sixth Ohio Regiment and hospital were in a palm grove and the railroad which goes to Havana went through camp. The water used in camp was brought from Santa Clara. Cuban trains are like everything else there—rather slow. It is said the trains stop when a buzzard is on the track. The best coaches are not as good as American immigrant coaches, the mail service is very poor. February 13, 1899 a cyclone struck camp and all the hospital tents were blown down. Nurses' tents were a total wreck and we could find very little of our wearing apparel. The officers were very kind and gave up their tents to us and patients were transferred to tents in the Regiment.

The First Battalion of Sixth Ohio was ordered to Santa Clara and five nurses sent with them. We had ten nurses remaining in camp. We attended the Cuban Jubilee and saw General Gomez. There was great preparation made for his coming, archways in streets, flags, and decorations galore. The lower class of people wear very little clothing and the children wore just a smile. The Cuban ponies are used as pack mules. Millet and sugar cane is tied on their backs until they are covered. All you can see is their nose and feet. They look like walking grass mounds. The pony has a halter on and it is fastened to another pony's tail. Sometimes there is [sic] four or five in a string. I went to a New York syndicate sugar plantation. It was wonderful. Oranges, palms, lemons, bananas and beautiful flowers. . . . They had a modern sugar mill and made two hundred and fifty thousand pounds a day. The soil is very fertile and everything seemed to grow. Even the fence posts take root and grow into trees. There was a hedge of sword cactus about one and a half miles long by the roadside from camp to Cienfuegos. The ties used on the railroad were of mahogany. On our side of camp was the famous tracks and blockhouses we have heard so much about. Lizards, scorpions, centipedes, tarantulas and snakes were often found in our tents but we became used to this and did not mind them very much.

The *Texas*, *Detroit*, and *Indiana* Battleships were in the harbor and one day we visited all of them, also *Bay State* hospital ship which was built to accommodate a hundred patients. The city hospital was more modern than I had expected to find. The superintendent, four physicians and an interpreter showed us through the hospital. They expressed a desire to have Uncle Sam's nurses in their hospital. We remained in Cienfuegos over four months.

Esther Voorhees Hasson
(1867–1942)
U.S. NAVY

Esther Voorhees Hasson of Baltimore, Maryland, served as a nurse with the Army on the hospital ship *Relief*, a passenger liner used to evacuate casualties from Cuba. Hasson was one of six nurses charged with caring for 1,485 sick and wounded men. After the war, she served as a nurse in the Canal Zone from 1905 to 1907. When the Navy Nurse Corps was established in 1908, Hasson became its first superintendent, but resigned in 1911 after the surgeon general questioned her leadership abilities and imposed what Hasson believed to be unfair policies for nurses. She then joined the Army's Reserve Nursing Corps and was called to active duty in 1917 for service as chief nurse of two Army base hospitals in Europe during World War I. This excerpt is from a professional article Hasson published in the *American Journal of Nursing* in 1909.

Early in May of 1898 four women graduate nurses left Washington for Key West, Florida, under orders from the Surgeon-General of the

Army to report to the medical officer in command of the military hospital at that place for such duty as he might assign to them. Little did the nurses of this country think, at the time, of the far-reaching results of this order and that these women were the nucleus around which would form, first the corps of contract nurses, and later on, in 1901, the permanent organization of the Army Nurse Corps as it exists to-day. Their plunge into this (to the average nurse of that date) unknown field of work was like unto the traditional pebble cast into the sea of military nursing. The tiny ripples set in motion have spread out in gradually increasing circles until the little group of women on the extreme outer edge who at present represent the nurse corps of the Navy are already beginning to wonder upon what shores the last ripples will break.

Although the Army Nurse Corps was distinctly the product of war, the Navy corps is the indirect outcome of its proven worth and efficiency, not only in time of great national emergency, but of peace as well....

All applicants will be required to pass a rigid physical and mental examination.... The examination is required in all cases irrespective of whether the applicant has had previous Government service, either civil or military.... The first few months of service will invariably be spent at the Naval Medical School Hospital in Washington, and after this term of trial, the nurses will be distributed to the various naval hospitals in the United States, Japan, the Philippines and Hawaii where it is deemed advisable to station women nurses....

During the period spent in the naval hospital in Washington, nurses will be expected to inform themselves in regard to the rules, regulations and etiquette of the service, also of the different degrees of rank with insignia of same, not alone of the commissioned officers, but of the warrant and petty officers as well. Head nurse positions will in all cases be filled by promotions from the grade of nurse.... We hope to make the nursing in our eighteen general hospitals somewhat uniform, so that when ordered from one to the other the nurse will know about the conditions she will encounter in regard to scope of work, hours of duty, duration and frequency of night details, personal privileges, etc....

One of the principal duties of the woman nurse in the Navy will be the bedside instruction of the hospital apprentices in the practical essentials of nursing, and for this reason she must be thoroughly conversant with the head nurse routine of a ward. When treatments, baths, or medication come due it is not expected or desired that she will always give these herself, but it will be her duty to see that the apprentices attached to the ward carry out the orders promptly and intelligently. This arrangement does not, however, absolve the nurse in any way from doing the actual nursing work whenever necessary, but is in a line with the general principle instilled into her from first to last, and which she is expected to always keep uppermost in her mind.... The improvement of the apprentices to whom the bulk of the nursing of the Navy afloat will always fall, for it is not the intention of the Surgeon-General to station women nurses on any but hospital ships.

The first few months of service is ... a period of probation during which the nurse will be under observation as to her suitability for naval nursing. To be dropped from the corps at the end of this time may not, and in most cases will not, imply anything derogatory to the character or even to the professional ability of the nurse, as it will usually merely mean that she is lacking in the peculiar qualities requisite in work of this nature, namely: the cheerful disposition that accepts the ups and downs incidental to changes of station; that adapts itself easily to new environment; that accepts the undesirable detail without complaint and confidently looks forward to the better luck that will surely come next time. Above all she must possess in the highest degree the quiet dignity of bearing which alone can command respect from the apprentices or male nurses whom she must instruct. Although she possesses all else, and yet lacks this one quality, she had best seek another vocation at once as she would be absolutely useless for the work we wish her to do. The ability to get on with others will also be a very valuable adjunct. Ample authority will be given the nurse in all that pertains to the nursing, but we all know that there are women who can produce good results and maintain discipline without keeping things constantly in a state of turmoil. In a training school when a pupil nurse proves unsatisfactory another can easily be found to take her place, but with the hospital apprentice it is different, for the Navy is always far short of the number required, from which it will readily be seen that the woman who can inspire the male nurses with a pride in their work and a desire to learn, and who at the same time can reduce to a minimum the friction always incidental to a change in the old order of things, will be the most valuable woman for naval work. . . . In other words, dignity, self-control and courtesy are the keynotes to the situation. . . .

It is too soon as yet to outline the scope of the work or to make predictions as to the future of the corps, but it is my most earnest hope to make it a dignified, respected body of women, governed largely by that feeling of esprit de corps without which no rules ever devised will be of avail to keep us free from all that approaches scandal or disagreeable comment.

Undoubtedly the future status of the Navy corps will rest largely in the hands of its members, and especially is this true of the first nurses. If they are content with low standards either professionally, morally, or socially the status of the corps will be fixed for all time. Future women will accept the standard set by us now without question; if it be high they will rise to it, if it be low they will with equal facility drop to its level.

We nurses who come into the nursing service of the Navy during this first year of its existence are the pioneers, and it rests with us to make the traditions and to set the pace for those who are to follow, and so upon our shoulders rests a great responsibility. I am sure that the nursing profession of the country will extend to us its hearty good wishes for success in our undertaking.

4

World War I

"Because We Knew We Could Be Useful"

Around 11 a.m. on November 2, 1918, German artillery soldiers retreating up the western bank of the Meuse set up a barrage of indirect fire intended for Allied artillery units emplaced above the bombed-out and abandoned village of Fromeréville-sur-Vallons, five miles west of Verdun. When the first shell landed near the hospital, officers and enlisted men of Evacuation Hospital No. 4 poured out of the ruined mill they had chosen as headquarters and male quarters. The second shell landed on the mill, killing off-duty enlisted men who were sleeping there. Shells began to fall at three-minute intervals in a walking barrage, the impact points leaving craters like the footprints of an invisible giant stomping up the hill toward the hospital tents housing soldiers wounded too severely to be evacuated farther behind the lines. Thirty-year-old chief nurse Cassie White realized that her patients must be moved to safety. She ordered the nurses in charge of each ward to prepare for immediate evacuation.

With too few officers and enlisted men to carry all the stretchers, White and two other nurses, Minna Meyer and Victoria Robinson, struggled in pouring rain and knee-deep mud to help carry patients to the top of the hill. Exposed to artillery fire, they took the stretchers to the far side of the ridge and ran back for more wounded.

An officer who had served with the British forces knew the sound of incoming artillery. When he heard the shriek of an approaching shell, he would call "Duck!" After the fragments had fallen, he gave the all-clear: "Go ahead!"

White and one of the men were carrying a patient when they heard the call to take cover. They ducked. But White stood up too quickly. A piece of shell casing knocked her stiff-brimmed rain hat off her head. She fell to the ground.

"Oh my God, Miss White, you're hit!" the enlisted man cried.

"No I'm not, either," she said. She stood up. "But catch hold of that stretcher and let's get out of here." Still calm, she picked up the fragment of shell casing and pocketed it for a souvenir.

Victoria Robinson paused to cover a patient with a blanket before moving him. When she bent down he panicked and shoved her under the bed. "Now you stay there until this thing is over," he told her. "If a shell comes in here it will have to go through me before it can get to you!" Robinson crawled out from under the bed and returned to work.

Later White said, "It really was remarkable that none of the nurses were struck. I guess it was simply luck. Certainly they were all exposed long enough. It was not a pleasant experience at all and yet, in a way, it was pretty to look at, pretty to watch the little groups scurrying up that long hill and running down."

During the bombardment the staff evacuated all the patients to another hospital. By 2 p.m., nothing remained of Evacuation Hospital No. 4 but shrapnel-riddled tents and some equipment. At three the nurses had a cup of coffee for lunch and relocated to Fontaine Routon for the night. The next day they helped patch up the hospital tents, rebuilt the operating room, opened a new headquarters, and once again began receiving patients.

After the Armistice, White, Meyer, and Robinson returned to their parent unit, Base Hospital No. 31. They carried a citation: The commanding general of the Armed Expeditionary Forces, Gen. John J. Pershing, had commended them for their "heroic conduct."

When Congress established the Army Nurse Corps in 1901, nurses had no military rank. They did not receive pay equal to that of men with similar duties or veterans' benefits. They were outside of the military chain of command: although they had the responsibility to maintain order on the wards, male enlisted corpsmen frequently contested or disregarded their orders. The Army Nursing Corps prohibited nurses from socializing with patients; supervisors continually scrutinized their personal conduct on and off duty. Nevertheless, women continued to enter the Army—and the Navy after the establishment of the Navy Nurse Corps in 1908. In March 1917, 403 professionally trained graduate nurses were on active duty.

In 1916 the Red Cross and the Department of Military Relief established fifty base hospitals staffed with doctors and nurses from large civilian university hospitals. Each staff trained together under Red Cross auspices in preparation for U.S. entry into the war. Base hospitals transferred to the Department of the Army when mobilized to federal service. Six of these units sailed to Europe in May 1917. The first American troops deployed in the Great War, they initially joined the British Expeditionary Force hospitals. Two nurses, killed on ss *Mongolia* when a gun misfired, became the first American casualties of the war. In Europe the nurses worked long hours in challenging conditions. Those sent to field and evacuation hospitals on "detached service" served with surgical, trauma, or gas teams. They treated soldiers under artillery fire and aerial bombardment.

The Army Nursing Corps finally permitted African American nurses to enroll during the influenza epidemic in fall 1918, but restricted them to treating mostly African American soldiers at hospitals on U.S. bases. All were released by summer 1919. Nineteen Roman Catholic nurses from the Sisters of Charity of Saint Vincent DePaul and other orders deployed to Vicenza, Italy, for seven months with Base Hospital No. 102. Graduate male nurses could only enlist as corpsmen despite their certification—a discriminatory policy that remained in place for another four decades.

By the end of the war, nearly 21,500 women served in the Army Nurse Corps and nearly 1,400 in the Navy Nurse Corps. Ten thousand served overseas. Several were wounded during the war; more than two hundred died in service, mostly of influenza or its complications. Three Army nurses were awarded the Distinguished

Service Cross; at least one was awarded a Citation Star (later the Silver Star); twenty-five received the Distinguished Service Medal. France awarded twenty-eight American nurses the Croix de Guerre, and Great Britain awarded sixty-nine the British Royal Red Cross and two the British Military Medal. Many stayed on with the Army of Occupation after the Armistice.

Business schools had begun training women in typing and other administrative skills by the early twentieth century. Secretary of the Navy Charles Bonaparte had suggested replacing yeomen at shore stations with civilian women in 1906, but officer prejudice stymied the initiative. His successor Josephus Daniels foresaw the need to expand the Navy rapidly if the United States entered the war, and he realized that recruiters would struggle to meet the demand for personnel.

In spring 1916, nineteen-year-old Charlotte Berry, a graduate of a two-year course at the Washington Business High School, called on Daniels. The record of the visit lacks detail, and Daniels credited no one but himself for the idea, but Berry later told family members that she had suggested during the call that the Navy enlist women typists and stenographers. Later that year, the Bureau of Navigation and the Office of the Judge Advocate General reported to Daniels that a loophole in the Naval Appropriations Act, passed in August, would allow the enlistment of women. On March 21, 1917, Loretta Perfectus Walsh enlisted in Philadelphia and became the first woman to enlist officially in the U.S. armed forces. Berry and her younger sister Sophia soon followed.

The yeomen (F) could not serve at sea. They worked at shore stations as typists, stenographers, radio and switchboard operators, messengers, chauffeurs and truck drivers, pay and supply clerks, and intelligence analysts. A few with prior training enlisted as electrician's mates. Yeomen (F) filled primers on torpedoes: men filled an average of 29 primers a week, but the women filled an average of 162. At least fourteen African American women enlisted to serve as yeomen (F) in the Navy Muster Office.

Twelve thousand yeomen (F) served, at rank and with pay equal to that of their male counterparts. Officers recommended four yeomen (F) for promotion to officer, but the war ended before the paperwork was processed. A small number even served overseas in Guam, Puerto Rico, the Panama Canal Zone, Hawaii, and Europe.

Pvt. Opha Mae Johnson enlisted on August 13, 1918, as the first of three hundred women Marines. The Corps insisted on calling the women "Marines" just like the men, though the nickname "Marinettes" was also popular. Most served as clerks, typists, and stenographers; others became recruiters or served in public affairs.

The Coast Guard enlisted only a few women in World War I to serve at the headquarters as yeomen. The first, nineteen-year-old twins Genevieve and Dorothy Baker of Brooklyn, had originally enlisted as yeomen (F) in the Navy and served as bookkeepers. On April 11, 1917, twenty-one light stations transferred to the Department of the Navy, and their keepers were tasked with keeping a lookout for the German U-boats that were sinking coastal shipping. Four women serving as keepers in the United States Lighthouse Service for periods of at least six continuous months were awarded the World War I Victory Medal.

In Europe, Armed Expeditionary Forces commander Gen. John J. Pershing found his operations hampered by the poor quality of the French telephone system. The Army enrolled 450 women into the Signal Corps beginning in March 1918. The women, nicknamed the "Hello Girls," purchased Army uniforms and insignia at their own expense. The Army trained them, paid them the same as their male counterparts, and subjected them to military discipline. In France, Chief Operator Grace Banker and six others were ordered to the headquarters of the First Army near the front at Ligny late September 1918. Six more women joined them to handle the volume of traffic, which included orders for troop movements. On October 30, 1918, under German aerial bombardment, the barracks housing the switchboards caught fire. The women refused to leave their posts until Signal Corps officers threatened to court-martial them for disobeying a direct order to leave immediately. They returned to the switchboards, only a third of which remained operational, within an hour. The Army awarded Banker the Distinguished Service Medal.

After the war, when the women requested their Victory Medals and honorable discharges, they found that the Army had only considered them contract workers. Had they been wounded, killed, or captured, they would have had no military status for internment under the rules of war, prisoner exchange, or veterans' benefits.

With the exception of a small number of Army and Navy nurses, military women were discharged from service within a year of the Armistice. The service of women who joined the armed forces or served abroad in civilian relief agencies like the Red Cross changed American society. They voluntarily took on the responsibilities of full citizenship despite not having the same rights as men. In part because of their service, Congress granted American women suffrage in 1920. After the war the Army granted its nurses relative rank, though they continued to receive less pay and to hold less authority than men of the same rank.

Many women who served in the Great War did not reintegrate into traditional domestic roles. They continued to work as civilian nurses and clerical personnel. A few became writers and journalists, though they rarely, if ever, mentioned their wartime experience. A few penned brief memoirs that remained unpublished, or wrote short articles for professional nursing journals and reunion societies.

The women were thanked for their service and told that they would never be needed in uniform again.

Beatrice MacDonald
(1881–1969)
U.S. ARMY NURSE CORPS

Beatrice Mary MacDonald of New York, New York, enlisted in the Army Nurse Corps in 1917 and went to France with the Second Evacuation Hospital. While on duty with the surgical team at the British Casualty Clearing Station No. 61 in France on August 17, 1917, she was wounded by shrapnel during a German air raid. Surgeons tried to remove the shrapnel, but had to remove her entire eye. MacDonald insisted on returning to duty six weeks later, declaring, "I've only started doing my bit." She returned to the front lines as the chief nurse of Evacuation Hospital No. 2 in May 1918, and continued to serve through January 1919. MacDonald and her tent mate, Helen McClelland, received the Distinguished Service Cross for extraordinary heroism during the air raid. Mac-Donald also received the Distinguished Service Medal, the Purple Heart, the Military Medal (awarded by Great Britain for bravery in a land battle) with an associated Royal Red Cross Medal, and the French Croix de Guerre with Bronze Star. The excerpt below is taken from an article she wrote for the *Quarterly Magazine*, the Presbyterian Hospital School of Nursing alumnae publication.

When I was asked if I would contribute an article [to this journal], I hesitated at first, for the reason that I felt there were many members of the Unit ... who were far better qualified to record their experiences in front line hospitals, than this humble "step-child."

On July 20th, 1917, when I was ... told that two surgical teams (a surgical team consisted of a surgeon, anesthetist, nurse, and orderly) were to be sent to the British front for the great offensive in Flanders, which was later known as the Paschendahl Battle, and asked if I would be willing to go on Col. Brewer's team, needless to say, I was thrilled. We were told to hold ourselves in readiness to leave at a moment's notice, and to take only sufficient clothing to last three days, or a week at the most.

After anxiously waiting for two days, orders came through for both teams to proceed at once, to report to the Gas School in Havre for steel helmets, gas masks, and instruction, which included entering chambers containing a certain amount of Phosgene and other gasses, in order that we should be able to recognize them in case of an attack, and to become adept in adjusting our gas masks in less than ten seconds....

We proceeded to Havre as per orders, received our instruction at the Gas School, and by eleven o'clock were winding our way through the lovely Normandy country.... We arrived at Abbeville about 8 p.m....

After leaving Abbeville, we began to see trenches, barbed wire entanglements, partially and totally destroyed villages, dire evidences of war. As we neared the front, we passed large numbers of British troops moving up, and my Scotch heart fairly burst when I heard the skirl of the bagpipes and saw the Black Watch marching along with every kilt swinging in unison.

Our destination was Dozingham (a code name), situated about three and a half miles northwest of Poperinghe, Belgium, which we reached about four o'clock on the afternoon of the 23rd.... These two hospitals [Casualty Clearing Stations 61 and 47] were located within three hundred yards of each other, and under canvas, except for the large operating theatres, which consisted of corrugated iron Nissen huts, containing seven tables, and one small theatre under canvas with two tables. The part of the hospital which handled the surgical casualties was divided in two parts by a broad duck-board walk. There were nine wards on either side, with smaller duck-boards between each ward; and woe betide anyone who was unfortunate enough to step off a duck-board, as I realized to my sorrow one night as we were hurrying from the operating theatre to snatch our much needed six hours' rest, when someone accidentally ran against me. I landed in the mud face down, and sank almost out of sight. Laid out on the ground in front of the hospital, plainly visible by day, and strongly illuminated at night, was a large Red Cross 30 x 40 feet. There were also one or two Red Crosses on top of the large tents; so we felt secure and had no fear of the enemy mistaking it for an ammunition dump, army camp, quartermaster's stores, etc.

No. 61 and 47 CCS were new hospitals established especially for this drive and within four miles of the front line. For some reason the offensive did not start as early as expected, and we were at the station a week without any active surgical work. Our days were occupied making supplies, helping to put the finishing touches to the operating room, watching the enemy observation planes, and when it was not pouring rain, making short trips to nearby places of interest. The nights during this first week were comparatively quiet. We could hear the enemy aeroplanes go over us to the back areas, but we paid little attention to them until the anti-aircraft guns began, when we would get up and watch the planes passing along in the light of the strong electric searchlights, and after watching for a time, would turn in again.

On the night of July 30th, all hell seemed to break loose, and we realized that the great offensive had started. From midnight on, especially when the barrage was laid down just before dawn, there was the most terrific bombardment. I must say that I got very little sleep that night, as I sat on my cot with the flap of the tent held back, simply fascinated watching the flashes of the guns in the sky, listening to the terrific explosions, and the whizzing of the shells from the heavy guns in our rear passing over our heads. At that time, I was sharing a tent with four British sisters who had seen nearly three years' service. Three of them slept through the whole thing, and I marveled that human beings could get so accustomed to it, that they slept as if in a peaceful English countryside. One sister, who was rather wakeful, said to me, "Sister, you had better try and get some sleep, here is some cotton, put it in your ears, we shall have some heavy days ahead." She was absolutely right. We began to receive wounded about ten o'clock on the morning of the 31st. The plan was for the three hospitals in the immediate neighborhood . . . to each receive 200; but it seemed that we hardly made a dent in the number to be operated upon before word would come that we were again receiving. The three hospitals had over 2,400 casualties in the first twenty-four hours. All operating teams worked continuously for twenty-two hours, then took four hours' rest; returned to duty and worked another eighteen hours, then took six hours' rest, and carried on in this manner until the battle was over. We then went on a regular schedule of eight hours on and eight hours off. No one ever grumbled at the long hours, we only begrudged the time we took for sleep; but this we knew was absolutely necessary in order to be able to "carry on."

By the end of the second week, and particularly after the heavy work, we were desperate for fresh clothing, my two operating dresses and service dress were filthy, and my cloth mess dress was hanging in my tent soaking wet, the result of slipping into a blind ditch filled with muddy slimy water nearly up to our waists, as we crossed the fields to attend a Sunday service in an old convent about a mile from the hospital. A British Tommy came to our rescue, helped us out of the ditch, emptied our rubber boots, brought us a pail of water and towel from his quarters nearby, and we washed our faces and hands, repaired as much of the damage to our dresses as possible, in full view of the Head-quarters of the Prince of Wales and the passing troops, then proceeded to service. The officers were pretty much in the same straits in regard to clothing; so Col. Brewer prevailed upon the Commanding Officer to send a camion to our base for fresh clothing for the two teams, as it was evident that our stay at the front was to be an indefinite one.

On the night of August 17th just as we had turned in after a heavy day's work, the anti-aircraft guns started. We could hear and see an enemy plane about 5,000 feet up with the searchlights on it, we could see the shrapnel bursting, but finally it went away and we went to bed. A few minutes later, we heard three explosions, which seemed to be almost in our compound, then the whizzing of another plane coming, coming. I remarked to my tent mate, Miss McClelland of the Philadelphia team, that I believed they were out to get us, and picked up my steel helmet to put it on my head, when suddenly without the slightest warning, there were three more explosions accompanied with the most violent concussions and our tent riddled with small frag-ments of bombs and debris. We were shocked, and I was soon aware of blood trickling down both cheeks, and totally blind in the right eye. I was taken at once to the operating room where it was decided to send me on the hospital train to Boulogne. Our night cook, who was standing outside the mess tent about twenty feet away, was blown to pieces, and one of the British officers severely wounded. There was also one British sister severely shocked, and one very slightly wounded.

I later went back to my base, where I remained until May 1, 1918, when orders came through for my transfer to Evacuation Hospital No. 2, A.E.F., as its Chief Nurse. My first impulse was to ask Col. Dar-rach, who was our Commanding Officer at that time, if he would request that I remain at Étretat. He asked me if I had any feeling about going back to the front after my experience in Flanders, and when I told him I had not, he replied, "Then I am afraid you will have to go." I had been so happy at Étretat, had made so many friends, that I was very loath to leave the Unit, and would have preferred a thou-sand times to go up again on a surgical team with some of our own officers, than assume the duties of a Chief Nurse for which I did not feel fully qualified.

[MacDonald then describes this post, including the help she receives from her commanding officer in relocating the nurses' quarters to the hospital compound so they can be nearer their work, and the difficulty of training staff who have had no previous wartime experience and who do not understand the need to conserve materials or to vacate the upper floors of buildings during air raids. Evacuation Hospital No. 2 then transfers to the Army of Occupation and advances into Germany.]

It was due entirely to the encouragement, consideration and patience of the officers and nurses with whom I was associated, that I was able to "carry on" as soon as I did after being wounded. At no time was I ever made to feel an outsider, and I look back upon those days spent with the Unit at Étretat as the happiest ones during my war service.

Joy Bright Hancock
(1898–1986)
U.S. NAVY

Joy Bright Little Hancock Ofstie, from Wildwood, New Jersey, served as a Navy yeoman (F) and courier at the Naval Air Station, Camp May. After the war, she took a job with the Bureau of Aeronautics. Her first husband, a pilot, died in the crash of a ZR-2 airship in 1921. Her second husband, also a pilot, died in a crash in 1925. Undaunted, Hancock learned to fly, but she preferred working on airplane engines.

During World War II, she joined the Navy as a first lieutenant in the WAVES (Women Accepted for Volunteer Emergency Service). She rose to the rank of commander by the end of the war. In February 1946, Commander Hancock became assistant director (Plans) of the Women's Reserve and then director of the WAVES five months later. She was promoted to the rank of captain in 1948.

Hancock retired in 1953 and married a vice admiral, a former World War I pilot whom she had known since 1920. She was widowed a third time a year later. Despite her enormous personal losses, Hancock continued to work to expand the roles of women in the military. The excerpt below is from her memoir *Lady in the Navy: A Personal Reminiscence.*

In 1917, I was attending business school in Philadelphia. My chief fear was that I would not be qualified in time for naval service. . . .

As soon as possible, I explored the possibilities of enlisting in the Navy. Since Captain Elmer Wood, a retired naval officer who had lived in Cape May Court House when I was a child, had been recalled to active duty and was in charge of the Branch Hydrographic Office of the Navy in Philadelphia, I had not too far to go for information. I had come to the right place, for he took me to the Philadelphia Navy Yard to introduce me to a friend of his, Captain George Cooper.

In response to Captain Wood's statement that I wanted to enlist, Captain Cooper said that, although no very formal organization had been set up to handle such a request, I could go to the Naval Home for a physical examination. If I qualified on that score, he would arrange for a test of my clerical ability.

Some consternation was clearly the reaction of the medical staff at the Naval Home when I appeared for physical examination. But since consternation did not involve prejudice, I passed both the physical and mental tests successfully and was enlisted as a yeoman first class.

Indoctrination was not the order of the day; one simply plunged into service cold. At the Navy Clothing Depot, I was outfitted with two uniforms and told to report to the office of the Navy Superintending Constructor of the New York Shipbuilding Corporation in Camden. . . .

No dormitory arrangements were made for the women in service; they simply lived at home and reported daily for work. Since I lived in Philadelphia with one of my mother's friends, I commuted to Camden, New Jersey, via the ferry across the Delaware River and thence a twenty-minute train ride from Camden to the New York Shipbuilding Corporation. Ferry and trains were so jam-packed with shipyard workers that it was not unusual to ride straddling the couplings. On this twenty-minute run, the men called me "Heavy Artillery," in teasing recognition of my five-feet, four inches and mere 102-pound weight.

Since I was assigned to the superintending constructor's office, one of my duties was to carry papers and plans to naval ships being built at the yard. As I walked on these errands, my friends of the daily train rides would spot me and call out cheerily, "Hello there, Heavy

Artillery." This practice was discontinued when an efficiency expert following me found that the time taken out to call greetings was a comparatively costly gesture. Thereafter, a sailor took over that task.

Some of my off-duty time I spent with other yeomen (F) who were assigned to sell Liberty bonds in theaters. At Keith's theater in Philadelphia, for example, we would go up and down the aisles during intermission to make sales.

We also participated in Liberty bond parades on Broad Street. Our training for this activity was acquired at the Navy Yard twice a week. There Marines taught us the rudiments of drill, but we learned hardly more than "forward march," "halt," and the necessity of maintaining straight lines and keeping in step. No instructions were ever given to the effect that we were not to break step for any obstacle that might be in the way, but sometimes there was sharp provocation for changing direction, as, for example, the time we marched behind beautiful, high-spirited horses that had not been housebroken. After a particularly shabby parade performance, our instructor gave us explicit directions: "You don't kick it, you don't jump over it, you step in it."

After a year, I was a seasoned yeoman. There being no designation for women signifying their sex on the rolls, I received orders to duty aboard a combatant ship. My commanding officer, a naval constructor, had never approved of women being attached to the Navy in a military capacity, so when I presented these orders to him, he was blunt, "Carry them out." Upon reporting to the Fourth Naval District in Philadelphia, I was told in no uncertain terms that the Navy had no intention of ordering women to sea for duty on combat ships. My orders being so endorsed, I returned to my job in the superintending constructor's office. Because assignments like these were also received by other women, an "F" was placed after the rate to alert assignment officers that the yeoman was a woman.

[Near the end of the war, Petty Officer Bright is reassigned to the Naval Air Station at Cape May, New Jersey.]

As personnel yeoman at the air station, I appeared at Mast daily with the commanding officer of the station. Upon my reading the charge, the master-at-arms would step forward, explain the situation and have the man tell his story. The captain would pronounce the sentence and I would record it. I was also the stenographer on Naval Courts and Boards. These assignments placed me in a position to be embarrassingly aware of some of the failings and misdemeanors of the men. But I was impressed by the way members of the courts would make every effort to assure that justice was done.

There was certainly no discrimination by reason of sex in the assignment of duties. On my second day at Cape May, a call came over the loud speaker, "All hands on the starboard watch, report to the hangar for sweeping down." I trooped over with the other office workers and was given a broom, learning the hard way what a huge space a dirigible hangar was....

Late in 1918, one of the coastal northeast storms that sweep the New Jersey coast regularly in the fall and early winter, hit the area. To transport personnel living ashore as well as to deliver material arriving by rail, the station maintained a truck. On this particular morning when the truck left for its regular six-mile run from the town to the air station, the wind was blowing a gale and a blizzard was under way.

After four miles, we could go no farther. At times, the ocean was running across the road, battering the houses between the road and the sea. There was nothing to do but start walking across the fields, heading directly into the wind, sleet, and snow which cut our faces. After the first mile, the men formed a double line abreast, and we three women fell in behind. I was nearly frozen. I had lost a rubber—there were no galoshes in those days—and my thin Navy cape kept slipping from my numb hands. The chief in charge finally told the women and men to fall in close and walk lockstep. I drew the leading chief, who was a foot taller than I, and, matching my step with his stride, I soon had my blood circulating. Upon reaching the station, we were sent to the dispensary to thaw out.

During the day, the road to the station was washed out, making it impassable even at low tide. A minesweeper was ordered to take us back via the inland waterway to Cape May....We rolled and pitched with such force that the warrant officer in charge was a worried man as he endeavored to get back to the protection of the breakwater.

I myself never got out of the galley. One of the yeomen (F) was very,

very seasick. The other, scared almost to the point of hysteria, helped me nonetheless as we made coffee and egg sandwiches for the men on deck. I have never been more frightened. Not only was there the angry sea to contend with, but the hot coals continually spilling out of the galley range had to be shoveled back. A heavy lurch of the boat landed me on a crate of eggs. From then on, we had scrambled egg sandwiches.

After fighting the storm for five hours, the crew managed to get us back to the air station at ten o'clock that night. The dock was gone, carried away by an Eagle boat which had rammed it in an attempt to tie up. The boathouse had landed on the forward deck of the Eagle.

Our minesweeper finally tied up at the marine railway and we got ashore by pulling ourselves, flat on our stomachs, along the elevated, open ties. The day ended as it began: in the dispensary. After hot drinks, we three yeomen were bedded down there for the night. . . .

As I look back to World War I, I need to stress the fact that the accomplishments of the more than ten thousand women who served as yeomen (F) were not limited to purely clerical duties. They served ably as translators, draftsmen, fingerprint experts, camouflage designers, and recruiters. Five of them, connected with the Bureau of Medicine and Surgery, served with naval hospital units in France; and one found her place in the operations of the Office of Naval Intelligence in Puerto Rico. Old records reveal that a few yeomen (F) were stationed at Guam, the Panama Canal Zone, and Hawaii.

Once all of the women had been released from active duty, on 31 July 1919 Secretary [of the Navy Josephus] Daniels sent the following message: "It is with deep gratitude for the splendid service rendered by yeomen (F) during our national emergency that I convey to them the sincere appreciation of the Navy Department for their patriotic cooperation."

Lela Leibrand

(1891–1977)

U.S. MARINE CORPS

Lela Leibrand was one of the first ten women to join the Marines in 1918. A divorcée with a young daughter, she used an eighth-grade education and a stenographer's course to get a job as a newspaper reporter in Missouri in 1911. By 1916 she was writing movie scripts in Hollywood. The Marine Corps assigned her to the Publicity Bureau; as a private, she wrote articles for the *Recruiters' Bulletin*, *Marines Magazine*, and *Leatherneck*. After her promotion to sergeant, she edited newsreels with footage of the war in Europe and the first military training film, *All in a Day's Work*. Discharged from the Corps at the rank of sergeant, she returned to Hollywood where she married John Rogers and managed the career of her daughter, Virginia McMath (Ginger Rogers). Leibrand wrote the following article for an unidentified publication in 1918 or 1919.

The Girl Marines

Cherchez la femme! (Find the woman!) It is no longer a problem down at Headquarters in Washington. Girls, girls everywhere! And the Marines might just as well accustom themselves to us for we've come down among them to stay four years!

The moment your Marine Corps sent out the call for girls we flocked to the recruiting stations in every village, hamlet and town, eager to be one of that splendid body of men who have rendered such excellent account of themselves "over there." And, we found they were most particular who they enrolled. "One hundred per cent men; one hundred per cent women," seemed to be the slogan resulting in about four hundred being chosen out of as many thousand applicants. Believe us, we who are in are mighty glad it was us! It's an enormous satisfaction to know you can rate such an organization.

Many of us have left splendid positions back home to answer the call of our country in her hour of stress, even as the boys, because we knew we could be useful. Others of us have come because the Marine Corps pays a better wage than most private concerns for the same kind of work, and the hours, 8.30 a.m. to 4.30 p.m., are especially light. Then, not the least inducement is that fascinating uniform,—enough to make any girl leave home. Have you seen them? Done up in one we have to salute officers and everything.

You see, we are here to attend to your official business while you go out to fight. Some of the officers and men are most skeptical as to our intentions and we've found we must convince them we mean business. . . . We are going to do it, too, by honest effort, rigidly applied. Our work is exacting, and the detail cruel, in a way, for it keeps us upon the tips of our mental toes every moment of each day. To trifle means an error; errors mean inaccurate records. It can't be done in the Marines! However, the men are kind and considerate and patient with us, though a bit dazed at the newness of it.

There's romance in the work; real, live, human romance. We keep in closer touch with you than you dream. If you are transferred we know where from and to. If you are hurt, we know when, where and how much. When you reach another step in progress of your training, marksmanship, promotion, we hear about it and see to it you get the proper credits on your records and—the additional pay! But, when we read "Ashore France, servg. With Army fr." stamped on your card—well, it is but a little hope, just a thought, but it is a prayer that God will watch over you and care for you, in the end delivering you safely home, truly glorified, to that little mother who writes us occasionally that we might know exactly where she may be reached the speedily "in case of emergency." Romance, did you ask? Each one of you is a special little story all by yourself. Sssh! We know when you're brigged, too!

Oh, I mustn't forget to tell you about our drills. You boys would turn dark green with envy to see us "right face," "left face," "salute" (at the heathenish hour of 8.30 in the morning). And, Corporal Lockout, who is in charge of our drills said (and these are his exact words), "Girls learn the drills much easier than men." He added he doesn't know why, but we do. . . . We do police duty in our offices, too, but we didn't have to be drilled to that.

However, Corporal Lockout whispers to me that the drilling is only a means to an end. Discipline is the goal! Military discipline, at that. Personalities and sex must be subdued. The girls must learn as the men have learned, they are privates in the Marine Corps; must learn to accept discipline as the men accept it, without a single consideration for the fact that in private life they were self-governing young ladies. There is to be no proviso to this discipline. We are Marines! That says it all! And, once our lesson has been told to us, I hear from various sources, in ominous tones, leniency will cease to exist. The chaff will be separated from the wheat. A sort of forewarning. Now, do you gather a bit of our importance among you? We are not a fad by any means. . . .

All this is just to let you know we are here, also to warn you that, whatever you do, remember the eagle eyes of the Marinettes are right upon you. Watch your step!

Kate Walker
(ca. 1850s–1931)
U.S. Lighthouse Service

Katherine Gortler emigrated from Germany to the United States in the 1870s. While working as a waitress to support her young son, she met John Walker, a retired sea captain who taught her English. After their marriage, John Walker kept first the Sandy Hook lighthouse in New Jersey, and then the lighthouse at Robbins Reef, a tower surrounded by water one mile from the tip of Staten Island that served as a key navigation aid in the approach to New York Harbor. John died of pneumonia in 1886; his last words to Kate were "Mind the light, Kate!" Walker did so for the next thirty-three years, boarding her daughter, Mamie, in Staten Island during the school year. She rescued as many as fifty people, most of them fishermen blown onto the rocks of Robbins Reef in storms. She rarely went ashore; her son, Jacob, served as assistant keeper and courier. Walker was seventy years old at the beginning of the First World War. She retired in 1919 at seventy-three, and in 1921 she and three other women lighthouse keepers were awarded the World War I Victory Medal for their service. The *New York Times* interviewed Walker for the article "Kept House Nineteen Years on Robbin's Reef," published March 5, 1905, from which this excerpt is taken.

> Lonesome? [Walker says in response to a reporter's question.] I have no time to be lonesome. There is as much housework to do here as—as—at the—the Waldorf.
>
> *[The reporter describes this as her "exploding," as if in indignation.]*

I have my meals to get regularly, although there is often nobody but myself here to eat them. Then there are all the beds to make, the floors to scrub, the windows to clean, and—ach, there is plenty to do.

[The reporter adds that Walker resents an unintentional implication that because she is a lighthouse keeper, she doesn't have the same household duties as other women.]

This lamp in the tower—it is more difficult to care for than a family of children. It need not be wound more than once in five hours, but I wind it every three hours so as to take no chances. In nineteen years that light has never disappointed sailors who have depended upon it. Every night I watch it until 12 o'clock. Then, if all is well, I go to bed, leaving my assistant in charge.

[The reporter notes that she always refers to her son as her "assistant" when discussing duties of the lighthouse.]

I am always up in time to put out the light at sunrise. Then I post my log from which monthly reports to the government are made out. We have to put everything down, from the amount of oil consumed to the state of the weather. Every day I clean the brass work of the lamp, and every month I polish the lenses. The latter is a two days' job.

Merle Egan Anderson
(1890–1986)
U.S. ARMY SIGNAL CORPS

Merle Egan Anderson, of Helena, Montana, joined the telephone operators of World War I known as the "Hello Girls" in 1917 and sailed to France. The Hello Girls discovered after their return from the war that they did not rate veteran status. For sixty years, Anderson campaigned to have them recognized as veterans. When President Jimmy Carter signed the bill granting the Hello Girls veteran status in 1977, only fifty of the women—thirty-three of whom had served in France—were still alive to receive their honorable discharges and Victory Medals. Egan was among them. The excerpt below is from her unpublished memoir, held in the collection of the Women in Military Service for America Memorial Foundation.

I was in a different world. Nothing was real. It was hard to believe that men were dying in a war a few hundred miles from us.

But at the office next morning life became real again. Sergeant Carr greeted me with, "We have a new job. Beginning Monday we are to train soldiers to operate front line switchboards. I hope you are familiar with magneto boards."

I said, "I certainly am. We have a lot of magneto boards in our small offices in Montana." So we spent the rest of the day outlining the procedure we would follow.

When I arrived at our office on Monday, the room had been transformed into a miniature battleground, wired with several magneto boards. We also greeted our first class of ten soldiers. They were all "casuals" having, somehow, become detached from their outfits. They were a sorry looking lot and their first greeting was, "If we have to be telephone operators, where are our skirts?"

I said, "Okay, fellows, before you start you must realize that this is a serious business. Any soldier can carry a gun but if you operate one of these switchboards in the front lines, a whole regiment may depend upon *you*." That seemed to sober them and I soon had willing students.

Most classes lasted a week or ten days since, in addition to operating the switchboards, they had to learn the regulation phrases for all operators as well as a few French phrases in case they connected with French lines. The Army needed soldier operators at some of the smaller exchanges so they were prepared for those jobs also. Since they were detached from their regiments, they were usually without pay checks so I spent my "small change" for sweets from the PX for their "graduation" celebration. They could always eat free Army food in the chow line.

One young redhead in my second class seemed so lost that he aroused my "motherly instincts" and I took him to La Central for dinner. Christie scolded me, accused me of "robbing the cradle." I told her I was adopting him.

She looked at me in amazement and said, "Have you lost your mind?"

I said, "The poor boy is lost in the Army. He is the son of a Pennsylvania minister, has been detached from his friends and is so homesick and lost that I told him I would be his sister and he could call me 'Sis,' which he proceeded to do." Somehow, the fact that I was around seemed to help, and when he was assigned to an operating job he wrote regularly.

In contrast, there was the "hard boiled" regular Army sergeant who took one look and stated, "I am not going to report to any woman." I asked Sergeant Carr what I should do.

He said, "Assign him to K.P. Duty."

So, when he again refused to cooperate, I said, "Okay, report for K.P."

He said, "Says who?"

I replied, "I do."

That set off the fireworks. I was treated to all of the cuss words in his vocabulary. I smiled and said, "Okay, go tell that to Lieutenant Hill." He reported to some officer, was assigned to K.P. and, in a few days returned somewhat subdued and became one of my best students. We parted friends. . . .

Just before the final Meuse-Argonne Drive I had been given the seemingly impossible task of training sixty-three men to operate switchboards for the front lines and a time limit of three days. Our hours were long and strenuous. I was fortunate in having a couple of experienced telephone men in the group who were able to explain the operations of the switchboards while I taught the needed operating technique. Somehow the job was accomplished and I have often wondered how many of those men survived.

About the same time, I learned that some of our Signal Corps women were operating switchboards directly behind the front lines, and, later, when Grace Banker, the chief operator of that group, was stationed in Paris, she told me she had been awarded the Distinguished Service Medal. After her death in 1968, I had the privilege of receiving her story of those front line experiences and had them published in *Yankee Magazine* (March 1974).

[Egan returns to the United States ten months after she deploys to France.]

I was back in the United States! At almost the same spot from which I had sailed ten months earlier, but was I that same person? I suddenly realized I was not. . . .

When we reached Army headquarters I received a shock. Although the Army owed me a month's salary plus "per diem allowance," totaling nearly two hundred dollars, I was informed I could have neither until I paid them the sixty dollars they had failed to deduct from my first two months' salary. Such deduction was to cover the thirty dollar a month allotment I had made to my mother.

When we enlisted we had been told we must have five hundred dollars to cover cost of uniforms and other equipment, so I had found it necessary to borrow one hundred dollars from my mother and stepfather to augment the money I had available. The allotment would repay them and also give me money I now needed so I went to a nearby telegraph office and wired for one hundred dollars. Then I proceeded to the Quartermaster Department to arrange for transportation.

[Egan later marries her prewar sweetheart, Hal, and tries to settle into the life of a Montana housewife.]

For the first week we had nothing but stew for dinner. Each day I added a new ingredient and by the end of the week my patient husband said, "Dear, can't we have something else soon?" So I began to study cookbooks and experiment and eventually became . . . a good cook.

There were other facets of housekeeping I didn't enjoy. There were no vacuum cleaners in those days and our house was on a busy street so I was constantly sweeping and dusting. Also, there was the washing to be done for two people that must be done in a wash tub in the basement and I had to learn to soak the clothes and use a wash board to get them clean. Then I had to pack them up some rickety stairs to hang them in the back yard to dry. Why had I wanted to marry anybody? Housekeeping was not only hard work, it was boring. I longed for the old days in the office when each day brought some new challenge.

5

World War II

"We Were Very Proud To Do Whatever Was Necessary"

Off the coast of North Africa, on the night of November 7, 1942, the staff of the Forty-Eighth Surgical Hospital assembled on board a transport ship near the coast of Algeria to receive instructions for going ashore with the American invasion force. The chief nurse, Capt. Theresa Archard, and the nurses under her command were to line up on the decks when ordered, packs ready with the front of the harness open, shoes unlaced, and helmets on their heads but unfastened. If they were hit, they would have to slip out of their packs, jettison their shoes and helmets, and swim for shore. Their musette bags contained three days' worth of D and C rations: canned hash, beans, stew, coffee, and three chocolate bars each. The women joked around, pretended they were not afraid, and tried not to think too much about what might happen to them.

When the large guns began to shell the small town of Arzeu the following morning, soldiers poured from the ships into commando boats with their guns and equipment. Others loaded tanks for transport ashore. The nurses were ordered to the boats a few hours later. Captain Archard, in the last group to board, watched as her nurses descended the swaying ladder with full packs and untied shoes, guns roaring in the background. They disembarked in waist-deep water and waded up the beach.

Cold, tired, wet, unarmed, and afraid, the nurses huddled behind a sandbank to take cover from sniper fire. They could hear the big guns booming in the distance and the ping of snipers' bullets nearby. After a while, they moved down the beach to a dirty, deserted house where they tried to rest on the cold tile floors. Soon a voice called for Archard and her deputy, Lieutenant Salter. One of the doctors had taken charge of a French and Arab hospital nearby and needed four or five nurses.

At the hospital, enlisted corpsmen held flashlights for the surgeons in the operating room, who worked without gowns or gloves. Wounded men waited in crowded stairways and halls. The nurses carefully rationed the small supply of sedatives. They worked through the night without stopping for food or coffee. The ships, still taking fire from shore, could not offload more supplies. For the next two days, the hospital staff divided their rations with the wounded men who could eat and gave their patients sips of water from their own canteens. They shared the few cigarettes they had with their patients and made cocoa from the chocolate bars.

In a second facility half a mile up the road in a filthy, verminous, abandoned French barracks, the nurses threw out lice-infested mattresses, covered the springs of wooden cots with capes, and sluiced down the floors with nonpotable water. They treated their patients while dodging bullets aimed into the windows of the barracks.

No nurses were wounded or killed during the North African invasion. Nevertheless, General Eisenhower decided that nurses could not go ashore with the landing force again: they would come ashore only after the beachhead was secure. A year later this precaution would prove ineffective. Several nurses were among the casualties on the beachhead at Anzio.

In 1920 the Army (but not the Navy) granted nurses "relative" officer rank, from second lieutenant to major, in recognition of their wartime service. They did not receive equal pay or equal privileges of rank. And except for the nurses, after the First World War the American armed forces never expected to need women's service again. In 1925 Congress rewrote the Naval Reserve Act of 1916, which had authorized the Navy to enlist "citizens"—the oversight that had permitted enlistment of women into the Navy and Marines—to limit enlistment to "male citizens" only.

Because of the close alliance between the women's suffrage and pacifist/antimilitary movements, in 1921 the War Department attempted to persuade women voters that a strong military was necessary. The secretary of the Army named Washington socialite Anita Phipps, the daughter of a brigadier general who had served as the director of the Pennsylvania-Delaware division of the Red Cross Motor Corps Service during the war, director of Women's Programs. The War Department gave Phipps no military status or support, and she lacked credibility with women's organizations. She also proved unable to respond effectively to a smear campaign linking women's activism to Bolshevism. Despite these obstacles, in 1926 she presented a plan for a 170,000-strong Women's Service Corps to serve as an auxiliary to the Army in time of war. The War Department rejected her plan, and in 1931 Gen. Douglas MacArthur abolished her position, saying that it was "of no military value."

In May 1941, Rep. Edith Nourse Rogers (R-Massachusetts) introduced a bill in Congress to establish the Women's Army Auxiliary Corps (WAAC). Rogers, who had inspected field and base hospitals with the Women's Overseas League and served in the Red Cross in Washington DC during World War I, believed that if women were again called to serve during wartime they should receive the same legal status and benefits as men. The Army disagreed: in an internal memo, Brig. Gen. Wade Haislip noted that the Army had "stopped her" by promising to study her proposal "so that when it is forced upon us, as it undoubtedly will be, we shall be able to run it our way." The bill languished in Congress until after Pearl Harbor.

When the Japanese attacked Pearl Harbor, dozens of Army and Navy nurses were serving in Hawaii and the Philippines. Two days later, Japanese troops captured five Navy nurses assigned to the naval hospital on Guam and imprisoned them in Japan for seven months before repatriating them. After the fall of Corregidor in May 1942, Japanese soldiers captured sixty-six Army and eleven more Navy nurses in the Philippines and incarcerated them in the Santo Tomas internment camp in Manila for three years.

By the war's end, nearly sixty thousand women had volunteered to serve as military nurses. More than half volunteered for service in combat zones; sixteen were killed by enemy action.

The attack on Pearl Harbor renewed congressional interest in Nourse's proposal. Congress established the Women's Army Auxiliary Corps, which did not offer women full military status, on May 15, 1942. Oveta Culp Hobby was sworn in as first director at the rank of major, and the first class of women officers graduated in August. Most had attended or graduated college and had work experience as teachers or clerical workers. On July 30, 1942, Public Law 689 established the Navy WAVES (Women Accepted for Volunteer Emergency Service) with Wellesley College president Mildred H. McAfee sworn in as the first director; as in World War I, Navy women had full military status. The Coast Guard followed suit with creation of the SPARS in November 1942, and the following month SPARS entered the Coast Guard Academy in New London, Connecticut—the first women to attend an American military academy. When senators argued that establishment of women's auxiliaries would "destroy their femininity and future standings as 'good mothers,'" the Marine Corps located women who had served in the USMC women's reserve in World War I to prove them wrong; they reestablished the Marine Corps Women's Reserve in November 1942 under the direction of Ruth Cheney Streeter. Training for the Women's Auxiliary Service Pilots (WASP), a civilian auxiliary of the Army Air Corps in which women pilots ferried aircraft military aircraft from factories to military bases and towed targets for anti-aircraft artillery students, began in 1943. All the women's services were to be disestablished six months after the war ended.

The Navy and Marine Corps, aware of the value of a smart uniform for recruiting and morale, engaged professionals to outfit women. Mainbocher, a former *Vogue* editor and fashion designer, volunteered his service to design uniforms for the WAVES. With minor modifications, the women's service dress blue uniform

Mainbocher designed is still worn by Navy women today. Navy officials insisted that the uniforms be trimmed with light blue braid instead of traditional gold; only when women achieved permanent status was gold authorized for women's uniforms. Capt. Anne Lentz, who had worked in a large civilian department store, designed the Marine Corps Women's Reserve uniforms. Elizabeth Arden visited Camp LeJeune in 1943, and after examining the shade of green of the uniforms, she created "Montezuma Red" lipstick, nail polish, and rouge to match the scarlet cap cord and chevrons. By contrast, the Army Office of the Quartermaster General developed uniforms for the WAAC and contracted their production to men's clothing manufacturers. Uniforms frequently required major alterations; shortages of women's uniforms required improvisation with men's items; and women lacked both cold weather gear and tropical uniforms that would protect against insects, as well as shoes that were resistant to tropical rot. Perhaps worst, civilian department stores sold WAAC uniforms: civilian workers and prostitutes seeking easier access to military clubs bought or copied them.

By the spring of 1943, when Army officials requested that the women's corps be granted "regular" instead of "auxiliary" status, a slander campaign against Army women was underway. Initial military investigations into WAACs' "immoral behavior" found that civilians often misidentified drunk and disorderly civilian women dressed in uniforms or copies as WAACs. Rumors led to recruiting shortfalls. In May 1943, Director Hobby asked the Army to investigate the possibility that the rumors originated with Nazi sympathizers.

The Army brought in the FBI when rumors surfaced that 90 percent of WAACs were prostitutes; 40 percent were being sent home pregnant from overseas assignments; virgins were not approved for enlistment; WAACs were engaged in public sex acts; and that the Army was issuing prophylactics to WAACs—normally only purchased by married women at that time—so that they could "keep the troops happy." When syndicated "Capitol Stuff" columnist John O'Donnell published the rumor about the prophylactics on June 8, 1943, Director Hobby, Secretary of War Stimson, President Roosevelt, and First Lady Eleanor Roosevelt all publicly denied the rumors and demanded that O'Donnell retract his story.

Army investigators and censors eventually discovered that the malicious rumors were originating from American servicemen, both officer and enlisted; soldiers' wives; civilian women; and "fanatics" opposed to women working outside the home. Eighty-four percent of letters from soldiers overseas examined by the Office of Censorship contained derogatory comments about WAACs— even when soldiers had never seen or served with any. Congress ordered Director Hobby to appear with statistics on actual cases of pregnancy and venereal disease; the rates turned out to be lower than those of civilian women. Many members of Congress and Army commanders, including Gen. George Marshall, then issued statements supporting the women's corps. But the damage was done, with lasting effects. When the WAAC was disestablished in July 1943 and replaced by the regular Women's Army Corps (WAC) only three-fourths of WAACs chose to remain, despite receiving equal pay with men and increased benefits. Most women who declined to reenlist gave the hostility of camp commanders and soldiers who followed their commanders' lead as their primary reason for leaving.

Despite the rumor-mongering, women signed up to serve in more than two hundred occupational specialties—not only in clerical jobs that "freed a man to fight," but also in finance, communications, supply, transportation, and intelligence. They repaired vehicles and aircraft, packed parachutes, analyzed intelligence photos, made maps, translated, and broke codes. Some worked on the Manhattan Project and in the "Battery X" experiment, in which WASP pilots towed targets that WAACs tracked with new anti-aircraft radars. Twenty thousand Army women served overseas: close to the front lines in Sicily and Italy; under threat of German V-1 and V-2 attacks in London; and in the tropical heat of Africa, Australia, New Guinea, Burma, and India. Navy nurses served on twelve hospital ships. WAVES, with their SPAR counterparts, served in Alaska and Hawaii and at then top-secret LORAN navigation facilities. WAVES were air traffic controllers, Link aviation simulator instructors, radio operators and repairmen, gunnery instructors, naval air navigation instructors, mechanics, aerial photographers, and targeteers for surface gunnery and naval aviation attacks. They also participated in a secret night-fighter training project. Navy flight nurses evacuated casualties from Guam, Tinian, Kwajalein, Iwo Jima, and Okinawa, sometimes while fighting was in progress. WASPs not only ferried aircraft and towed targets but also tested aircraft after repair.

From the start of the war, women of color who attended the first officer and enlisted classes petitioned Congress, the secretary of war, the president, and the First Lady to be allowed to serve to the full extent of their abilities. The Army accepted their service reluctantly and restricted their assignment. Black nurses deployed to Liberia to treat malaria cases in 1943, but they were sent to Europe only near the end of the war. Black WAACs attended racially integrated classes but were assigned to segregated units commanded by black women, where they lived and ate in segregated facilities. Most often they served in areas where black men served or there was a significant African American community. White commanders requested black WAACs for the "morale" of black troops. The Navy recruited few black women; the Marines recruited none until desegregation laws forced the services to integrate after the war.

The Army was authorized to recruit Nisei women in the fall of 1943. It inducted some directly from internment camps. Most with language proficiency were assigned as document translators. One worked with an Australian army major to identify members of a secret Japanese society that tortured and killed prisoners of war. Two Asian American women joined the WASPs: one, Chinese American pilot Hazel Ying Lee, died in an airplane crash.

By the end of the war, approximately 350,000 women—all volunteers—had served in the armed forces: 150,000 in the Army; 80,000 in the Navy; 20,000 in the Marines; and 12,000 in the SPARS. Some 1,100 served as WASP pilots. Around 17,000 WACs served overseas. More than 500 military women were killed in the war, including more than 200 nurses and 38 WASPs who died in accidents caused by bad weather and mechanical failure. Around 1,600 nurses received decorations, including Distinguished Service Medals, Silver Stars, Distinguished Flying Crosses, Soldier's Medals, Bronze Stars, Air Medals, Legions of Merit, Commendation Medals, and Purple Hearts. WASPs flew 60 million miles, ferried 12,650 aircraft, towed hundreds of gunnery targets, and instructed hundreds of male pilots.

At the end of the war, both the Army and the Navy wanted to make the women's corps permanent. Opposition came from members of Congress; society expected women to return to their homes and release jobs to men. The League of Women Voters declined to support women veterans' claims to veterans' benefits, access to Veterans' Preference, and the GI Bill; Mrs. Robert Gordon, legislative chair, argued that women veterans' use of benefits would result in discrimination against disabled male veterans and working women who had remained in the civilian sector. WASP Director Jackie Cochran refused to serve in an organization in which she would be subordinate to WAC Director Hobby, and she argued to disband the WASP if it was not integrated into the military. Even the directors of the women's services were reluctant to seek permanent status. They noted the reluctance of military men to accept women; treatment of women's concerns as frivolous, not worth the bother, or seeking favoritism and special privileges; and the reluctance of women to complain of maltreatment due to feelings of powerlessness and fear of reprisal.

Demobilization was set for September 1, 1946. Later that year, a Veterans Administration study, "The Woman Veteran," noted that "many of the women were experiencing the same readjustment problems as the enlisted men separated around the same time . . . and that, in addition, women veterans had to deal with problems and bias against women in the military and women veterans." Many women felt that the government and the American people failed to value their contributions.

In the years that followed, few women veterans commercially published memoirs of their service. Only as the fiftieth anniversary of VE Day and VJ Day approached did more accounts begin to appear in print. Most were self-published or published in limited print runs by university presses.

Avis Schorer
(1919–2016)
U.S. ARMY NURSE CORPS

Avis D. Schorer, from Iowa, served as an Army nurse at evacuation hospitals in Africa and Italy from 1942 to 1946. She and twenty-five fellow nurses landed on the Anzio beachhead under constant bombardment from German artillery. They set up a field hospital, nicknamed "Hell's Half Acre," on the beach. The following are excerpts from Schorer's memoir *A Half Acre of Hell: A Combat Nurse in WWII*, published in 2000.

> We went ashore on D-day plus five—January 27, 1944. . . . The terrain was flat, unlike the mountains near Naples. Little did we realize that our first thirty-six hours ashore would be a foretaste of what lay ahead.
>
> Instead of a hero's welcome, men on shore shouted, "What the hell are women doing here? This place is hot. Take the first vehicle you can and get out of here."
>
> We rushed aboard [an open truck waiting to take the nurses to the hospital site], but the sirens immediately blasted their warning—German planes overhead. Everyone jumped from the truck and pressed against the last remaining wall of a bombed building. American planes swooped in, guns blazing, and chased the intruders back to their territory.
>
> *[Red crosses on a white background mark the hospital site, a few tents set up on the beach. The commander, Colonel Blesse, gives the nurses a pep talk and assures them that there is no need to dig foxholes.]*
>
> The pep talk did little to soothe our shattered nerves when German planes appeared overhead with American fighter planes in pursuit. The planes dived and swooped with guns blazing. Puffs of black smoke filled the sky and the rat-a-tat-tat of antiaircraft guns sent up a deafening roar.

"Get him! Get him!" we shouted, even though the gunners could not hear us.

We saw an American plane spiral downward, leaving a trail of smoke. "Oh! That Jerry got our plane!" we cried in anguish. The pilot ejected and slowly drifted to earth. We ducked the dirt and flames that shot skyward when the plane plummeted to earth two hundred yards away. A German plane fell across the road from where we were standing at about the same time. The other German planes disappeared into the morning sunshine....

Even though Colonel Blesse told us foxholes were unnecessary, many of the officers and men started to dig anyway.... The bank of the ditch [that bordered the camp] soon resembled a prairie dog village. Nurses could not find the time or did not have enough strength to dig a hole. We always wore a steel helmet. Those without one received a twenty-five dollar fine. The order was enforced easily.

Air raids continued for the next two days. The big railroad gun that the Germans pulled from a tunnel in the mountains shelled all night. We learned that the gun fired one-quarter-ton missiles that made a bone-chilling whistle when they traveled overhead. We soon referred to it as the "Anzio Express." The gun terrorized us and caused much loss of life and valuable equipment during the seventy-six days we were on the beachhead....

In our first thirty-six hours, the hospital admitted 1,129 battle casualties. The 750-bed hospital expanded to 1,200 by adding more tents.... Despite being on duty for thirty-six hours, I felt quite well physically. I again went to bed fully clothed and slept despite two air raids and the shells, too numerous to count, that screamed overhead.

[More hospitals arrive on the beachhead, including the 93rd Evacuation Hospital, the 33rd Field Hospital, and the 95th Evacuation Hospital. The hospitals are set up in a group to enable the Germans to identify them more easily as off-limits.]

The Germans shelled the 33rd Field Hospital just after they arrived. The compound was between the harbor and the Alban Hills behind us occupied by the Germans. It soon became known as "Hell's Half Acre" because it was one of the most feared places on the beachhead.

Ammunition dumps, motor vehicle pools, fuel dumps, and artillery surrounded the hospital compound. The navy trained their guns on the German lines and the Germans shelled the harbor. Shells and bombs fell short a few times and landed in the hospital, but they did not injure anyone. Most managed to carry on without a great deal of panic and fear despite shattered nerves and sleepless nights. Less seriously wounded patients continued to plead for a discharge to the front because they felt safer in their foxholes there....

One of the first mornings, after a night of duty, I went outside for a breath of fresh air before I found my tent for some much-needed sleep.... I again thought about the 95th Evac in the same area and wanted to look for [my friend] Gertrude.

[Eventually Schorer returns to her tent and falls asleep. The date is February 7, 1944.]

I had been asleep for several hours when I heard planes overhead and gunfire close by—or was I dreaming? I slid deeper into the sleeping bag and covered my head. I shifted and turned, trying to block out the noise.

Mary burst into the tent. "Thank God, Avis! You're all right!"

"What was all that noise? I could hardly sleep."

"Oh, I'm so glad you're all right," cried Mary, her words spilling out hysterically. "It's so terrible—the 95th was bombed. We don't know how many are killed. We're working on the wounded and surgery is swamped."

"Was anyone we know killed?" I asked, afraid to hear her answer.

"The chief nurse and a Red Cross worker were killed instantly. Most of the patients in the post-op ward were killed. Your friend, Gertrude, is critically wounded. The doctors don't think she'll survive. She's in surgery now." ...

I lay on my cot for an hour and stared at the top of the dark tent. I fought choking emotions of grief, fright, and anger. I was angry at Hitler, the Germans, and the war that put us here. My heart ached and it was hard to breathe. I realized any breath could be my last.

I learned later that the carnage happened when German planes flew over the beachhead. Allied planes were in hot pursuit. Jerry, trying to lighten his load and escape, jettisoned his anti-personnel bombs. The bombs landed on the hospital, killing twenty-six and wounding sixty-eight. The bombs killed or wounded everyone in the pre-op area, including many already wounded while fighting on the front. The Allies shot down the plane when it tried to get away. . . . I was sleeping about 150 yards from where the bombs fell. . . .

A tap, tap on the tent brought me to my feet. It was Jon.

"I just wanted to see if you're all right," said Jon.

"How is Gertrude Morrow?" I asked anxiously.

"She died."

I wanted to cry, but the hurt was so deep, tears would not come. I was numb and did not want to believe what I heard.

"Couldn't they do anything to save her?" I cried.

"The bomb blew her leg off at the hip," said Jon. "She also lost her kidneys. Her life wouldn't have been worth living."

I found little comfort in his words.

[Jon helps Schorer dig a shallow foxhole in the sand, which makes her feel safer. She notes that medical personnel do not spend much time in the mess hall because mealtime is a favorite time for German attacks.]

The Germans unleashed their heaviest raid after dark on February 12. I was outside my tent when the red alert sounded. . . . I ran to the air-raid shelter and was just inside when planes dropped flares over the hospital. They lighted the whole area brighter than day. Planes made pass after pass over the hospital, unleashing a deadly load of antipersonnel bombs. Jagged fragments of metal tore into the flesh of anyone near the explosions.

Bombs screamed earthward and landed with a thud. Above the chaos and bedlam, someone shouted, "They're falling on the nurses' tents!"

A soldier ran to the air-raid shelter shouting hysterically, "Is there a doctor in there? We need a doctor!" Before anyone could answer, he said, "Ellen's been hit!"

Ignoring the falling bombs, two soldiers ran out, found a litter, and carried Ellen [Ainsworth] to the pre-op ward. [A piece of shrapnel about the size of a quarter had pierced her chest and she had a sucking chest wound.] Bomb fragments riddled my tent, which was about six feet from Ellen's. I found a jagged hole in my metal sewing box that was deep inside my barracks bag. We learned later that the Germans flew about two hundred planes in the raid.

The wound in Ellen's chest appeared small. The white hot metal passed through the lung into her abdomen and internal injuries were massive. Stomach contents spread through her lungs and abdomen, which made her condition grave. . . . She detected my alarm when I approached her bed.

"Don't worry, Avis," she said. "I'm tougher than anything Jerry can throw at us." . . .

Ellen lost ground each day. She was aroused only when the percussion of a shell was near or the red alert sounded. I believed much of her lethargy was due to heavy narcotics we gave her regularly. Her abdomen was distended and we gave her oxygen through a mask. She remained so mentally alert that I could not dismiss her fighting spirit. I refused to think she would not recover.

We attached the chain with her dog tags, rabbit's foot, four-leaf clover, lucky-seven dice, and St. Christopher medal to her medical record. Captain Sloan, the ward officer, and I were at the desk when he picked up the chain loaded with charms. He said, "She might as well throw this away." I then realized how grave her condition had become.

On February 16, her breathing was shallow and her pale skin ashen. I tried to moisten her parched lips. She waved me away weakly. I could see her life slipping away. At [10 a.m.] she reached to remove the oxygen mask.

"Ellen, we'd better leave the mask on," I whispered. She rolled her eyes back and took her last breath. . . .

Shocked and numb, I couldn't comprehend what had happened. Tears did not come. . . . Why couldn't I cry when it hurt so much? . . . Why hadn't I insisted she go to the air-raid shelter with me?

[Schorer goes on to describe dressing Ainsworth for her funeral service; she is buried in the cemetery at Anzio. Schorer also describes gathering Ainsworth's personal effects to be sent home to her family.]

While shells from the Anzio Express screamed overhead, I went to bed and prayed I would see another day.

Maude Denson "Denny" Williams
(1907–1997)
U.S. ARMY NURSE CORPS

Williams was one of sixty-six Army and eleven Navy nurses taken captive by the Japanese in the Philippines and held as prisoners of war in a civilian prison camp for three years. The Japanese did not permit them to care for military patients, but the nurses continued to care for interned civilians in the camp hospital throughout their imprisonment. Because of shortages, the Japanese rationed the prisoners' food and finally suspended rations altogether in December 1944. From that time until they were rescued by soldiers of the First Cavalry Divison of the Sixth Army in February 1945, the prisoners subsisted on about five hundred calories a day. The nurses lost an average of more than forty pounds each and nearly died of starvation. In 1985 Williams published her memoir *To the Angels*, from which the following excerpts are taken.

> I went to the Main Tunnel just before the surrender. The dirty, hungry, and exhausted men filled the passageway. Some asked for water, some for food, and the pity was that we had very little of either. Some of them were swearing, some were staring into space. A Filipino had shot his brains out. I tried not to show any emotion; I hurried back to our lateral to be alone. Such a sad, sad day—the Japanese were everywhere on the island, except in the tunnel.
>
> Late in the afternoon *they* came.
>
> Our officers conducted their officers with swords hanging from their waists, and their soldiers who had guns with bare bayonets and camouflage netting strung with leaves on their helmets, into the tunnel.
>
> Standing in uniform, my face to the wall as instructed, I glanced sideways as they peered into the lateral. Arrogant little men puffed and strutted in their moment of victory. They did not harm me, they didn't speak to me, they didn't even come close to me. But now the enemy had a face, a body, an evil intention toward me.
>
> In my anguish I remembered God's telephone number—Jer. 33:3. "Call unto me, and I will answer thee, and shew thee great and mighty things, which thou knowest not."

Frequently I had used the Episcopal prayer book. If ever I needed God's phone number it was now.

"O merciful and compassionate God! You're ever ready to hear the prayers of those who put their trust in you, help us in our need. I humbly ask, in your goodness to comfort and help all prisoners. Look on us with mercy."

At this time a Japanese guard shuffled into the nurses' quarters. I bowed and turned again to talk to God.

• • •

In the presence of any member of the Japanese Imperial Army, you will bow from the waist. The first rule handed down from our military captors and the one we hated most.

Immediately after the surrender, innumerable groups of the enemy prowled through the Hospital Tunnel, talking loudly and coming close to be sure we bowed from the waist. I obeyed, and if we had to bow from the waist, at least the enemy couldn't dictate what we thought.

Following the first inspection tour, the Japanese Tunnel Commander ordered the hospital to function as usual. Back on duty, we shared with our eight hundred patients bits and pieces of food squirreled away in the diet kitchen and mess, plus a supply of cracked wheat, destined early in the war for China until General MacArthur had commandeered it six months ago.

All able-bodied men not needed in the hospital were marched out of the tunnels at bayonet point late on the afternoon of surrender, and our doctors were ordered to discharge all patients as quickly as possible for work outside. Almost at once signs went up announcing that everything was the property of the Japanese Imperial Government and nothing was to be removed. We were not permitted outside, and we were forbidden to talk with our patients except on medical matters—a rule we broke whenever our soldiers came in under guard to remove the dead, and when new patients arrived. In broken sentences and muttered phrases, we learned that in two days they had buried three or four Japanese to every one of ours; and for three days they had been held in the sun without food or water or even shelter. Enemy soldiers had robbed them of all their possessions, even eyeglasses; and for the first two weeks they were considered hostages rather than prisoners of war, since U.S. Forces elsewhere had not yet surrendered. Gaunt, unshaven, dirty, and risking a beating to whisper to us, these men stubbornly maintained their dignity and self-discipline in the face of defeat and brutal treatment. I thought them all heroes, and asked God to bless them. . . .

The enemy surgeon in charge told Colonel Cooper that sanitation and our basic human needs were matters of indifference since Japan's standards were lower than ours. Repeated pleas for us to leave the tunnels were refused for two or three weeks; and when finally we were permitted out into the sunshine, we had to stay within twenty-five yards of the tunnel entrance.

While I desperately craved fresh air, I didn't go often because groups of chattering captors clustered around us to stare and whisper and take pictures.

• • •

Colonel Menzie and his wife Mary, a nurse, occupied the back room [in one of the lateral tunnels off the main tunnel] until the surrender, at which time Colonel Menzie was taken out of the tunnel with all the other men. After he had gone, Mary asked another nurse, whom I shall call Kate Clark, to join her, while two other nurses occupied the adjoining room. . . .

One night late in May a Japanese officer entered the end room where Mary and Kate were sleeping. In the semi-darkness, Mary was aware of a presence. Half asleep and confused she made out the faint outline of a Japanese officer looming over her. Then she glimpsed the dagger in his hand above her. At this she came wide awake. Terror-struck at what she saw, she screamed like a banshee and sat up in bed. Her voice had a wailing, piercing shriek. The Japanese drew back in surprise, and in this instant she scrambled to her feet, giving him a hard push in the stomach with her elbow. She used these precious seconds to hoist herself over the partition. Once in the adjoining room she ran through into the nurses' lateral, screaming hysterically.

Kate had been sleeping soundly across the aisle from Mary; she awakened and watched frozen in terror as Mary climbed the partition. She knew that she could never escape that way, for her legs were shorter than Mary's and she was farther away from the partition.

The Japanese officer turned toward her brandishing his dagger and indicating that she would do instead of Mary. He forced her back down on the bed from which she was attempting to rise and despite her cries, he held her while lowering himself over her. She struggled and tried to kick him in the groin, moving her face from side to side to avoid his seeking lips. He was bigger than she was, and strong. Enraged and thwarted, he almost flattened her and hissed in Japanese; she could not understand but the tone further alarmed her. Unable to break his hold and helpless under his weight, she felt him tearing at her pajamas. A faint tearing sound and she felt his hand on her naked flesh. Her skin cringed, and she struggled more. A desperate heave shook him partially off her; she freed herself with phenomenal strength to roll away slightly from him. The Japanese was panting and sweating: his odor was revolting to her. She felt his bare thigh against her. Waves of disgust almost impaired her thinking. At last she remembered the Kotex pad. Thank God, she thought, maybe this will save me. As the Japanese once again fumbled toward her in the semi-darkness, she took his hand—already a bare inch or so from her legs— and moved it toward the Kotex. She felt him hesitate, then examine what it was he was feeling. His fingers moved over the Kotex, over her legs. A few tentative movements over her stomach and then nothing. Kate lay perfectly still, praying, "Lord Jesus help me, don't abandon me."

After what seemed hours, but in reality was only minutes, he grunted something in Japanese and removed his hand and rolled away from her. Kate lay perfectly still, afraid to breathe. How long she lay, she did not know. At long last, exhausted and drained, she quit sobbing; she pulled herself together and got out of bed. She stumbled to her feet. Unaware of her appearance, and like a zombie, she staggered out of the room and into the nurses' lateral.

We had heard all the screaming, and knew too well what was probably happening. Afraid to act, and filled with horror, we stood in the center of the room, unsure of what to do. "Kate, what in heaven's name, what happened to you? Are you hurt?" Someone rushed toward her, and led her quietly to a bunk. Dazed, Kate allowed herself to be set down. Her hair was wild in disarray, her pajamas ripped on top, the trousers hung in shreds. Her legs were bleeding. Her breasts and stomach which were mostly uncovered were bruised and scratched.

The next day the Japanese command interviewed those living in this lateral and intimated that perhaps the man was an American or a Filipino and not a Japanese.

Looking at a bespectacled Kate, who registered a cool and calm appearance, I said, "Kate, this situation really burns me up. Not only are we prisoners; because they got their feathers ruffled about the embargo, they starve us, beat our men, and try to rape us!"

"Yes. I feel like I'd been bitten by a venomous snake. . . . I have clammy skin, a dry mouth, faintness, tremors, heart palpitation and sometimes nausea. I'm sure the horrible creature's Wasserman was higher than his IQ."

"I admire you, Kate. You've managed to regain your composure and you haven't lost your sense of humor. I guess we'll keep on keeping our guard up; whatever that includes."

"I hope our men in POW camps never hear of this incident," Kate said. "They have heartaches by the million. They're starved and forced to work as slave labor. Just think of the anxiety they have about their families and loved ones."

Kate joined the rest of the nurses in the crowded lateral [tunnel] and seemingly slept well from then on.

[February 1945. The nurses hear shooting close to the camp.]

I leaned toward the window. Outside it was darker than it had been, but not yet black night. I could see a little, and it looked quiet enough down the drive to the main gate with its guardhouses on either side. "I hear a rumble. Can't you all hear it? Can you see anything?"

"I hear it," Josie breathed. "But I don't see anything. Could it be tanks?"

"Ours, do you suppose?" Shack asked. "Or theirs?"

"Theirs," someone said. "They've come to kill us off and have done with it."

"Oh, no," I said. "You're wrong again."

"How do you know, Denny?"

"I feel it, that's how! Hush now, let's just listen."

The rumble persisted, grew louder, filled the air with a clanking rattling rolling grinding roar as it advanced inexorably toward us. Relentless doom for the enemy? Or annihilation for us? Would the Japs dare? Of course they would. Hadn't they already stopped our food entirely?

The rumble stopped. Dead silence at the gates. Dead silence in the building. Full darkness now, and not a light showing this side of the glare on the horizon. Dead silence and black darkness while our whole world held its breath.

"Where the hell is the front gate?"

A good American male voice that made me tingle all over, brought me to my feet pounding somebody's shoulders, all of us screaming, joining our voices to others which rose all over the building.

"It's the Americans! God bless America! The Yanks are here! Our boys have come!"

Mary Ellen "Liz" Graydon
(1918–2000)
U.S. WOMEN'S ARMY CORPS

Mary Ellen "Liz" Graydon served three years as a WAC during World War II. A published poet, she was a member of the Southern Poetry Association in Mississippi, the Georgia Poetry Society, and the Disabled American Veterans. She graduated from Oglethorpe University in 1975 and published two books, *My Time in Rhyme—and More* and *Love and War: One WAC Remembers World War II*. The following excerpts are from *Love and War*, published in 1998.

One of the most vicious rumors ever started about the WACs surfaced in late 1942 or early 1943. The rumor appeared in the newspapers and on the radio that 250,000 WACs were being sent home from overseas because they were pregnant! [There were only 16,000 WACs serving overseas at that time, and approximately 140,000 WACs total.]

Parents of the WACs went ballistic! They wrote and/or called their senators, congressmen, lawyers, and even the President of the United

States, which at the time was Franklin D. Roosevelt. They demanded that the WAC be disbanded and all the girls be sent home.

To make the situation even worse, a well-known, highly visible woman made a suggestion to the Army that all the WACs be issued condoms! In the 1940s the word "condom" was not even mentioned in polite society. The public was astounded and horrified, and "the lady" had to apologize via radio, saying that her suggestion was inappropriate, but the damage was done. . . .

Who started the rumor? We never knew, but recruitment of WACs fell off for a few months, and our reputation suffered terribly as the result of an awful lie!

A columnist, John O'Donnell, claimed "a super-secret War Department policy authorized the issuance of prophylactics to all WACs before they were sent overseas." He said Director Hobby knew about it and agreed with the policy. The charge was a lie, and O'Donnell had to retract his allegation. WACs and their families were very angry, but the harm had been done.

Congress told Director Hobby to give them statistics on WAC pregnancies and their supposed venereal diseases. Congress learned that the percentage was very small, and they turned their efforts toward praising the WACs.

I was there with the women, and I know the truth. Not one WAC became pregnant in my company during my three years of service, and if anyone contracted any disease, we were not aware of it.

The WACs were human, but they were ladies, and they wouldn't dream of behaving in such a way as to disgrace the Women's Army Corps.

• • •

WACs were supposed to take over the clerical duties of the men, although these were considered menial and uninteresting. But those were the jobs familiar to a large percentage of working women in the 1940s. So, if WACs could do the work *and* free the men for combat, we would all be doing our duty, and the war would soon be over. Right? Wrong!

Some of the men were very comfortable in their jobs and resented the WACs who would depose them. The men did not want combat and neither did their families and fiancées. They believed that the WACs were to blame for the threat of overseas duties. The women who joined the military meant change, and men did not want change. Therefore, they believed the worst rumors about the women, and passed them on (elaborately embellished) to their fellow soldiers, families, and friends.

In the 1940s, there were still many men in the United States who wanted their wives "barefoot and pregnant," as gross as that sounds. It was a repugnant idea but true. The egos of those men must have suffered a terrible defeat when the WACs were neither barefoot nor pregnant but soon learned skills never allowed for women previously, work that had been dominated by men. . . .

Thousands of men tried very hard to stay out of the Army, Navy, or Marines. They sought help from congressmen, senators, lawyers, friends, and anyone who could secure a deferment for them. Many of them were successful and remained at their civilian jobs throughout the war. . . . However, some were drafted in spite of the "strings" that had been pulled. I do not blame anyone for avoiding death in some war zone, but it has always been the duty of every male to defend his country from the enemy. To do otherwise would have branded him a coward, and few men could live with that badge.

Some men could, however, and they wanted the women out of the WAC. They wanted to remain safe and secure on U.S. soil. If the WACs took over the menial tasks the men were doing, servicemen had no reason to remain in the States, and overseas duty was inevitable.

But, were we to blame? We *volunteered* for overseas service when the Army needed us, knowing that our lives could be at risk. . . . We (the WACs) wanted to serve our country anywhere the Army needed us. What does that say about some of the men?

[Graydon serves in London during the German v-1 and v-2 bombings in 1944.]

Our company of WACs gathered our gear, disembarked, and wearily climbed aboard a train bound for London. Arriving at our long-awaited destination, we went directly to our "billets" which were two five-story English houses, now joined together (on the inside) to house 150 WACs.

We carried our barracks bags up the long flight of stairs to a room on the fifth floor assigned to four WACs, and I was one of them.

Now, at last, we were ready for sleep, the windows of our rooms darkened by blackout curtains. The trip from Boston to London by ship, train, and Army trucks had left us all exhausted, and the hard Army cots felt like eiderdown.

The silence was shattered by deafening explosions. Ear-splitting sounds came from every direction. Other loud noises, which we could not identify, penetrated the night. We had heard some of those sounds before—back home in the newsreels. But something strange and different from anything we had seen or heard before was raining on London, and the antiaircraft guns stationed just two blocks away in Hyde Park were firing in staccato-like bursts of flame.

• • •

German planes, with their bombs, had been quiet over London for many weeks—had they begun again? The WACs had little time to contemplate Hitler's war strategy. We scrambled out of our beds and ran down the five flights of stairs to the basement with the air raid warning signal screaming in our ears. The sound was loud, alarming and frightening.

The dark basement was much too small to allow a hundred and fifty WACs to lie down, and the hard cement floor was cold and damp. In sitting positions, we huddled together for warmth and comfort, and I prayed harder than I ever had before. The thought uppermost in my mind was the fear that June 12–13, 1944, would be my last night on earth.

The booming sound of the antiaircraft guns and the screaming air raid warning signal continued, and so did the explosive sounds—screeching, thunderous, deafening, and terrifying. We heard falling objects like pieces of metal raining from the sky. Something was disintegrating, and the debris was flying through the air. Walls of the buildings shook from the impact, and bricks tumbled down the chimneys. Throughout the seemingly endless night, our stunned, frightened women remained awake, still praying for our safety and, strangely enough, for silence—silence that would reveal the end of that nightmare.

In the early dawn, news came to us from our officers that the explosions, which we had not been able to identify, were from Hitler's first buzz-bombs: v-1 robot bombs he hoped would bring an end to the long war with Great Britain.

[Graydon summarizes the design and some of the effects of the v-1 and v-2 bombs on London.]

There were few visible signs of fear after the first weeks of our visit from Hitler's buzz-bombs. There were no hysterics, no fainting or tears from the WACs.

[She goes on to talk about how many of the WACs learned to smoke cigarettes in the basement during air raids.]

After many sleepless nights, our Commanding Officer called a meeting to ask all of us a question, "Do you want to die in the cold basement or in your bed?" We voted unanimously to die in bed. It posed a greater threat to me because my room was on the top floor, the place where a bomb would hit first. I could easily be killed at that instant or fall through the five stories and be buried beneath the rubble. Not much of a choice. However, all of us had to work, and we needed to sleep and rest. For the remainder of our stay in London, we slept in our beds and prayed every night that we would live to see the morning.

The other girls and I closed the blackout curtains at our window each night just before dark. When we put out our one light in the room and opened the curtains, we looked with fear and also with a sense of excitement, toward the English Channel and France. We talked very little but just waited to see the buzz-bombs coming toward us. The sound was much like that of an outboard motor on a boat. A flash of flame could be seen coming from the tail. We held our breath as we waited to see if it would continue on its path. If the motor cut out directly over us, our lives were in jeopardy. A direct hit could destroy our building and the company of WACs inside. Night after night, we were quite lucky because the bombs flew over us, and we were safe for a time.

When we left London, the buildings on all four sides surrounding our billets had been damaged or completely demolished. Our "homes" stood alone, almost untouched by the enemy bombs. We all felt that God had watched over us throughout our months at 72 Upper Berkley Street.

• • •

We were soldiers in the U.S. Army, and we were trained to steel ourselves from the usual feminine emotions. We were very proud to do
whatever was necessary to bring the war to an early victory over the
enemy. The discipline the WACs had acquired gave us the courage to
say, "Soldiers do not cry."

Later, however, after the war was over, some veterans would learn
that our discipline and our war experiences would lead to life-altering
physical and mental conditions, later to be called "post war syndrome."

Psychologists believed that veterans had held their muscles, nerves
and minds as tight as steel. They were taut over a long period of time
but, when the war was over, men and women relaxed completely.
They were like rubber bands that had been would up so tight that
sooner or later the bands had to snap, and snap they did. Some veterans developed ulcers, chronic diarrhea, spastic colitis and irritable
bowel syndrome (IBS). Others suffered from psychological problems
and were unable to adjust to civilian life after the trauma they had
experienced. . . .

Back home in the United States, our citizens slept snug in their
beds but complained of the shortage of silk stockings, gas, coffee,
sugar, and a few other items. They still had plenty to eat, warm clothing, heated homes and hot water, alcohol to drink, cosmetics to wear,
and most of the necessities of life, and they enjoyed the most important thing in their lives—peace on United States soil.

Charity Adams Earley
(1918–2002)
U.S. Women's Army Corps

Charity Adams Earley, from Columbia, South Carolina, was the
first African American officer in the Women's Army Auxiliary
Corps. During World War II, Earley commanded the first battalion of African American women serving overseas, the 6888th Central Postal Directory. By the end of the war, Major Earley was the
highest-ranking African American woman in the Army. According
to Black History Now, Earley "was dressed down by a racist colonel,

had her rank questioned by MPs in civilian settings, and once, at home on leave, defended her father's house with a shotgun by her side during a tense standoff with members of the Ku Klux Klan." The following are excerpts from her memoir *One Woman's Army: A Black Officer Remembers the WAC*.

21 Mar.–5 May 1945

On my frequent trips to London, I had come to know many of the Red Cross staff members, especially those in the operations office. In fact, I had several dates with one member of the staff. He was white, and perhaps that black-white combination on dates may have been the reason for what happened next. I received a call from Red Cross Headquarters asking me to "please" come into the city next day if at all possible. It was possible, and I went.

At the Red Cross office I was presented with a piece of news that was supposed to excite me. It made me angry. The director said, "We realize that your colored girls would be happier if they had a hotel all to themselves so we have leased a hotel from the British government, and we are in the process of renovating and furnishing it now."

"Did the white girls complain?" I asked.

"Oh, no, we just know that your girls would rather have a place of their own."

"More important to me, I have not had one single complaint from my 'colored girls.' My advice is to leave well enough alone."

"Oh, please," the director persisted. "Won't you let us take you out to see it?"

We climbed into a vehicle and went to the hotel. Later, I summed up my reaction to the hotel to my officers as follows. "It will make a lovely hotel, but it is as far off the beaten path as it could be and still be a nice place and in the city, and it is the most blatant segregation and discrimination I have ever encountered."

Warning the Red Cross director, one more time, that this was a shameful waste of volunteer contributions, I returned to Birmingham. Over the next several weeks we watched and waited and planned. Finally, the call came. The hotel was ready, and would I please come see it before the women arrived? The next morning I was off to London again. I did have a vehicle and chauffeur assigned to me for official business, so I could make these one-day trips into London, as well as to other military locations on short notice. When I arrived in London, I was rushed out to the hotel for my "colored girls." For war times, the hotel was quite nicely furnished, the kitchen was complete and stocked, supplies adequate, and staff sufficient. Everyone was beaming and waiting to know what I thought of it. I toured the entire place, room by room, before I made my comment.

"I am sorry that you have gone to so much expense and trouble. I advised you that the Negro WACs had had no problems with the white WACs, so this hotel is not necessary. I promise you that, as God is my witness, as long as I am commanding officer of the 6888th Central Postal Directory Battalion, not one member of that unit will ever spend one night here."

Back in Birmingham I prepared to put our plan in operation. The following morning for the first and only time I shut down the eight-hour shifts and had every member of the unit (the only ones excused were the ones in the hospital) assemble in the gymtorium, and I laid out the strategy. All this took place after the unit was at full strength, so there was not enough room for nearly a thousand people to be seated. I had prepared my remarks carefully.

"Since we have been here, those of you who have had passes to London have stayed at the WAC hotel for enlisted women. Not one of you has every complained about sharing a hotel with white WACs. Whether white WACs have complained about you is not my problem. Several weeks ago I was informed that the Red Cross was going to prepare a separate hotel for members of the 6888th because that organization feels that you would be happier in a segregated building. They described it as your own private hotel.

"Yesterday, I visited the hotel. It is very nice, but it is very segregated. What it does is to create a segregated hotel when we already have an integrated situation, which is working. Yesterday as I stood in that hotel, I promised that not one of you would spend a night in that hotel. I cannot force you to support me, short of not granting any overnight passes. I will not do that, but I do ask your support.

"We have worked out several options that we hope you will use. First, since transportation is free, you can take your pass to London by going in the morning and returning here in the evening to your regular sleeping quarters. For this, we will make adjustments in curfew hours based on the train schedule. Second, if you want to stay overnight in London, you may go to any hotel and pay your own bills. Third, if you want to stay overnight in London and you want approval of the family with whom you want to stay, you'll get approval with a minimum of trouble."

I am very proud of my service as CO of the 6888th, but one of the proudest times was when the women of that unit supported me in this action. I have never deluded myself that this support came out of love for me. What we had was a large group of adult Negro women who had been victimized, in one way or another, by racial bias.

Josette Dermody Wingo
(1924–)
U.S. NAVY

Josette Dermody Wingo, from Detroit, joined the WAVES in 1944 for the remaining eighteen months of World War II. She served in an elite WAVES unit that taught men how to shoot down enemy aircraft. After the war, Wingo used the GI Bill to complete a master's degree. When she retired from teaching, she began writing about her war experiences. The following excerpts are from her 1994 memoir *Mother Was a Gunner's Mate: World War II in the WAVES*.

Shooting the big guns is actually kind of fun, but breakdown is awful. When the sun sets, we have to take our guns apart and stow them securely before the guys can finish theirs and stand around teasing. Worst part of the day on the gunnery range. Worst part of my life. Taking the guns apart isn't all that hard, Lord knows we practiced it enough with the wooden mockups that are easy because they have the firing systems painted red. We can all, by this time, break down a machine gun blindfolded and race some instructor's stopwatch to put it back together. Nothing to it. Easy as pie. Just remember that the sear pin is in the correct position if it looks like a highchair; and don't mention it out loud when the guys are around. It drives them nuts when we use a feminine image like a highchair for remembering. Too bad.

The problem is, the real guns, the Oerlikons, are heavy machined blue steel. It takes me and Corman, one at each end, to carry the long barrel. Atkinson struggles awkwardly with the shoulder harness, leather half-moons that catch her legs as she walks toward the gunshed. Tolliver carries the empty magazines, big as bowling balls and twice as heavy. Dombrowski is the fifth member of our guncrew, she's clumsy and always in a hurry, so she treads on Tolliver's heels as she lugs our five helmets. "Shake a leg," she grumbles to Tolliver.

"Kee-rist. I'm hurryin' as fast as I can." Too late. The sailors have secured their guns and are waiting for us. They chant, "Release a man for active duty. Har har. It takes five of you broads to do what two guys can do." We have to walk right by them, looking as confident and unwinded as we can. Let me tell you, it's not so easy to look dignified and ladylike under these circumstances. Only thing to do is ignore them, but I'd sure like to have a word with the genius who dreamed up that slogan, "Release a Man for Active Duty," for the WAVES. The guys won't stop. "The WACS and WAVES will win the war. What the hell am I here for?" Holy Mary, I could be home, doing my part by serving cookies and jitterbugging in my aqua prom dress at the USO with our brave boys who have to behave nicely there. Too late, megirl. You'll never get the gun grease out from under your fingernails.

• • •

What happened yesterday is all my fault. Lately I've been crawling into the sack at night and falling right asleep without saying my evening prayers; transgressions like that always catch up with you sooner or later. Sooner, in my case, why else did he pick my workbook to check, first thing as we slouched into the classroom, still half asleep?

"Kee-rist, Jee-zus H. Kee-rist on a raft." He flung the workbook, with the last two mimeographed pages not filled in, at my head. I ducked. Good reflexes are important in a career in the Navy. Remind me to put that in a recruiting brochure. "Dermody, you dum-dum. You've been gold-bricking long enough. Do this over. Do it right. Ya hear me? Otherwise you'll find yourself a civilian with an Unsuitable Discharge. Out on yer ear. O-U-T spells Out-Goes-You. Crazy broads anyway. No job for a man, teaching dumb stupid broads. Nothing but bitches and lezzies."

A proper fit he'd worked up to. Do the medics know he's over the edge? They probably don't care. I turned back to my desk, not saying anything.

"Can we help it if you can't get sea duty?" Tolliver muttered in a semiaudible way.

"You, Dermody. Repeat what you just said." Spit sprayed out in a fan in front of his little pointed teeth.

"I didn't say anything."

• • •

"I'm never going to take his stupid class again, ever." I heaved a great breath and tossed my workbook into the trash barrel. I felt a great, crazy sense of freedom, watching my future life arc into the innocent wire barrel. I strode ahead, ignoring the others and their gasps.

Corman grabbed my shoulder, turned me around to face her. "You get that workbook back. Hear? Right this instance, Josette Dermody. Move it."

"Won't."

She shoved her exasperated face into mine. I looked away.

"What do I care?" The others gathered around as we stood arguing where the walkway branches off toward the mess hall. Corman handed her books to Dombrowski.

"You all go ahead. Me and Miss Priss here have got something to talk over." When they were out of earshot she says, "Okay, Dermody. Time to grow up. You're in the Navy. Fish that out."

"I thought you were my friend."

"Knock it off, Dermody. You'll give all of us a bad name if you act this way and get into trouble. Don't you ever think of anybody but yourself? Honestly. Look alive now." She had her arms on her waist, elbows out. If I ever remember Corman when I am an old lady, I'll think of her, standing pigeon-toed, arms akimbo, pretty face flushed with exasperation, chivvying me, willing me, saving me, actually, from totally messing up.

"I still hate him."

"Hate away, kiddo. Only two more weeks and we never see that handsome face again. If you don't foul up, Dumbo, we'll all be off to our new duty stations in another month. C'mon, pal, there's a war on."

I walked back the way we had come, retrieved the duotang-covered notebook, and brushed it off. "The next time I get a notion to enlist, I hope my mother ties me to the bedpost."

"Me, too." She tagged my arm. "Race you to the mess hall."

• • •

We aren't bored, not at first. It isn't hard. Easier than Great Lakes. Groups of sailors are shepherded into the stark gunsheds all day long. Double rows of Oerlikons, 20-millimeter antiaircraft guns, are bolted to the deck. Mounted on top of the guns, where the cylindrical magazines of shells would ordinarily be, are suitcase-shaped metal boxes containing the projectors. A GI imitation of an arcade shooting range. Our job is to thread the projectors with a large reel of film of incoming Japanese planes, know how to turn the machine on, encourage the reluctant boys in blue to use the ringsight to hit the planes. Then we must write the score on each sailor's hand-carried scorecard.

Corman is spokesman—our head teacher. As each group arrives she stands in front and explains the drill. She doesn't look much like a recruiting poster. They always have their full dress blues on, including hats, no matter what they are doing. Corman is as pretty as a recruiting poster, but she is wearing exactly what the rest of us are wearing, neat blue wool slacks, dark-blue rayon long-sleeved shirt, and a sky-blue butterfly tie, exactly the color of her eyes. No hat, no jewelry—none that shows, anyway. She stands by the charts of the silhouettes of the planes. She always amazes me, with her way of batting her eyelashes and using her honey-toned voice so disarmingly. She never lets on that she notices the guys are unhappy about a girl instructing them. Especially instructing them to shoot guns. A girl who never would see combat.

"The most important thing is to estimate how far you must lead him," she says. "Calculate how fast he is probably going, allow for the angle, and use the farthest ring you can."

A sullen, square-faced sailor in the front row raises his hand and says mincingly, "Miss, how can we tell how fast the little bugger's going?" I had seen the sailor behind him give him a shove; looks like Square-face lost the draw today about who's going to give the WAVES a hard time. Usually they have a bet they can fluster her or make her mad before the petty officer knocks them off. Dumb broads don't know nothin' is what they want to prove. Corman is unflappable.

"Simple." She gives him her homecoming queen smile and continues, "You know, I assume, that the top speed of a Zero is approximately 300 knots, a Betty 250 knots, and so on. A dive bomber usually comes in at an angle of 70 knots." She waves her hand at the charts on the wall.

He isn't through. "But mate," he says, looking all boyish and earnest like he really cares, "sometimes they mush the planes, pull back at an angle to fly slower, and fool the gunners." He looks around at his sniggering buddies with satisfaction.

"I'm sure they wouldn't fool you, Seaman," she says, pulling a little rank on him. She looks at the rest of the class, "Remember, they're most likely to be coming in fast and dirty. If you aim right at them, by the time the shell gets there it will be behind him. Never, never aim right at him. Just remember that and you'll be okay." She smiles encouragingly and flies her left hand gracefully in a glide pattern and uses her right hand to demonstrate a shell passing way aft.

"What kind of frigging way is that to shoot?" the blue-jawed guy who had shoved Mr. Interlocutor before ventures impatiently. "We din't do it that way at Guadalcanal."

Corman pauses for just a minute, letting the "frigging" sort of hang in the air, then ignores it. With a tiny little frown she says, "Nobody here needs to be told, I am sure, just how close we came to losing Guadalcanal. Man your guns."

Berneice Herron
(1916–1988)
U.S. MARINE CORPS WOMEN'S RESERVE

Herron and her sister Eleanor, schoolteachers in southern Minnesota, worked in the defense industry after the Japanese attack on Pearl Harbor. They enlisted in the Marines and served almost three years. They taught aircraft and ship recognition to Marine fighter pilots at El Toro Marine Air Base in Santa Ana, California, and then as rehabilitation interviewers helped to discharge women Marines from the Corps after vj Day. During their enlistment they wrote home almost daily. Their mother saved their letters, which served as the basis for Herron's 2006 memoir *Dearest Folks: Sister Leatherneck's Letter Excerpts and World War II Experiences*, from which the following excerpts are taken. After the war, Herron completed a forty-seven-year career in education.

[The pilots] were expected, by their Commanding Officers (cos), to attend one hour of recognition each day. We taught the same syllabus each hour, for six hours per day, so the pilots could attend any hour that fit best with their other classes. We had to keep close records of their attendance as their cos felt it was, or could be, a matter of life, or death, for the pilots to learn to recognize the planes that they would so soon be dealing with, out in the Pacific....

When our training school had burned down, at Cherry Point, we had received about three weeks of training. The rest of our learning was up to us!! We REALLY had to study!!! We were determined to be good teachers and we realized that what we were teaching could well mean life, or death, to our pilots! We did NOT take our responsibility lightly!!! No one was going to stand up in front of a class of fifty-sixty Marine fighter pilots and give them any "bum steers." You would not have lasted, as their teacher, more than a minute. They were SHARP, in intelligence as well as looks!!! ...

It was not long before Eleanor and I were the only Recognition Instructors on base. What a *Challenge, Honor, and Workout!* When one of us would be in the classroom presenting a lesson, the other would be in our next door office helping Ruthie [their officer in charge, who preferred administrative work to teaching], studying, preparing future lessons, and digesting the messages from Washington!! It was a *very* busy schedule and very demanding, but we *LOVED* doing it.

We taught mostly by slides that would project a very small image on a screen. In a matter of a tenth of a second the pilots had to discern whether the flash was a Japanese plane, an American plane, or a British one. They further had to tell whether it was a bomber, a fighter, or another type plane. . . . They also had to be able to distinguish ships . . . and finally they had to study and be able to identify submarines and Japanese Merchant Shipping Tonnage. . . .

We fully realized that many of our pilots would leave our class, fly to San Francisco, then to Pearl Harbor where they would board their carrier and in a matter of two or three days they would be right out in combat.

Many times pilots who had been in combat, and returned to our base, would come in and thank us and tell us that what they had learned in our classes helped save their lives. What SUPER news! . . .

I am very sure that the number of enlisted females that taught fighter pilots could be counted on both hands, if even that many. Fewer male enlisted did the same thing. We were really *fortunate* to be selected for such an interesting and exacting experience!!!

Our new classes would be varied in size depending on many circumstances. . . . Very often even though a pilot had finished his required hours he could continue coming, as material kept changing all the time. Plans were either being added or deleted. . . . They wanted to be kept up to date. Because of all these changes our class never became "dull"—everything was very dynamic and changing all the time. Whenever the Allies sank one of the Japanese ships, we had that ship immediately deleted from our syllabus. It almost was a "race" between our sharpest pilots and ourselves, as they would try to "catch us" with a sunken ship still on the syllabus. We were very determined to keep ahead of "Our Boys."

Many times we would have as many as sixty-seventy pilots per hour. Often times the entire flight of five would attend class the same hour. . . . In the sixteen months that we taught our pilots, we had hundreds and hundreds of pilots go through our classes. To add a little "spice" to our class, on Saint Patrick's Day we told our pilots that anyone who didn't "sign in" as "Irish" on that one particular day would not be recognized as having attended class that day. You should have seen all the "O's" and "Mc's" that were added to their names that day.

Although we worked harder than we had ever worked in our lives, we also had many highly unusual and exhilarating experiences, due to our being Women Marines *and* being instructors in aircraft and ship recognition. . . .

Our officers were very polite, very understanding, very sharp, and really listened while in class. Once in a while we would have a very high ranking officer attend a class or two. We recognized that he was in there to check on what type teaching we were doing and how well the officers paid attention. We must have "filled the bill" as we were never replaced, never demoted, our teaching capabilities were asked for in several Squadrons, and we were often told that we knew more about recognition than anyone on the base. To this day I am most grateful, to God, for such an interesting, most unusual, dynamic and challenging position we had in the Corps.

Cornelia Fort
(1919–1943)
U.S. Women's Auxiliary Ferrying Squadron

On the morning of December 7, 1941, civilian instructor pilot Cornelia Fort was airborne with a student pilot in an Interstate Cadet monoplane over Pearl Harbor. She saw a military aircraft flying directly at her. She took the controls and pulled up over the oncoming plane. Only then did she see the Rising Sun emblem on its wings. Moments later, she realized that Pearl Harbor was under attack. Japanese Zeroes strafed her plane, but she landed and ran to safety with her student pilot.

In 1942 Nancy Harkness Love invited Fort, then twenty-three, to join the Women's Auxiliary Ferrying Squadron (later merged with the Women Airforce Service Pilots, or WASPs). On March 21, 1943, she led a flight of six new male graduates of a ninety-day flight training program ferrying BT-13 trainers to Dallas. Although ferry pilots were forbidden to fly in close formation, pilot Frank Stammes began flying close to Fort's plane and then pulling up. On one pass his landing gear collided with the tip of Fort's left wing. The wing tip broke away with six feet of leading edge attached. Fort's plane went into a vertical dive and impacted the ground nose-down. When Fort became the first woman pilot to die on active duty, she was one of the most accomplished women pilots in the United States. She had logged 1,100 hours; Stammes, only 267. The following is an article she wrote for *Woman's Home Companion*, published posthumously in June 1943.

At the Twilight's Last Gleaming

I knew I was going to join the Women's Auxiliary Ferrying Squadron before the organization was a reality, before it had a name, before it was anything but a radical idea in the minds of a few men who believed that women could fly airplanes. But I never knew it so surely as I did in Honolulu on December 7, 1941.

At dawn that morning I drove from Waikiki to the John Rodgers civilian airport right next to Pearl Harbor where I was a ... pilot instructor. Shortly after six-thirty I began landing and take-off practice with my regular student. Coming in just before the last landing, I looked casually around and saw a military plane coming directly toward me. I jerked the controls away from my student and jammed the throttle wide open to pull above the oncoming plane. He passed so close under us that our celluloid windows rattled violently and I looked down to see what kind of plane it was.

The painted red balls on the tops of the wings shone brightly in the sun. I looked again with complete and utter disbelief. Honolulu was familiar with the emblem of the Rising Sun on passenger ships but not on airplanes.

I looked quickly at Pearl Harbor and my spine tingled when I saw billowing black smoke. Still I thought hollowly it might be some kind of coincidence or maneuvers, it might be, it must be. For surely, dear God ...

Then I looked way up and saw the formations of silver bombers riding in. Something detached itself from an airplane and came glistening down. My eyes followed it down, down and even with knowledge pounding in my mind, my heart turned convulsively when the bomb exploded in the middle of the harbor. I knew the air was not the place for my little baby airplane and I set about landing as quickly as ever I could. A few seconds later a shadow passed over me and simultaneously bullets spattered all around me.

Suddenly that little wedge of sky above Hickam Field and Pearl Harbor was the busiest fullest piece of sky I ever saw.

We counted anxiously as our little civilian planes came flying home to roost. Two never came back. They were washed ashore weeks later on the windward side of the island, bullet-riddled. Not a pretty way for the brave little yellow Cubs and their pilots to go down to death.

The rest of December seventh has been described by too many in too much detail for me to reiterate. I remained on the island until three months later when I returned by convoy to the United States. None of the pilots wanted to leave but there was no civilian flying in the islands after the attack. And each of us had some individual score to settle with the Japs who brought murder and destruction to our islands.

When I returned, the only way I could fly at all was to instruct Civilian Pilot Training programs. Weeks passed. Then, out of the blue, came a telegram from the War Department announcing the organization of the WAFS (Women's Auxiliary Flying Squadron) and the order to report within twenty-four hours if interested. I left at once.

Mrs. Nancy Love was appointed Senior Squadron Leader of the WAFS by the Secretary of War. No better choice could have been made. First and most important she is a good pilot, has tremendous enthusiasm and belief in women pilots and did a wonderful job in helping us to be accepted on an equal status with men.

Because there were and are so many disbelievers in women pilots, especially their place in the army, officials wanted the best possible qualifications to go with the first experimental group. All of us realized what a spot we were on. We had to deliver the goods or else. Or else there wouldn't ever be another chance for women pilots in any part of the service.

We have no hopes of replacing men pilots. But we can each release a man to combat, to faster ships, to overseas work. Delivering a trainer to Texas may be as important as delivering a bomber to Africa if you take the long view. We are beginning to prove that women can be trusted to deliver airplanes safely and in the doing serve the country which is our country too.

I have yet to have a feeling which approaches in satisfaction that of having signed, sealed and delivered an airplane for the United States Army. The attitude that most non-flyers have about pilots is distressing and often acutely embarrassing. They chatter about the glamour of flying. Well, any pilot can tell you how glamorous it is. We get up in the cold dark in order to get to the airport by daylight. We wear heavy cumbersome flying clothes and a thirty-pound parachute. You are either cold or hot. If you are female your lipstick wears off and your hair gets straighter and straighter. You look forward all afternoon to the bath you will have and the steak. Well, we get the bath but seldom the steak. Sometimes we are too tired to eat and fall wearily into bed.

None of us can put into words why we fly. It is something different for each of us. I can't say exactly why I fly but I know why as I've never known anything in my life.

I knew it when I saw my plane silhouetted against the clouds framed by a circular rainbow. I knew it when I flew up into the extinct volcano Haleakala on the island of Maui and saw the gray-green pineapple fields slope down to the cloud-dappled blueness of the Pacific. But I know it otherwise than in beauty. I know it in dignity and self-sufficiency and in the pride of skill. I know it in the satisfaction of usefulness.

For all the girls in the WAFS, I think the most concrete moment of happiness came at our first review. Suddenly and for the first time we felt a part of something larger. Because of our uniforms which we had earned, we were marching with the men, marching with all the freedom-loving people in the world.

And then while we were standing at attention a bomber took off followed by four fighters. We knew the bomber was headed across the ocean and that the fighters were going to escort it part way. As they circled over us I could hardly see them for the tears in my eyes. It was striking symbolism and I think all of us felt it. As long as our planes fly overhead the skies of America are free and that's what all of us everywhere are fighting for. And that we, in a very small way, are being allowed to help keep that sky free is the most beautiful thing I have ever known.

I, for one, am profoundly grateful that my one talent, my only knowledge, flying, happens to be of use to my country when it is needed. That's all the luck I ever hope to have.

Mary C. Lyne
(1916–2001)
U.S. Coast Guard Women's Reserve

Mary Catherine Lyne of Shenandoah Junction, West Virginia, graduated from Madison College (later James Madison University) in 1940. Although she had studied high school education, she wrote for and edited the award-winning school newspaper *The Breeze* under the pseudonym "Mike Lyne," worked on the "Schoolma'am" yearbook, and participated in college literary societies. She was working as an editorial assistant at a trade organization when the United States entered the war; in 1943 she joined the first class of SPAR officers and served in a New York City public information unit responsible for coverage of the Coast Guard in national magazines. She was discharged in 1947 as a lieutenant. After the war she wrote for the U.S. Public Health Service and then the State Department, where she pursued a twenty-year career as a newswriter in the Near Eastern, South Asian, and African branches of the U.S. Information Agency. She retired as the chief of the Publication Section of the International Press Service Africa Branch. A fifty-year member of the National Press Club in Washington DC, she co-authored several books. The excerpt below is taken from *Three Years before the Mast: The Story of the U.S. Coast Guard SPARS*, which she co-authored with fellow lieutenant Kay Arthur.

Battle of the Sexes

Men, all men, regarded as one great big awkward group, protested longly and loudly that they didn't care for "women in uniform." We knew that, and didn't expect them to care for us collectively. What man cares for women as a group anyway? Individual men cared for individual women in uniform, and that was all that mattered to us.

Men's prejudice often took the form of what in civilian life would be called slander. Attacks upon the morals of SPARs were common, and where there was little basis in fact for the charges, tales were invented and improved upon in the telling. Others, less aggravated and more literate cases, blew off steam by drafting letters to magazines and newspapers, secure in their knowledge that the general public, all too suspicious of any innovation, would applaud. Either we had to grin and bear it or fall into the trap of becoming embittered ourselves.

The Men

And how did the men take this infiltration of women? The attitude toward us ranged from enthusiastic reception through amused condescension to open hostility.

We felt that one important factor in determining a man's attitude was his own desire for sea duty. If he were eligible and wanted to shove off, he was not inclined to frown with disfavor upon his deliverer, even if she appeared in SPAR clothing. On the other hand, it was natural that the swivel-chair commando should rail against the presence of the little lady who had come to release him for the briny deep. Fortunately the proportion of the latter was low compared with the Coast Guard as a whole.

Men with axes to grind because of personal disappointments seldom took a shine to us either. Perhaps the greatest reason for resentment in this category involved ratings and rank. If they had not been advanced as rapidly as they thought they should have been, seeing a SPAR go ahead of them was adding insult to injury, and they refused to believe that they were not being discriminated against. In some cases this feeling may have been justified; in others, it was pure bilge.

There was many a man whose ego was punctured when he found his place could be so easily taken by a woman. There was many a man who believed that women should not venture beyond the rose-covered door of the oven. And there were men who, resplendent with ribbons and beyond reproach, were pointed out to us as "a man who doesn't like SPARS." No reason. These were the really fascinating individuals who stalked in solitary splendor and made the same impression upon us as a virile civilian bachelor who "doesn't like women."

Not all the objections to us were personal or petty. Some were purely objective. Many men sincerely failed to see the necessity for SPARS in the Service; others felt the expense was unjustifiable, and so on. There was nothing surprising in any of the objections. Any woman who tries to become part of a man's world even in a time of a great national emergency is automatically placing herself at the beginning of an obstacle course.

Often the fault was our own. Just as in civilian organizations, friction between men and women working together in the military can be caused by minor irritants, easily avoided.

A little tact will go a long way with a man. Wise indeed was the SPAR officer, married to a male chief who answered the barbed inquiry of an acquaintance: "Does he have to salute you in the office?" with "Oh yes, indeed. But when he gets me home, he beats me." Some SPARS even wore their raincoats when out walking with gentlemen of lower rank "so the seniority wouldn't show."

On the whole, if we did our part and proved equal to the job, the men, both regulars and reserves, were willing to give us our due. And we, in turn, gave our heartfelt thanks to those men—no small group— who, from the beginning, backed us with their unqualified support, taught us the ropes, encouraged us, worked with us harmoniously and made us feel that we belonged and were doing a job, even as they. We will always remember them with the deepest appreciation.

6

Unconventional Operations, Espionage, and the Cold War

"We Had Observed So Much"

Just hours after Claus von Stauffenberg and some German military officers tried to assassinate Hitler in July 1944, U.S. Army Pvt. Barbara Lauwers rode across the Italian countryside in a Jeep. The next day, prim and correct in her WAC uniform, she introduced herself in fluent German to eighteen carefully screened prisoners of war in the camp at Aversa. From among those dissidents, deserters, impressed laborers, and conscientious objectors, she chose sixteen men who met her exacting standards. Her colleagues issued American army coveralls to the men and loaded them in a truck for transport to a two-story, tile-roofed villa near Rome. There, Lauwers created false identities and cover stories for the men that closely matched their true backgrounds. For the next four days she trained them on their new mission.

Operatives issued the men forged identity papers and passes, German uniforms and field gear, pistols, rifles with forty rounds of ammunition each, compasses, quality watches, thousands of Italian lira of mixed denominations, Italian cigarettes for barter— and thousands of propaganda leaflets printed with an "official" denunciation of Hitler's policy of destroying the German army for the sake of the Nazi party. Then the men followed OSS officers across the German lines in two waves: the first at midnight, the second at dawn. They crossed the Arno River, made their way three miles into German-held territory, and began nailing the leaflets on trees and scattering them in buildings, on vehicles, and in the streets. All sixteen returned safely two days later, carrying vital intelligence about German defensive positions and troop movements. Operation Sauerkraut—intended to undermine the morale of the German army by circulating rumors, fake orders, and leaflets about growing unrest among German military leaders—was a success.

"Zuzka" Lauwer, who had emigrated from Czechoslovakia to the United States in 1941, spoke five languages (English, German, Czech, Slovak, and French) fluently and held a doctorate in law from Masaryk University in Brno. Her husband joined the Army after Pearl Harbor; Lauwer became an American citizen on June 1, 1943, and joined the WAC a few hours later. She and two other women singled out in basic training were ordered to the U.S. Office of Strategic Services (OSS), a new unconventional warfare organization subordinate to the Joint Chiefs of Staff. Lauwer became the only woman in the Rome branch of the OSS's Morale Operations Division.

Early in 1945, Lauwer learned that several hundred Czech and Slovak soldiers impressed into the German army to do menial service tasks were serving at the Italian front. She designed a morale operation targeting her former countrymen. She created dual-language leaflets in Czech and Slovak urging the soldiers to desert, cross over to the Allies, and fight to reclaim their homeland from the Nazis. OSS infiltrators crossed the front lines to distribute her leaflets, and the BBC broadcast the message along the Italian front. On the morning of April 29, 1945, more than six hundred Czech and Slovak soldiers marched across to the Allied side while their band played the Czechoslovak national anthem. They carried Lauwer's leaflets in their pockets.

Lauwer received a promotion to corporal and a Bronze Star for her work.

In the later years of the Second World War, the WAC became a recruiting ground for the OSS, the forerunner of both the modern Central Intelligence Agency and Special Operations Command (SOCOM). OSS counted around 4,500 women among its thirteen thousand employees. OSS gave some civilian employees "assimilated rank"—military precedence and circumscribed command authority. Nine hundred of these women deployed overseas during the war, most in clerical roles. Those with unique language or other required skills served in the Secret Intelligence (espionage), Morale Operations (psychological warfare), or X-2 (counterintelligence) divisions. OSS trained a very small number, probably fewer than forty, to parachute behind enemy lines, coordinate with local partisans, sabotage infrastructure and factories, and arrange for the escape of downed pilots.

The most famous of these, civilian Virginia Hall, came to the OSS after serving early in the war with the British Special Operations Executive (SOE) in France. Hall had lost the lower part of her left leg in a prewar shooting accident, and she acquired a wooden leg she called "Cuthbert" that left her with a permanent limping gait. Early in the war, while America remained neutral, Hall worked for SOE undercover as a *New York Post* reporter. But when German troops entered Vichy France in November 1941, she became an enemy alien. Known to German intelligence only as the "Limping Lady," she fell under suspicion and was forced to escape to Spain over the Pyrenees Mountains on foot in severe winter weather. When her amputation site became painful, she sent a message to SOE Headquarters: "Cuthbert is giving me trouble but I can cope." A colleague unaware of "Cuthbert's" identity replied: "If Cuthbert is giving you trouble, have him eliminated."

Hall continued to work for SOE in Madrid, finding safe houses on the Allied escape routes and serving as a courier for SOE. But she wanted to return to France, and in November 1943 she transferred to the OSS.

Hall reentered France by boat prior to D Day and worked as a courier and radio operator—the most dangerous position on an infiltration team, requiring constant relocation so that German radio detection equipment would not find her and her suitcase-sized radio. In a one-month period after D-Day, she transmitted thirty-seven intelligence messages to London describing German troop movements. With the help of a three-man "Jedburgh" infiltration team, Hall organized, armed, and trained three battalions of Forces Françaises d'Intérieur (FFI) to conduct guerrilla warfare and sabotage operations to slow the German retreat. Her teams destroyed four bridges, derailed freight trains carrying supplies to the German army, severed an important rail line in several places, downed telephone lines, captured nineteen members of the pro-German militia, killed 150 Germans, and took 500 more prisoner.

The British government awarded Hall the MBE (Member of the Order of the British Empire) for her service; President Truman awarded her the Distinguished Service Cross, second only to the Medal of Honor. She declined to have the president present it, saying that she was "still operational and most anxious to get busy."

President Truman disestablished the OSS in October of 1945, but rising Soviet influence in Eastern Europe and Soviet intelligence-gathering activities convinced him of the need for continued intelligence operations. OSS's functions were divided between the military departments and the Central Intelligence Group (later the Central Intelligence Agency) in 1946. Hall remained in the CIA at a headquarters desk job for nine more years, retiring as a GS-14. Despite her record and desire to continue in clandestine operations, the CIA failed to use her expertise. Many other women of the OSS also continued to work in one of the postwar intelligence activities.

Women in the armed forces were no longer desired for clandestine operations, and institutional memory of the women of OSS faded. Over the course of the Cold War, however, thousands of women in uniform filled military intelligence billets. They translated documents, managed the flow of classified material, analyzed reports, processed sensitive signals, broke codes, studied the profiles of leaders in Eastern Europe and China, interpreted intelligence photography and video, trained pilots to recognize enemy assets, and monitored Soviet submarines in the Atlantic and Pacific Oceans. Many of their stories remain classified and some will never be told. A few are presented here.

Stephanie Czech Rader
(1915–2016)
WOMEN'S ARMY CORPS/OFFICE OF SPECIAL SERVICES

Stephanie Czech, the daughter of Polish immigrants and a Cornell University graduate with a degree in chemistry, was one of the first eighty women to enter the Women's Army Corps in 1943. After she received her commission, OSS recruited her because of her proficiency in Polish.

Czech began clandestine work in October 1945 under cover as an embassy secretary. She traveled throughout Poland to collect information on Soviet troop movements and the activities of the Soviet intelligence services, and to build an espionage network that would play a significant role in subsequent decades of the Cold War. The American naval attaché in Warsaw had disappeared without a trace in southern Poland where Czech also operated; he was never found. Czech, operating in civilian clothing, could expect a similar fate if detained by the Soviet forces occupying the country.

The chief of station in Berlin asked Czech to carry top-secret documents to the embassy in Warsaw even though a superior in Paris had negligently compromised her cover.

Returning to Warsaw on January 15, 1946, she saw Soviet security agents at the German-Polish border checkpoint. She quickly handed the classified material to a man walking next to her— someone she knew would be unlikely to raise suspicion—and told him to whom it should be delivered in Warsaw. When she reached the checkpoint, the Soviets detained her briefly. The classified material arrived safely at the embassy.

Senior OSS officers recommended her for the Legion of Merit for her "unusual coolness and clear thinking" during the incident. The War Department, failing to understand the risk of her actions and the courage she displayed, downgraded the award to the Army Commendation Ribbon. The Army posthumously upgraded her award to the Legion of Merit on June 1, 2016.

Czech left the Army and the OSS at the rank of major; she married an Air Force officer and earned a master's degree in chemistry. She died on January 21, 2016.

The following excerpt is transcribed from a September 2006 oral history at the Women in Military Service for America Foundation; Col. Jane Maliszewski, USA (Ret.), interviewed Rader.

I was in X-2. That was counterintelligence. That's what they recruited me for.

When I got there [when she reported to OSS headquarters], 'cause I was in uniform, they . . . gave me a jumpsuit, said, "Don't bring anything with you except your clothes, there's no IDs, nothing." They gave you a name, and said, "This is you, and don't ever tell anybody who you are."

[The OSS sends Captain Czech to a two-week school. They give her a jumpsuit and a fake name and tell her not to bring identification. She is driven to the school with four men in a car with blacked-out windows. Men and women train together.]

We were all dressed alike, in jumpsuits. . . . It was sort of a nice house . . . and that's the way we trained. They showed me how to take a gun apart and put it together—like I needed that!—and they showed you how to shoot a machine gun; I needed *that* [she says sarcastically]. . . . They taught us stuff about the intelligence in Germany and Japan, and what we were supposed to do, and the things that you have to look out for, so somebody doesn't recognize you as an American, like how you smoke a cigarette, which—I never smoked—how you eat, all your mannerisms and all, you've got to watch all that. . . . Never did figure out where the school was. One guy was a Marine sergeant, one a naval officer . . . that was the class. We were all being trained for different areas. I never saw them again in my life.

[After training, she reports to Fort Dix and then travels with Army nurses on a ship to Glasgow. She has orders to Warsaw, via Salzburg; her colleague Agnes is destined for Czechoslovakia.]

I didn't go to Warsaw right away. We went to Salzburg . . . we went to the office every day. . . . It was a different way of life.

We were doing research. Corrections. We read magazines, anything

FIG. I. Portrait of Deborah Sampson Gannett by self-trained artist Joseph Stone of Framingham, Massachusetts. The portrait greatly resembles biographer Herman Mann's description of Sampson and depicts her in a fashionable dress with a fichu inserted at the neckline for modesty. Symbols of femininity (flowers), military masculinity (weapons and flags), and patriotism (an eagle and stars-and-stripes medallion) decorate the frame. Oil on board, dated 1797. Image courtesy of the Rhode Island Historical Society, RHi x5 25.

FIG. 2. Sarah Osborn Benjamin (ca. 1745–1858). At the time this photograph was made, she claimed to be 109 years old. Photo courtesy of the Wayne County Historical Society, Honesdale, Pennsylvania.

FIG. 3. Dr. Mary Edwards Walker in "reform dress" (shortened skirt over trousers) and wearing her Medal of Honor. Photo #p2101 dated January 1, 1870, courtesy of Legacy Center Archives, Drexel University College of Medicine, Philadelphia.

Fig. 4. Harriet Tubman in Civil War scout attire. This woodcut, by J. C. Darby of Auburn, may have been based on a photograph taken during her service with the Union Army. Tubman's grandnephew Harkless Bowley claimed that someone took the photograph and never returned it. The woodcut was used as the frontispiece for Sarah Bradford's 1869 biography *Scenes in the Life of Harriet Tubman*.

FIG. 5. (*left to right*) Susan Bordeaux (Rev. Mother Mary Anthony Cloud Robe); Josephine Two Bears (Rev. Sr. Mary Joseph); Rev. Francis M. Craft; Ellen Clarke (Rev. Sr. Mary Gregory/Gertrude); and Anna B. Pleets (Rev. Mother Mary Bridget) of the Congregation of American Sisters, possibly taken in Cuba in 1898. The four Lakota Sioux nuns, who served as Army contract nurses in the Spanish-American War, were posted to five different hospitals in Florida, Georgia, and Cuba in just four months. Mother Mary Anthony died in Cuba of complications from pneumonia and was buried with military honors at Camp Egbert in Pinar del Rio; however, her remains were not transferred to Arlington after the war with those of the soldiers buried there. Photo courtesy of the Marquette University Archives, Bureau of Catholic Indian Missions Records, ID #07436. Harmon & Shaw, photographer.

Fɪɢ. 6. Loretta Perfectus Walsh (1896–1925) of Philadelphia, a 1915
graduate of the Scranton Lackawanna Business College, worked as
a clerical assistant for the wife of recruiting officer LCDR Frederick
Payne at the Philadelphia Navy League. She became the first woman
to enlist in the U.S. Navy on March 21, 1917, at the recruitment office
of the Fourth Naval District, Philadelphia. She held the rank of chief
petty officer on her discharge in 1921. Walsh died of tuberculosis after
contracting influenza during the war. Photo courtesy of the Loretta
Perfectus Walsh Collection, Gift of James Walsh, Women's Memorial
Foundation Collection.

FIG. 7. Cohan, France. ANC nurses Jennie Conn, Blanche Feister, Lucy Raeter, Mary Conyord, Mary Swain, and several officers look at a German aerial bomb that dropped within fifteen feet of a ward tent containing about fifty wounded soldiers on the night of August 12, 1918. Photo by Private R. P. Antrim, U.S. Army Signal Corps. Photo III-SC-21795, dated August 13, 1918, courtesy of National Archives.

FIG. 8. (*above*) Army Signal Corps "Hello Girls" at a switchboard three kilometers from the trenches in France during the Battle of St. Mihiel Salient, October 15, 1918. They have helmets and gas masks in bags on the backs of their chairs. Photo III-SC-21981 courtesy of National Archives.

FIG. 9. (*opposite top*) Army nurses freed from imprisonment in the Santo Tomas Internment Compound climb into trucks to leave Manila for repatriation to the United States. They wear new uniforms given to them to replace clothing worn out during their three years as prisoners of war. The nurses lost an average of forty pounds each while imprisoned. Photo III-SC-200726, dated February 24, 1945, courtesy of National Archives.

FIG. 10. (*opposite bottom*) WACs of the 6888th Postal Battalion sort packages taken from the mail sacks by French civilian employees at the 17th Base Post Office in France, 1945. Arriving in Birmingham, UK, in 1945, the women found unheated warehouses stacked to the ceiling with a backlog of mail. Rats gnawed through care packages to reach cookies and cakes. Working eight-hour shifts around the clock for seven days a week, the women processed an average of 65,000 pieces of mail each shift. They maintained information cards for seven million individual soldiers and cleared a six-month backlog of mail in three months. Moving to Rouen, France, they cleared a two- to three-year backlog in six months. Photo III-SC-3337995-1 courtesy of National Archives.

FIG. 11. (*opposite top*) Women Airforce Service Pilots (WASP) talk shop, 1943 or 1944. Photo courtesy of the Dorothy Nichols Collection, Gift of J. D. Nichols, Women's Memorial Foundation Collection.

FIG. 12. (*opposite bottom*) Specs. (Gunnery) Third Class Florence Johnston and Rosamund Small are the first WAVES to qualify as instructors on electrically operated .50-caliber machine gun turrets. Naval Air Gunners School, Hollywood FL. Photo 80-G-45240, dated April 11, 1944, courtesy of National Archives.

FIG. 13. (*above*) In November 1943 thirteen flight nurses, thirteen medics, and four air crew from the 807th Medical Air Evacuation Transport Squadron were stranded behind German lines in Albania when their C-53 went off course and crash-landed. For the next nine weeks, Albanian partisans and a British Special Operations agent helped them evade German patrols while they crossed the Albanian mountains on foot, often in blizzard conditions and sharing the Albanians' meager food supplies, to reach the coast. The nurses' shoes wore out on the 800-mile trek. In this photo, taken after their rescue, they display the wear and repairs on the soles. Photo #342-FH-3A13649-59824AC, dated January 9, 1944, courtesy of National Archives.

FIG. 14. (*opposite*) Ens. Susan Ahn (1915–2015) at the pistol range at Naval Air Station Pensacola in 1943. Daughter of the first Korean couple granted permission to emigrate to the United States, Susan Ahn (Cuddy) was commissioned in the first class of WAVES officers and assigned as an aviation gunnery instructor. She was reassigned to the Office of Naval Intelligence, where her security clearance was delayed for months because of her Asian heritage, and then to the National Security Agency. When released from active duty in 1946, she remained at NSA and became director of the Central Research Facility, where she worked until 1959. Still active past her 100th birthday, she gave a presentation to college students in June 2015 and died peacefully the following day. Photo courtesy of the Lt. Susan Ahn Cuddy Archives.

FIG. 15. (*above*) Ten of the "Lucky Thirteen" nurses from the First Mobile Army Surgical Hospital who survived a night under fire in a ditch during an ambush near Seoul on October 9, 1950. (*left to right*): Capt. Mary Ward, Capt. Eleanor Faust, Maj. Eunice Coleman, Lt. Marie Smarz, Lt. Olive Rockabrand, Capt. Marion Benninger, Lt. Clara Kehoe, Lt. Ann Haddock, Capt. Jane Thurness, and Capt. Margaret Zane. The other three nurses (1st Lt. Faye Sullivan, 1st Lt. Winifred Jensen, and 2nd Lt. Cornelia Newton) are not pictured. U.S. Army photo by Cpl. George Dunn. Photo SC358193, dated February 14, 1951, courtesy of National Archives.

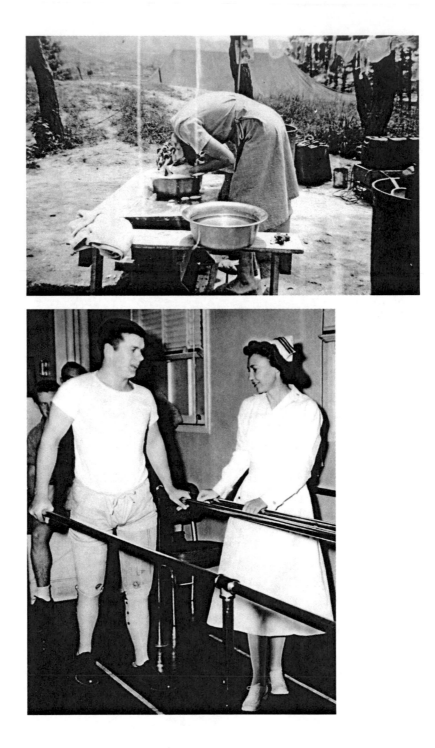

FIG. 16. (*opposite top*) Frances Bradsher Turner (1918–2009) from Durham, North Carolina, washes her hair in a bowl at the Second Mobile Army Surgical Hospital in Korea, ca. 1951. She wears the Army Nurse Corps brown and white striped seersucker overseas hospital dress. Turner served as an Army nurse during World War II, Korea, and Vietnam. After her retirement in 1971 at the rank of lieutenant colonel, she served with the American Red Cross. Photo courtesy of the Frances Bradsher Turner Papers (WV0236), Betty H. Carter Women Veterans Historical Project, Martha Hodges Special Collections and University Archives, University Libraries, University of North Carolina at Greensboro.

FIG. 17. (*opposite bottom*) Navy Nurse Corps Lt. Sarah Griffin Chapman, an amputee, works with an injured Korean War veteran as he learns to use his two artificial legs at the Rehabilitation Center, Naval Hospital, Oakland, California, 1951. Photo courtesy of the Naval History and Heritage Command, #NH 94946.

FIG. 18. (*above*) Diane Kay Corcoran, Army Nurse Corps, with Vietnamese civilians during a MEDCAP, a medical civic action providing outpatient health services to South Vietnamese. Photo courtesy of the Diane Kay Corcoran Papers (WV0526), Betty H. Carter Women Veterans Historical Project, Martha Hodges Special Collections and University Archives, University Libraries, University of North Carolina at Greensboro.

FIG. 19. WACS Marilyn Roth, Vicki Lapinski, and Lee Wilson (*left to right*) pose together in field uniforms in Long Binh, Vietnam, ca. 1968. Photo courtesy of the Lee Wilson Papers (WV0449), Betty H. Carter Women Veterans Historical Project, Martha Hodges Special Collections and University Archives, University Libraries, University of North Carolina at Greensboro.

FIG. 20. Lt. (j. g.) Beverly Kelley requested sea duty when she completed Officer Candidate School in 1976. When she received orders to shore duty at the Marine Safety Office in Portsmouth, Virginia, she began sending letters up the chain of command to policymakers in Washington DC. Four months later the Coast Guard changed its policy for assignment of women. Kelley was ordered to the cutter *Morgenthau*, homeported in San Francisco, as navigator and gunnery officer. She became the first woman to command a U.S. military vessel, the Coast Guard cutter *Cape Newagen*, in 1979. U.S. Coast Guard photo.

Fig. 21. (*opposite*) Lt. Col. Victoria Hudson with her wife, Monika Poxon, and their daughters at Hudson's retirement ceremony, October 18, 2013. Photo courtesy of Victoria Hudson. Photographer: Barbara Hartford.

Fig. 22. (*above*) Capt. Linda Bray, commander of the 988th Military Police Company, takes in the Panama scenery. In 1989 Bray led her company through a firefight to capture a kennel holding Panamanian Defense Force guard dogs and a cache of enemy weapons. But news of this groundbreaking event also led to a public and congressional debate regarding the leadership role of women in combat. Photo courtesy of Linda Bray.

Fig. 23. (*above*) M.Sgt. Linda Cox, USAF, took advantage of the Air Force's failure to ban women from serving in explosive ordnance disposal and became the first woman to graduate from the demanding and highly competitive Naval EOD School in 1974. A master sergeant when Iraqi troops invaded Kuwait, she volunteered to deploy when a male colleague found a reason not to go. In January 1991, Cox led a team of two intelligence airmen and another EOD technician into occupied Kuwait to survey the condition of runways and to search wrecked tanks for booby traps. Here she stands on her Humvee near the King Fahd Air Base, near Dhahran, Saudi Arabia, during Desert Storm in 1991. Cox received the Bronze Star for her work in Desert Storm. She retired as a chief master sergeant, the highest enlisted Air Force rank, and continues to work in ordnance disposal. Photo courtesy of Linda Cox.

Fig. 24. (*opposite*) Sgt. Lauren Nowak, USMC, of Fremont, Ohio, helps a local Afghan student with his alphabet during a class at Ekra Elementary School in Helmand Province's Nawa District on November 29, 2011. Nowak served as a team leader with a Female Engagement Team attached to Weapons Company, First Battalion, Ninth Marine Regiment during a seven-month deployment to Afghanistan. U.S. Marine Corps photo by Cpl. Alfred V. Lopez.

FIG. 25. Sgt. Leigh Ann Hester, team leader, 4th Platoon, 617th Military Police Company, 503rd M P Battalion, 18th M P Brigade, stands in front of a captured weapons cache after her squad repelled an insurgent attack on a Coalition supply convoy southeast of Baghdad on March 20, 2005. When approximately fifty fighters ambushed the convoy with A K-47s, R P K machine guns, and rocket-propelled grenades, Hester's squad flanked the insurgents and cut off their escape route. She and her squad leader, S.Sgt. Timothy Nein, assaulted a trench line with hand grenades and M 203 grenade launcher rounds. Twenty-seven insurgents were killed, six injured, and one captured. Hester was awarded the Silver Star, becoming the first woman to receive the medal since World War II. U.S. Army photo by Sgt. First Class Marshall P. Ware.

you might pick up in newspapers, and filing. . . . Then we were scheduled to go to . . . Salzburg. So we went to France first, and it was just like a tour. . . . We report to the embassies, we were not in any unit. Agnes and I were in it by ourselves, and we were attached to headquarters, because they had to put the military [people] *somewhere*, but they had no control over us. Nobody did. That was the beauty of it, nobody did. We were on our own schedule.

So we went to France. We left our stuff there. . . . I went to Switzerland, went skiing. . . . There was Agnes, and me, and a civilian girl. . . . And there was an enlisted man . . . he knew French.

[In Salzburg, OSS gives her a command car and Jeep trailer and picks up a GI to be their driver.]

He was out the night before, and he had a hangover that was terrible, and he could barely make it! So we started out with this entourage, just us, down the highway, and they just kept saying, "Don't ever pick anybody up"—see, there were a lot of these Germans running around, and young people in American uniforms, and a lot of kids got killed because they picked them up. So we go down the highway, and this kid's getting sicker and sicker, so we had to stop, I remember stopping somewhere—we were still in France—and there was a woman out there who had water in a pump, so we almost gave him a bath, sobered him up. And there was a question, "Who's going to drive?" This kid can't drive. You drive, Agnes. No, Stephanie's not going to drive. And [a third woman, name indistinguishable] isn't going to drive, so we're back to that kid again. We went for a while . . . we had a destination, we were supposed to get pretty far, but we were loitering with this kid not doing too well, and then he got us in a ditch. I thought, *Now that's dandy, we're going to park here all night!* We could hear this noise—whooping and hollering and singing and yelling—I said, "I think that sounds like a bunch of Americans." They were coming toward Paris. And I guess they stopped. They got out there, and they got that old car out of the hole and off they went, they gave us some gas, even.

So we made it to Luxembourg. Luxembourg wasn't expecting three women. There weren't too many women out there floating around. So Agnes and I—I don't know where the French girl went—we went to a convent! ... And off we went the next day, back on the road with that guy again, though he was sober by now.... We got as far as Nuremberg.... We were sticking to the main roads. You don't go off of them, and you don't pick anybody up.... The bridges were out. The superhighways were built for landing [airplanes]. We saw a lot of these makeshift airplanes, from the air they look like airplanes, but some of them were dummies.

[*She describes some incidents from her temporary assignment in Salzburg, and then the colleague for whom she works in the embassy in Warsaw.*]

[The other OSS agent, a man,] worked directly for the ambassador.... They were going to send him into Warsaw, working for the ambassador.... And Chad knew him from times before, he worked for him, so his cover was easy. And my cover was, I was his secretary. So we were together. Now, Chad could speak French, and Italian, and English, but he couldn't speak Polish. So I did. He got there a little before I did ... we were at the Polonia Hotel. He had a room across the hall, and that was our office, technically, because there were no offices or anything like that [because of the bombing] ... it was terrible, terrible.

I had two passports, a civilian passport and a military passport, and I had a military ID, and a civilian ID. So when I was assigned to go to Warsaw, I had to leave that. I had to change clothes, and I had my civilian clothes with me. So when I got to Berlin, I checked into the Embassy again, and I got some gals there, they kept my stuff, and I changed clothes, and I was a civilian! I used the same name—and then when I traveled, I traveled from then on as a civilian. But that's not too healthy, you know, when you're a "double."

We flew in a C-47 ... he flew us around that city. It was unbelievable. You can't even imagine. You looked and every house in the whole area, down to the basement.... The Germans were blowing it up street by street. And the question was, Why is this hotel Polonia still standing? And they said it was [Gestapo] headquarters. And they were managing to save that for last, but they had to leave so fast that they didn't get to blow it up. All the Embassy people were in there—one floor was American and another was French, and so forth.... It was beyond belief. The piles of stuff ... the women ... there were no men! They [the women] were tearing down buildings, and moving bricks, and you didn't get close to anybody because you didn't know if he was a Russian, a German, or what have you, so you had to be careful. And never answer anybody if he asked you the time, because the next thing you knew, you didn't have a watch! [Laughs.] It was unbelievable.

[Rader is in Warsaw about a year.]

There was no reason to be coming home, then all of sudden we got orders for me to go, because back here they decided they didn't need the oss, and they shut it down and said bring everybody back, bang. When I got back, I was not even oss, I was uss—United States Service they even dropped the name. It was 1946. I could have stayed in, and I could have gone back to my job, or get married. I decided to heck with all of this, I'd get married. And that's why I got out. There was a lot of confusion going on [the oss/cia reorganization], and I missed it all because I was in Poland. Agnes [came] back . . . she never got to Czechoslovakia. She got into cia, and they sent her to Czechoslovakia. She stayed in cia and she met somebody in the cia and got married and that was the end of her career too.

Jeanne Holm
(1921–2010)
WOMEN'S ARMY CORPS/U.S. AIR FORCE

Jeanne Holm, from Portland, Oregon, began her military career in the waac in 1942 and continued with the wac in 1943. She commanded a wac basic training company; the wac training regiment at Fort Oglethorpe, Georgia; and the 106th wac Hospital Company at Newton D. Baker General Hospital in West Virginia. She left active duty in 1946 to attend college and was recalled to active duty in 1948. In 1949 she transferred to the U.S. Air Force, where she served in Germany as assistant director for Plans and Operations at the 7200th Air Force Depot Wing and War Plans Officer for the 85th Air Depot Wing during the Berlin airlift. After subsequent tours in Washington DC and Europe, she was appointed Women's Air Force director in 1965. During her appointment, which was extended twice, she updated women's policies, doubled the number of women in the Air Force, and expanded their opportunities. She became the first woman general officer in the Air Force when promoted to brigadier general in 1971, and in 1973 became the first woman promoted to major general. She retired in 1975 and went on to serve as President Gerald Ford's special assistant in the Office of Women's Programs. She wrote two comprehensive, scholarly histories of women's contributions to the American armed forces in the twentieth century: *Women in the Military: An Unfinished Revolution* (1982, updated in 1994) and *In Defense of a Nation: Servicewomen in World War II* (1998). Mary Jo Binker, then the director of the Oral History Program of the Women's Memorial in Arlington, Virginia, interviewed Holm in January 2003. The following is excerpted from the interview. Binker's questions have been edited for length and narrative flow.

I flew over to Europe with a group of Air Force officers. I knew nothing about the Air Force. And I met these nice Air Force officers who were on this plane. And they—we talked about where they were going. They were all going to this little base called Erding Air Force Base, a depot in Germany. When I got off the plane, I went . . . to ask Headquarters U.S. Air Force over there about an assignment.

They said, "Where would you like to go?"

Well, I'd never been asked that before. So I said, "Well, how about Erding?"

So they said, "Fine. There's a seat—" [on] a DC-3, we call them gooney birds, "—and they're taking off from the airport out here tomorrow morning, get on it."

The next day I got up at the air base, got on this gooney bird and flew down to Erding Air Depot, and that was the start of my Air Force career.

They had no idea what to do with me. I just arrived there as a captain, and a fairly senior captain at that point. There were about five women officers who [were called WAF at the time]. I was the senior captain. But there were also about three or four nurses there who were in the medical facility. Then there was a detachment of enlisted women there of about 100 women who were assigned, and all these women were assigned to various places throughout the base.

And when I arrived fresh out of the Army, they had no idea what to do with me. I had not even been in the Army Air Corps, whereas the rest—most of these women had served in the Army Air Corps.... I didn't even know the terminology within the Air Force, so I was really a neophyte. But they were very nice. They said, "Well, do you have any idea what you'd like to do?"

I was being interviewed by a lieutenant colonel in headquarters in the base. And this was a depot, the largest and the only—actually the only Air Force depot in Europe, which serviced all the U.S. Air Force activities in Europe, in terms of supplies and maintenance, aircraft maintenance, and all of this. Huge facility. So they said, "Would you like to go in supply or maintenance, we'd be happy to train you?"

Well, that sound[ed] interesting.

[He] said also, "We have a job—a war plans officer job, would you be interested in that?"

"Oh, that sounds interesting. Yes, I'd like that." That's . . . how I became a war plans officer. It [wasn't the] Cold War yet. This was during the occupation [of Germany], and the Berlin airlift was on. And at this point in time of course we were beginning to think that we might go to war, because the Russians—the USSR was making moves against the U.S. forces in Berlin. And they had closed off the City of Berlin. And the only way into Berlin at that point was by air. And the U.S. Air Force and our—what became our NATO allies, the British and the French also were flying in the Berlin airlift, but it was mostly U.S. Air Force. And we provided most of the supplies that—from Erding Air Depot. It went into Berlin and serviced and maintained all the aircraft that were flying in the Berlin airlift.

Well, this was a very exciting time. And Germany itself was a rubble. Erding Air Depot was right outside of Munich. The City of Munich was 98 percent rubble. All of the cities of any magnitude in Germany were destroyed, Austria as well. A few of the cities were still standing, but most of them were destroyed. Also when the SS troops were evacuating areas, they destroyed all the bridges on the autobahns. So it just shut everything down. There were no airlines. There were no airports.

The only thing[s] running were the trains, and the trucks that were provided by the occupation forces. And Germany was just destroyed, barely eking out an existence. And we were there at that time.

And the black market was rife. It was rife with all kinds of illegal operations, but it was the only—only economy that was really working.

We were allowed to barter with the things that we were able to buy, mainly cigarettes, coffee, those kinds of things. The medium of exchange essentially was cigarettes, and candy bars, but cigarettes mostly. We had what we called funny money. It was occupation currency. We were not allowed to use American money. We had to use these scrip, it was called, money. And initially we were not even allowed to use German money. But the Germans were just now going into a new—a new currency system from the Reichsmarks to the Deutschmark. And so there was a lot of growing pains at this point. And of course the Air Force itself was going through growing pains.

The Air Force itself was going through a very confused period, having just broken away from the Army. And many of the ways they were doing things were Army ways of doing things, but they didn't like that. And they were trying to establish their own identity—their own organizational concepts. And this was all in the process at the time I arrived there. And so I was on the ... bottom floor of the new organization of the United States Air Force. In addition to being war plans officer, I was always—also doing manpower officer, doing manpower officer work, working with manpower documents.

[Binker asks Holm to tell her about war planning.]

Well, that was kind of Mickey Mouse, really, because the truth of the matter was that the Air Force at the local levels didn't really know much about war planning. The Army had usually done base defense planning, the Air Force was flying airplanes, they thought in terms of airplanes, rather than in terms of base defense, and that kind of thing. They didn't quite know how to cope with this yet. And so when I was offered this job, the job entailed my going to an office that was right inside—to get to it I had to go through the wing commander's office.

The wing commander's office had a bookcase that had to be pulled back, a secret bookcase, that I had to pull back. I had to go there before he got to work in the morning, go in, and only his secretary, and the executive officer knew why I was there. I would go in, pull this bookcase back, and I had this huge set of keys to this great big vault door. It was not—it was not a combination lock, it was keys. And so I would open this huge vault, go in there, close that, and the door, and then the bookcase would close. And there was a light over my door, when I worked in there, a set of lights. The red light was—meant that the commander's office was closed, and I could not leave. And when the green light was on, I could go and come as I pleased.

So I would go into this little office, little bitty office with a large set of files and a big safe, for which I had the combination and one window, and large desk and a table where I can draw maps, and work with these war plans. And very little had actually been done on these war plans before. And so I just dove into them, and got copies—got out copies of the top—and I was cleared for top secret. So I had all these—all these top secret documents were in my office, in my—my big safe. So I would get these top secrets documents out that came from our higher headquarters in Wiesbaden, and from the local Army headquarters. And I would go through those and pick out those portions that were assigned—made assignments to this depot, and this wing, to accomplish in the event of war. I pulled those out, the material out of those and inserted them in the Erding document war plans. And then I would go visit the various organizations on the base, and tell them what—show them their portion of this war plan, the things that they were to do in the event that the USSR decided to attack us.

[Binker suggests that the threat of a Soviet attack is an ever-present reality for Holm and the Air Force.]

It was daily. I got out and drove all around all the local roads to find [out] if we were attacked. You see, this depot was the closest base to the Russian lines. So we were the most vulnerable, and certainly the most important target for them. There were fighter bases there, but they were on the other side of Munich. We were between the fighter bases, and the border with the USSR. But when all this was set up, we didn't know that the USSR was going to become a threat. And it wasn't until the Berlin airlift that we really realized that we could go to war again, and that's when things began to heat up. And so I was at the very beginning of the planning for this—this possible war effort with the USSR.

Ruth M. Anderson
(1943–)
U.S. AIR FORCE

Ruth M. (Ellis) Anderson served in the Air Force as an intelligence officer and became the first woman in the Air Force appointed to the post of defense attaché at a United States Embassy abroad. Her three-year appointment to the U.S. embassy in Budapest, Hungary, coincided with the disintegration of the Warsaw Pact and the establishment of Hungary as a free nation. She also served as chief negotiator in bilateral agreements with NATO nations concerning ground-launched cruise missiles in 1979–83; and in 1986–87 she was deputy director of the Multinational Programs Office, Strategic Defense Initiative in the Office of Secretary of Defense. The following excerpts are from her 1999 memoir *Barbed Wire for Sale*, which she wrote with her husband, J. M. Anderson.

> March 15, 1989, left no doubt that "the times, they were a changin." This date, uncelebrated under the Communists, commemorates the day in 1848 when the Hungarians rose up against their Austrian overlords in a short-lived attempt to gain independence from the Habsburg reign. In 1987, antigovernment demonstrations on this day had been put down with the use of clubs. In 1988, the militia had scuffled with would-be celebrants. A year later, we learned that crowds of demonstrators would mass, seeking the kinds of freedom and justice embodied in our Bill of Rights. . . .
>
> JD Call [the Army chief warrant officer who was the defense attaché office operations coordinator] and I decided to join the demonstration, not sure what might happen and more than a little apprehensive about the day's events. . . . We stationed our support staff in my office as a mini command post. In addition to looking out on the Soviet memorial, my office also faced the street containing the national television station (Magyar National TV—MTV). Plans had been laid by the

demonstrators to symbolically take over the station, which occupies an attractive building used as the stock exchange before World War II.

People began massing, and presently a representative of the demonstrators stepped before a microphone hooked up to outdoor speakers. As the crowd hushed, the speaker declared that the people were symbolically taking over the station. He read the same twelve points the heroic young poet Sándor Petőfi had recited from the steps of the National Museum in Pest in 1848. The litany included freedom of speech, assembly, and property rights—standard liberation fare.

The loud affirmation from the peacefully assembled crowd both thrilled and concerned me, but the few police in the area stood back, weapons holstered. After the speeches and readings, the crowd headed for the Parliament building. We tagged along, and once the large square in front was filled, a band began playing the Hungarian national hymn. Men quickly doffed their hats, people began to sing along, and the occasion took on a solemn, if a bit unnerving air. A similar crowd had been gunned down in the same location during the 1956 Revolution.

A thoughtless youth directly in front of us had failed to remove his cap, and around my shoulder came a long arm. An old, gnarled hand thumped the kid on the back, and when he turned around, his elder pointed to the cap, which the kid quickly yanked off. Everyone around squared their shoulders and stood a little taller. It had been thirty-three years since Hungarians had met together, not as members of a Communist country, but as ordinary citizens to honor their past and cheer for their future.

What might have been an opportunity for the government to thwart political change passed, and Ambassador Palmer and all of us began to believe with great certainty that democracy was on its way. There would be more events like this one, but March 15, 1989, will live on as a watershed event in the life of the transition.

• • •

In October [1989], the Hungarian Socialist Workers' Party essentially fell apart. Holding their final Party Congress, the majority agreed to form the Hungarian Socialist Party, while a few diehards clung to their Communist underpinnings. Hard-liners such as Károly Grósz were effectively booted from power, and with little fanfare the starch went out of the Party that had ruled the country since 1948.

The government announced that on October 23, the date of the previously uncelebrated anniversary of the commencement of the 1956 Revolution, a ceremony would take place at Parliament Square. Long before the appointed hour, crowds began arriving, many of them spilling out of the subway stop near the building. Of all ages, nervous and excited, the Magyars assembled shoulder to shoulder in front of the sprawling seat of their soon to be changed government. While some still struggled down side streets for a view of the proceedings, the interim President of the Republic, Mátyás Szurös, who had replaced Bruno Straub, stepped before a microphone. He declared that from that day, Hungary would be known as the Republic of Hungary, no longer the People's Republic. As he spoke, huge Hungarian flags affixed to the building teased the sky, furling and unfurling in the autumn breeze.

Andy and I stood among the crowd as silent witnesses, biting our lips as the people cheered, cried and doffed their hats when the Hungarian Army Band played the national anthem. Here lay proof of prayers answered—the army band playing the salutes to the redefined nation. There was a God, and a gentle One, for not a shot had been fired, not a rock thrown, not a fire set. This was the silk revolution. This was the role model. We in the West, along with all the members of the former Soviet Bloc, owe much to this small, daring nation that celebrated its first taste of freedom in over four decades that bright fall day.

• • •

The most memorable and instructive ceremony we witnessed involved the departure of the [Soviet] tank division headquarters at a caserne in Esztergom, northwest of Budapest. Ceremonies were scheduled for February 1990. . . .

We arrived mid-morning on a brisk day, and were treated to a well-orchestrated parade, complete with band, dancing and speeches. An English-speaking officer escorted us through a barracks and company-grade officer family quarters. This experience began to reveal why our fears of the Soviets had been justified. It wasn't their weaponry, which, while formidable was not as . . . technologically up-to-date as ours; nor were their tactics of high concern if the exercises we had observed were to be believed. Rather, the answer to the question of which side might have won a ground war could be found in the soldiers' open-bay barracks.

Hungarian winters can be cold and damp, with frequent high winds eliciting stinging tears, and promulgating frightful chest colds. Yet here in one of the damper areas of the country, near the Danube River, Soviet soldiers slept in a cold barracks on cots covered with one small wool blanket each. In the latrine, only cold water was available for shaves and showers. This was a headquarters barracks, and had obviously been cleaned and readied for foreign observers. How much more crude the accommodations in the outlying areas must have been, we thought. Western military forces might have had the technical edge, and the flexibility factor might have worked in our favor, but I believe we'd have been hard-pressed in a long-term endurance test. . . .

The officers' quarters, crammed into cheap, concrete block buildings, by our standards were very cramped, badly maintained and poorly furnished. Yet the wives had no desire to return to their homeland, for they knew there would be no accommodations anywhere to equal the quality they enjoyed in Hungary. In some casernes, families shared bathrooms and kitchens. Andy and I recalled how many problems American military families had sharing laundry facilities, and couldn't imagine how more forced togetherness would work in a rank dominated community. . . .

When the Soviets were vacating the MiG-29 base on Csepel Island, we drove around the perimeter and were amused to see Soviet troops selling tires, tools and gas to the Hungarians. We had heard rumors that no funds had been forthcoming from Moscow for the withdrawal, which meant that commanders were having to sell off what they could to pay for their departure operations. But we suspected a great deal of black-marketeering was going on as well. I cautioned my folks not to stop to buy anything near the bases. We didn't need to get ourselves in trouble. However, most of the Western attachés came home with some souvenir—an old bent red star, a length of barbed wire, a rusty tool—our booty for winning the cold war.

[At a unit withdrawal at an army installation near Szeged, an attaché from another NATO country harasses the Soviet commanding general so much that the Soviet military issues no further invitations to observe troop withdrawals.]

But we had observed so much. We had been among the first Western military personnel to get inside the great Soviet war machine, to see how the soldiers and officers lived, to touch their equipment, to talk with the staffs, and to raise glasses to a peaceful future. I'm very grateful to the Soviets for allowing us this privilege. It came at a considerable personal price to the senior officers, who nevertheless endured the withdrawals, and our intrusions, with dignity and good-will. I hope Russian officers know that the majority of us didn't gloat over the changes that dictated their removal from Hungary. Rather, we respected them, we learned from the experience, and were extremely glad we hadn't had to face them in battle.

Anne Visser Ney
(1958–)
U.S. COAST GUARD

Anne Ney, Coast Guard and USCG Reserve veteran, served from 1979 to 2010. She grew up in Ohio and makes her home in Saint Petersburg, Florida. She holds a BS and MS in biology from Georgia Southern, a BA from Eckerd College, and an MFA from Vermont College of Fine Arts. Her work has appeared in *Rosebud*, *Tea Party*, the *St. Petersburg (Tampa Bay) Times*, and other venues. Her work "The Theory of Everything" received a National Institutions for Military Education Services Student Spotlight Award, and her essay "Middle Passage, Morning Watch" is anthologized in *Red, White, and True: Stories from Veterans and Families, World War II to Present*. She is currently refining a collection of essays about her military service and geopolitical borders. The following is an original essay submitted for inclusion in this collection.

Ice Curtain

"*Chicken* shit?" the Captain of the Port said.

"No, Sir. Chicken *ship*, with a *p*. She's an old Soviet trawler converted to carry frozen poultry." I paused my brief as the COTP and Task Force Officers cleared throats and shifted behind gray metal desks, our temporary furniture. Burnt coffee, fresh drywall, and aftershave scented the makeshift conference room. *Twenty-three years later and still I'm the only woman around*, I thought.

I was under Coast Guard recall orders to serve as intelligence officer to Charleston's maritime security project, hurriedly formed after 9/11 to "detect, deter, and destroy" terrorism in and through South Carolina's ports. The TFOs were loaners from federal, state, and local enforcement agencies. I was a counternarcotics and migrant interdiction intelligence type. The COTP was a shipping safety guy. We eyed each other nervously.

"Chicken ship," the COTP repeated.

"Yes, sir, a fishing trawler built to double as a surveillance platform for the Soviet intelligence machine. Former Ice Curtain vessel."

"Ice Curtain?" a sheriff's deputy said with an *ain't-she-cute* affect.

I ignored him. "The US-USSR Convention Line of 1867. They fished their side of the Line and, when possible, fished the Donut Hole."

"Donut Hole?" Krispy Kreme-and-cop jokes rippled across the desks.

I moved on. "The former trawler claims to be carrying chickens to market in St. Petersburg." I paused for the deputy's benefit. "Russia, not Florida. Recommend a dockside boarding." I reasoned that the Russian ship's electronics completely overpowered its humble cargo. "Plus, she's been anchoring off Groton and Norfolk for days, sometimes weeks, at a time."

"Waiting for chickens?" he said.

"Or to catalog fleet movements to Kuwait," I replied.

The COTP slowly digested the new thought food dumped onto his already overflowing plate.

The Russian ship moored at North Charleston's former Navy base on a chilly, windless morning good for photography. I studied its red hull from two quays downriver then readied my camera. Her hull cast a dark reflection. Between us lay the Coast Guard Cutter *Dallas*, her crew mustered at quarters on her flight deck.

I had history with Dallas and her sister ships *Mellon, Munro,* and *Chase. Dallas* was my last floating unit; *Mellon,* my first. *Dallas* carried me across the Atlantic, beyond the Mediterranean through Istanbul, and into the Black Sea. It was a show-the-flag cruise mostly, in 1999, after the Soviet breakup and before the Global War on Terror. *Mellon* carried me across the International Date Line, into the Bering Sea, and nearly to the Arctic Circle. I loved sailing aboard the 378-foot cutters: fast, highly maneuverable combatants built for Coast Guard operations during Vietnam.

I studied *Dallas'* graceful lines, universally recognized red-and-blue racing stripe, and U.S. COAST GUARD boldly stenciled on her white hull. With care, I framed a shot of *Dallas* and the Russian. I imagined the old adversaries' surprise at their sudden proximity. It occurred to me that I knew the Russian ship.

On Good Friday 1980 I reported to the *Mellon,* the eleventh enlisted woman on a cutter billeted for ten, plus its 150 men. I was a young Seaman Apprentice Quartermaster newly schooled in basic navigation, seamanship, and flag and flashing-light signaling. The following Monday *Mellon* sailed for Pearl Harbor and Navy training.

For four weeks *Mellon* and her crew navigated fake minefields, tracked and torpedoed pretend Soviet submarines, shelled nonexistent enemy ships, and fueled at sea from a very real Navy oiler. We survived nuclear war by packing into the cutter's hull where we waited cross-legged and shoulder-to-shoulder in a grown-up version of 1950s duck-and-cover drills. Someone cut a fart when the bridge piped the warning, "Nuclear attack imminent!" Dutifully, we tucked heads between knees. A Boston accent said what most of us thought: "Everyone bend over and kiss your ass good-bye."

By the time we sailed for June's routine Alaska Patrol, I played the old salt, charting *Mellon*'s northerly progress through the heaving grey Pacific. I felt powerfully connected to the ocean's expanse and fantastically insignificant under deeply starred night skies. A week after leaving Hawaii we entered the Bering Sea, one of the world's richest fishing grounds, through Unimak Pass.

Two-thirds of the Bering's pollock- and crab-rich area falls under

U.S. jurisdiction, although its fish are harvested mostly by foreign trawlers and longliners carrying U.S. State Department permits to operate. For weeks *Mellon* threaded the large foreign fleet's nets, lines, and factory ships to deliver and recover Coast Guard boarding teams enforcing federal law and international treaties on the huge foreign fleet. I scrutinized what I could through binoculars from *Mellon*'s bridge wings, envious but too junior to review the permits, compare catch logs to fish-hold counts, or inspect fishing gear for rule compliance. I stood watches: maintained the navigation plot, wrote ship's logs, and monitored bridge radios for Mayday calls breaking through the fleet's working patois, a rich mix of German, Polish, Korean, Japanese, and occasionally Russian chatter.

Between watches I haunted the flying bridge to survey my horizons with the ship's Big Eyes, yard-long binoculars mounted on a pedestal, gimbaled to correct for ship pitch and roll, and yoked to revolve through 360 horizontal degrees and from nearly overhead to the deck. Through them I searched the Bering as I imagined the Arctic Ocean beyond the far-off strait, western Alaska's small settlements, and the Aleutians' volcanic islands arcing from Unimak toward Russia's desolate Kamchatka peninsula. The Ice Curtain hung from the Strait southwest to the western Aleutians, a geopolitical boundary between Soviet and the West, democracy and totalitarian regime.

The chart called the boundary the US-USSR Convention Line. It is the outer limit of Seward's Folly—Alaska—acquired by the US under the 1867 Treaty of Cession. It unevenly divides the Bering into Russian (one-third) and American (two-thirds) waters. During the Cold War, the Convention Line was the maritime answer to Europe's Iron Curtain.

Mellon's chart also marked the two-hundred-mile wide Exclusive Economic Zone. Under United Nations Law of the Sea agreements, a coastal nation controls resources in or under the ocean within two hundred miles of its coasts. The Donut Hole, which would draw Krispy Kreme jokes during my future brief, is beyond any nation's 200-mile reach.

I struggled to understand the implications of these two competing boundaries until my mentor, a happy Hawaiian petty officer, showed me on the chart how Soviet trawlers had to cross a slim section of

U.S. Convention waters to reach the Donut Hole's 48,000-square-mile, wide-open fishing ground. "It's an accident of nature. They can fish if they're there, but they can't get in without State Department permission," he said. I studied the chart and its prioritized boundaries until I understood. It was only by permit that the Soviets could expand their fishing operations. By dumb luck, Seward's Purchase included what would become a coveted high-seas fishing ground.

And, possibly, a place where Soviet intelligence could reach a thousand miles closer to the U.S. coast.

"So what are we doing?" I asked the Hawaiian. *Mellon*'s turbine engines were whining loudly and we seemed to be flying, not toward the Arctic Circle for sightseeing as previously announced, but west, toward the Convention Line.

"State pulled Russia's permits."

I wondered why.

"Afghanistan," he said. He saw my blank look. "They invaded Afghanistan. We cut them off."

I relieved the next morning's watch to find *Mellon*'s captain, ops boss, and deck watch officer glued shoulder to shoulder and eyes to oculars with binoculars pressed to the bridge windows. The off-watch section lay below to spread the news about the Soviet trawler the electronics picked up on the midwatch. Even without binoculars it now loomed off of *Mellon*'s bow, four miles dead ahead according to the radar, two miles outside U.S. Treaty waters.

The DWO did not lower his gaze but ordered the helm to come right. I logged the course change as *Mellon* fell in step with the Soviet. The old man lowered his binoculars and nodded, uncharacteristically somber. He left orders to maintain a two-mile buffer between *Mellon* and the Ice Curtain.

The Coast Guard has served in every U.S. armed conflict from the Revolution through the Southwest Asian wars. But its true expertise lies in wielding the instruments of peace: enforcing laws and treaties. Of the nation's five armed services, only the Coast Guard performs this service without violating civil rights or waging an act of war. If the Soviet ship violated the 1867 Treaty, it would fall to *Mellon* to defend America while defusing tensions with the world's other nuclear superpower.

Off watch, I climbed to the flying bridge and watched a tumble of seagulls trailing nets four miles off our port beam. The lookout stepped back from the Big Eyes and whistled, "Wow. Commie." In the stiff wind, my ponytail lashed my face as I took a turn magnifying the red hull, yellow sickle and hammer, and Cyrillic letters announcing a Kamchatka Peninsula homeport. The chill down my spine came from more than blown sea spray.

• • •

Twenty-first-century ports possess lucrative terrorist targets: power plants, storage tanks brimming with oil, chlorine, and poisons jokingly called methyl-ethyl-death. Thru-port vessels, trains, and trucks drive the global economy. Charleston was also an outload port from which tons of military materiel departed 24/7, bound for U.S. operations in the Middle East.

Could the chicken ship be collecting information about the outloads? I stowed my camera and joined the boarding teams in the shadow cast by the Russian ship's superstructure. My team conducted crew interviews, inspected ships' charts and logs, and interviewed the vessel's master.

He was older than I and spoke fluent English. I guessed he once trained as a Soviet naval officer. I questioned him closely. Why were they hauling a low-value commodity like chickens? He shrugged. Russia's economy, fisheries collapse, inefficient managers in St. Petersburg. He did not know. I asked about the ship's antenna field. He shrugged again. I asked to see the radio room. Reluctantly he unlocked it then stood aside with palpable discomfort as I surveyed machines older than *Mellon*'s 1980 Navy hand-me-downs. The equipment was ancient, analog, and dustily disused.

Back on the bridge, spring sun poured through the windows. He watched me with heavily-lidded, marine-blue eyes. I looked at him more closely. He was neither tall nor short, stout nor thin, enthusiastic or indifferent. He seemed resigned. I felt in company with someone I once knew but could no longer place. I asked if he had sailed in the Bering. "Of course." He almost smiled. "Ship is from Kamchatka." I nodded, thanked him, and went ashore.

The wind had picked up. A passing gray-hull threw a broad, deep wake from its heavy load of Humvees, assault helicopters, and machine guns. The Russian caught its wake first and began to rock. A moment later *Dallas* began to move. I framed the scene mentally: the two old girls falling in step. And the gray-hull bound for Kuwait and its cargo headed beyond, to Afghanistan.

7

Women's Integration and the Korean War

"I Had To Make the Girls Go Off Duty"

In the early morning hours of September 26, 1950, 1st Lt. Jonita Bonham awoke from a three-hour catnap at Tachikawa Air Force Base, west of Tokyo. She and her teammates had just completed two hundred and forty-five nearly consecutive hours aloft, and had evacuated more than six hundred wounded American soldiers from Korea back to hospitals in Japan in a C-54 cargo plane converted into an airborne emergency room. Bonham, at twenty-eight, had served in World War II and in the Philippines and Japan during the postwar occupation. Although she had accepted a discharge, when the Korean War erupted she volunteered for service as a flight nurse in the Air Force.

Bonham drank two cups of coffee and joined the other members of her medical team, Capt. Vera Brown and a male corpsman, for a predawn flight. Their C-54 would carry fifty replacement troops to Kimpo and return with more wounded. The pilot suggested that Bonham and Brown get additional sleep, but the women chatted through takeoff into a stormy sky. The plane turned east over the Sea of Japan.

Half a mile from shore, the engine stalled. The C-54 plummeted to the ocean. The impact broke the plane into three parts. It began to sink.

Bonham regained consciousness underwater, in total darkness, still inside the plane's fuselage. She fought her way to the surface and kicked clear of the sinking aircraft. Around her, men battled wind and waves to stay afloat. Those who had drowned or died on impact floated around them. Bonham grabbed a floating barracks bag as it drifted by.

In the darkness a man's voice called, "There's a life raft here! How do you inflate it?"

Bonham called back, "Yank it out of the case and it will inflate itself!" Moments later, she saw the raft and swam to it. She grabbed the trailing rope with one hand and the nearest soldier with the other. She guided the soldier to the rope. Then she reached for another man. Saw a second raft. Grabbed another soldier. Seventeen men climbed into the raft; Bonham remained in the cold water until every survivor she could see had entered one of the two rafts. Only then did she allow the men to pull her aboard.

The pilot and copilot were dead. Captain Brown, the senior flight nurse, was missing. Knowing that she was responsible for the safety of the survivors, Bonham took charge. She ignored a broken left wrist and pain that suggested other serious injuries. She directed the soldiers to lash the two rafts together. Some of the men panicked and wanted to try to swim ashore. She reminded them of the danger from sharks and the likelihood of being swept out to sea by the storm, and then ordered them to remain in the rafts until help arrived.

Controllers at Tachikawa did not realize that the C-54 had gone down. Several other aircraft flew overhead but did not see the two rafts due to poor visibility. Japanese fishing vessels sighted the rafts after daybreak. Bonham managed to remain conscious while the men attached the rafts to a fishing boat, which towed them safely to shore.

Bonham spent nine months in the hospital recovering from a broken right shoulder, broken left wrist, broken cheekbone, and a skull fracture that required three surgeries. The Air Force awarded her the Distinguished Flying Cross, its second highest decoration for valor.

Initial plans for the women's components of all the armed forces created in the Second World War had called for the discharge of all women six months after the completion of hostilities. By the middle of 1946, most women who had served in the WAC, WAVES, Marine Corps Women's Reserve, and SPARs had demobilized. But facing the expansion of Soviet influence in the postwar period, the Navy requested in January 1946 that Congress authorize the establishment of a women's component. The Army did the same a month later. Supporters included Secretary of Defense James Forrestal, Chief of Naval Operations Fleet Adm. Chester Nimitz, Army Chief of Staff Dwight D. Eisenhower, and Gen. Douglas MacArthur. Admiral Nimitz stated that "the Navy's request for the retention of women is not made as a tribute to their past performance. We have learned that women can contribute to a more efficient navy. Therefore, we would be remiss if we did not make every effort to utilize their abilities." Eisenhower argued that "the women of America must share the responsibility for the security of this country in a future emergency as the women of England did in World War II." MacArthur called women his "best soldiers." They, and the directors of the women's components, felt that retention of women would reduce the need for a peacetime draft and create a corps of trained personnel who could be mobilized rapidly in the event of a conflict. But others opposed creation of a permanent women's component. One congressman claimed that legislators received daily complaints from enlisted men who didn't want to take orders from women; some military leaders and congressmen debated how best to keep women from serving in combat.

Representatives Edith Nourse Rogers and Margaret Chase Smith, working independently to avoid the perception that they aimed to create a so-called women's bloc in Congress, first sponsored legislation to authorize permanent commissioned status for military nurses in 1946. Congress failed to act on Rogers's bill prior to adjourning. Representative Smith revived the bill the following year, and President Truman signed the Army-Navy Nurses' Act on April 16, 1947.

Legislation to create permanent women's components in the line faced greater opposition. Thanks to Rep. Margaret Chase Smith's contacts in the armed forces and her understanding of the intricacies of legislative process and committee work—in events described below—President Truman signed the Women's Armed Services Integration Act on July 12, 1948.

Although both Rogers and Smith believed that women should receive equal rank, authority, pay, and benefits for doing the same jobs as men, they never intended the two laws to integrate women fully into all areas of the armed forces or to advance abstract ideas of women's rights. They aimed rather to reflect and codify the terms of women's service established in practice in the Second World War, and to ensure America's ability to mobilize women rapidly in a future national emergency. The laws also reflected the contemporary understanding of women's abilities and roles in society. Although the Women's Armed Service Integration Act granted permanent military status to all women, regular and reserve, Congress set a cap on women's participation at 2 percent of the regular component of each service. The highest rank a woman could hold was colonel (Navy captain); only one woman, the women's component director, could hold the rank—temporarily, for a maximum of four years. Upon completion of her term as director, a woman either resigned her commission or reverted to the paygrade of 0-5. Except in the newly formed Air Force, each service maintained separate promotion lists for men and women. These provisions prevented women from becoming top-level military decision makers and limited their influence on policy to some, but not all, aspects of women's matters.

The law set the minimum enlistment age for women at eighteen, with parental consent required before age twenty-one. Men could enlist with parental consent at seventeen and independently at eighteen. A woman could claim a husband and children as dependents only if she could prove that she contributed at least half of the family income, while a man automatically received dependent benefits for wives and children even if their wives were employed outside the home. The law explicitly prohibited women from assignment to naval vessels other than transports and hospital ships, and from flying aircraft engaged in combat missions. Finally, the law granted the service secretaries the authority to prescribe women's duties and occupations, and to terminate their service "under circumstances and in accordance with regulations proscribed by the President." This provision permitted the services to expel women who became pregnant or who acquired minor children through adoption or marriage.

These restrictions, and the prevailing expectation that women should return to domestic life after the war so that returning servicemen could find work in the civilian sector, kept the number of women serving in the armed forces low. When the North Korean army crossed the Thirty-Eighth Parallel and invaded South Korea on June 25, 1950, twenty-two thousand women (about 1 percent of the total military force and only about half the authorized number) were on active duty. Fifteen thousand of those serving were in the health professions and seven thousand in line assignments.

Only one Army nurse, Capt. Viola McConnell, was stationed in Korea. She organized and supervised the evacuation of 643 American dependents and foreigners who were ill or infirm on the Norwegian ship *Rheinholt*, which had only twelve berths available. Four evacuees were women in advanced stages of pregnancy; one had a skull fracture; and 277 evacuees were children under a year old—several of them seriously ill. Only one of the seven men evacuated assisted McConnell; the other six were elderly, ill, intoxicated, or unwilling to help. Seven civilian nurses and a civilian missionary physician worked with McDonnell until the ship arrived in Japan two days later; McConnell immediately requested to return to Korea. The Army awarded her the Bronze Star with oak leaf cluster for her wartime service.

Although 46,000 women had served by the war's end in 1952, only some 650 nurses saw service in Korea. WACS, WAVES, WAF, and women Marines remained stateside because of concerns for their safety until late in the war, when a few were assigned to billets in Japan and elsewhere in the Pacific. A handful served in support billets in Europe but did not participate directly in the war effort.

Korea rapidly became the "forgotten war." Congress never issued a formal declaration of war; most who fought overseas reintegrated into society as quickly as possible and seldom talked about their wartime experiences. The women who served during the Korean War era knew that many in America perceived them as girls who were "not nice," or they felt that their service had not been significant. None published memoirs. The National Archives and Records Administration in College Park, Maryland, holds a few unpublished recollections. Nurse Jean Kirnak became a journalist and wrote some short articles about her service experiences. A few women from the other service components contributed oral histories to various archives or gave interviews about their wartime service.

Senator Margaret Chase Smith
(1897–1995)
U.S. Air Force

Margaret Chase entered politics in Maine in her late teens. She married a much older Republican newspaper owner and politician, Clyde Smith, who eventually was elected to the House of Representatives. Upon his death, she took his seat and was reelected to represent Maine numerous times. She developed close ties with the Navy through Maine's shipbuilding industry, served on the House Naval Affairs Committee, and inspected Navy facilities during the boom years of World War II on a subcommittee investigating vice (specifically prostitution) around naval bases.

Smith cosponsored the WAAC bill with Edith Nourse Rogers in 1942–43. Late in 1944, a tour of Pacific theater bases convinced her that Navy nurses needed regular permanent status. In 1947 she introduced legislation that led to the Army-Navy Nurse Act.

In May 1946, the House Naval Affairs Committee met to consider a permanent women's component for the Navy. Naval Affairs chairman Carl Vinson (R-Georgia) felt that women needed only a permanent women's reserve, subject to unlimited active duty at the discretion of the secretary of the Navy. Smith amended the proposed legislation to create a permanent women's component, but Vinson refused to call a vote on the bill and the Seventy-Ninth Congress adjourned without resolving the issue.

The Senate heard testimony on creation of a permanent women's component for the armed forces in summer 1947. Senior military leadership enthusiastically supported the proposal. The Women's Armed Services Integration Act reported out of committee on July 16, 1947. It passed the full Senate on a voice vote a week later. However, House Armed Services Committee Chair W. G. Andrews (R-New York) and Representative Vinson refused to consider the bill in the House for six months.

Smith learned that in off-record executive sessions, unnamed members of the Navy Department and Andrews had reached an agreement to jettison the bill. The subcommittee once again amended the bill so that women would serve as reserves subject to indefinite recall to active duty. Andrews put the amended bill on the Consent Calendar, implying falsely that it had been uncontroversial and unanimously approved. Smith objected. This forced the bill onto the House floor for lengthy and heated debate. The excerpt below is taken from her testimony to members of the House.

From "Women in Armed Forces—Regular Versus Reserve: Extension of Remarks of Hon. Margaret Chase Smith of Maine in the House of Representatives, Tuesday, April 6, 1948"

Mrs. Smith of Maine. Mr. Speaker, the gentleman from Michigan [Mr. Shaper] has charged me with the responsibility of killing S. 1641 [the Women's Armed Services Integration Act].

If a bill as important as this is to be considered only on the Consent Calendar, then I unhesitatingly accept that responsibility.

In the first place, I would call the attention of the House to page 48 of the Consent Calendar . . . wherein it describes S. 1641 as "An act to establish the Women's Army Corps in the Regular Navy and Marine Corps and the Naval and Marine Corps Reserve and for other purposes."

The Members of the House will note that the words "Regular Army" and "Regular Navy" are predominant in the description of the bill. This is grossly misleading as this bill in the form it was reported out by the Committee on Armed Services in no respect establishes the Women's Corps in either the Regular Army or the Regular Navy. Make no mistake about it, it is a temporary one-year Reserve bill.

The Senate voted to give women Regular status as well as Reserve Status in passing S. 1641.

The House Armed Services Committee refused to give Regular status.

The House bill definitely dodges the issue. The issue is simple—either the armed services have a permanent need of women officers and enlisted women or they do not. If they do, then the women must be given a permanent status. The only possible permanent status is that of Regular status—not Reserve status, which at most is temporary. There is no such thing as a service career for a Reservist.

This issue was squarely met by the Senate, which granted the request of the armed services to give women Regular, as well as Reserve, status in the armed services—and rejected the attempts to deny women Regular status.

This legislation does not give women any security in their military service because it discriminates against women, and it will result only in not getting women of desirable caliber for the armed services.

I am convinced that this is extremely unwise legislation. I am further convinced that it is better to have no legislation at all than to have legislation of this type. I am, therefore, unalterably opposed to it and I objected.

I would point out in answer to the charge . . . that I have killed the bill, that there is nothing to prevent the Committee from seeking a rule on the bill so that the House can fully discuss the bill—and so that amendments to the bill may be offered. Therefore the responsibility is clearly that of the House Armed Services Committee—for it is up to the Committee to request a rule— and that means specifically the chairman of the subcommittee, the gentleman from Michigan [Mr. Shafer] and the chairman of the full committee, the gentleman from New York [Mr. Andrews].

When there is such a radical difference between the Senate version and the House version, it is extremely surprising that an attempt would be made to get this legislation railroaded through on the Consent Calendar.

During the debate on the House floor, Smith learned that unnamed service legislative liaisons had privately told representatives that so-called biological differences, including temperament, pregnancy, and menopausal disability and illness, would make a regular women's component too costly. When the bill moved to a joint House-Senate committee to work out a compromise, Smith contacted Secretary of Defense James Forrestal and demanded that he investigate and expose the duplicitous collaboration of Navy officials with Andrews, Vinson, and other congressmen to prevent establishment of a regular women's component:

April 22, 1948

Honorable James V. Forrestal

THE SECRETARY OF DEFENSE
WASHINGTON, D.C.

My Dear Mr. Secretary:

Yesterday the Honorable Dewey Short in opposing the proposal to grant women Regular Status in the Armed Services stated:

"We were told that because of certain biological differences in the sexes when they reach the age of menopause or go through the change of life, with the physical disabilities or illnesses that result, the cost of the program would be stupendous if not prohibitive. Those are a few of the fundamental and essential facts, unpleasant as they might be, which we must as legislators wisely and soberly consider." [Smith enclosed a clipping of the statement from the *Congressional Record*.]

This statement, coupled with reports that I have received, that although the civilian and military heads of the respective Armed Services had unanimously urged Regular status for women in the Armed Services, the Legislative and Liaison officer representative of the Armed Services had "behind closed doors and in executive session" opposed Regular Status for women.

Mr. Short's statement on the floor of the House confirms these reports that the Armed Services had officially through their legislative and liaison representatives opposed Regular Status for women at least on a cost basis.

This, to say the least, is duplicity that gravely questions the integrity of the administration of the National Military Establishment. I believe that it is incumbent upon you as the head of your department to determine and identify the Armed Services representatives whose statements were the basis for Mr. Short's statement. The basic question is whether we are to accept the official "on the record" statements of the executive and military heads of the Armed Services or the "behind closed doors" statements of your legislative representatives to individual members of the Committee.

Since S. 1641 is now in conference, I believe that immediate action and reply on your part is imperative.

Sincerely yours,
Margaret Chase Smith, M.C.

Forrestal immediately sent members of the joint committee messages of support for the Senate bill authorizing an active women's component. The joint committee merged the bills for the Army and Navy women's components into one favoring regular status for women. President Truman signed the Women's Armed Services Integration Act into law on July 12, 1948.

Smith, having developed close ties with the Air Force during her earlier efforts to help establish it as a separate service from the Army, was commissioned as a lieutenant colonel in the Air Force Reserve in 1950. She served in manpower and administration for eight years, concurrent with her service in the Senate. Although she is most remembered for her courageous stand against the excesses of the McCarthy Commission, which she expressed in her famous 1950 "Declaration of Conscience" speech, she remained a strong advocate for military women throughout her career.

Eunice Coleman

(1903–1983)

U.S. ARMY NURSE CORPS

Maj. Eunice Coleman, chief nurse for the First Mobile Army Surgical Hospital, and twelve other Army nurses landed on the beach
at Inchon, Korea, September 26, 1950—eleven days behind the
invasion force. After treating Korean civilians there for just over
a week, the hospital moved to Pusan with the Seventh Infantry
Division. Battle lines moved rapidly and the MASH units were
close to the front; early on the morning of October 9, the convoy
in which the nurses were traveling came under attack. Coleman
and her nurses took cover in a roadside ditch for several hours, and
then treated the wounded in place before continuing to Pusan.
After the ambush, the nurses began calling themselves "The Lucky
Thirteen." This excerpt is taken from Coleman's personal letters.

15 November 1950

On 22 September 1950, we sailed from Yokohama on the *General
Mann* and arrived Inchon Beach 26 September. This was our first
experience in going down the side of a ship in what seemed to
be mid-ocean, onto a small boat that carried us to the sand on
the beach. Even though it was a first experience for most of the
nurses, not a trip or slip was made and no delay in debarking
was caused by the nurses.

After we were secure on land, the possibility of a place to live
seemed for a while to be narrowed down to our pup-tents, but
without too much delay we were told that an old school building
would be used to accommodate the entire hospital unit. And so,
through one of the most disagreeable sand storms, we put all our
gear on backside again and hiked to where we had been told that
transportation would take us to the school. Sure enough, the truck
was there and did take us about three miles to the designated
place. Perhaps the narrative should stop here lest I not give the
school credit for any good points it might have had. It really was
pretty awful. Our work began that day by opening wards in the

school and within two days we had over 300 South Korean civilian casualties of the worst type. Much surgery was needed to save lives, so for six days we were very busy. We had no beds or cots because our equipment was still on the ship and our priority was low on the list for unloading. Matter of fact, we never did get our hospital equipment until we finally reached the Iwon Beach. Anyway we did what we could with what the Marine Corps gave us and when we left there 6 October we had all of the patients (civilian Koreans) in civilian hospitals or homes. Many infants and children we placed in Christian Orphans Homes.

I wish I could really tell you about some of those poor people and their wounds and burns. The nurses showed themselves to be real soldiers by working until late if not all night. There was no time to feel that you could "go off duty." I had *to make* the girls go off duty after 16 to 20 hours of caring for these people. We had all the patients on the floor so you can imagine how our knees and backs felt after hours of bending, stooping, and jumping in and around the sick and dying.

From Inchon we convoyed to Pusan on 7, 8, 9 October. On the morning of the 9th at 0300 our convoy was attacked and the nurses spent the remainder of night in a ditch. Without a single word being spoken or a light on, when the First Sergeant opened the back of the ambulance we were in and whispered that we were attacked every nurse quickly put on her gear, grabbed a blanket, and moved quietly until we found a ditch not too far away. About 0430 I decided to check on everyone under my charge so with my blanket completely over my back and head I crawled down the ditch, calling the roll, so to speak, in whispers. Everyone except one girl answered me back and most of them asked how I was making out. I kept feeling about and calling this one nurse who had not responded but still no answer; so then I decided to count for 12 and by elimination could locate her if she were still with us. This I did and when she was located and found to be O.K. I inquired why she had not answered. Her reply was that she was afraid the enemy would hear her!

The entire sky was lit up from gunfire and burning vehicles. About sun up we got out and started treating the wounded who, by this time, were coming in pretty fast. All that day until about 3 p.m. we worked on the roadside giving blood, operating, etc.—treating for shock and putting the wounded in ambulances for care. We lost 8 men and quite an amount of supplies and vehicles. After all was clear, the convoy started out again and arrived in Pusan around midnight. We were put up with the 64th Field [Hospital] and worked several days with them caring for POW patients. The stay there was uneventful and on 17 October we boarded ship, the *E. Patrick*, which planned to sail next day for Wosan, North Korea. Something changed this and not until 29 October did we move from the Pusan Bay. So we had almost two weeks of clean comfortable living again—eating from a table and sleeping in a bed. It was really wonderful and it seems now as I look back on those days that we washed our hair every day.

On the 29th we sailed and arrived Iwon Beach 4 November. That night we nearly froze. We were in a building that had been a house once but now it had no doors or windows or furniture— the worse though is that it had no stove. Next morning we were mighty glad to start out again. This we did about 6 a.m. And arrived here in Pukchon where we are doing an active business for the 7th Division. All three surgical teams are working steadily, and the postoperative section is just as busy. Our main problem now and since we opened here is getting the patients evacuated to the 121st Field [Hospital]. We are having to keep them four or five days due to bad weather or poor roads or enemy activity. All this cannot be avoided so the crowded wards and personnel shortage is made the best of under the circumstances.

As for clothing, we are wearing the same winter issue that the men wear and the smallest shoe they have for the soldier is an eight. We put two or three pairs of socks under these and do fairly well. Have heard very few complaints about this and none of the nurses have asked to go back to Japan. Our food has been good. Cannot say that anyone has gained weight but no noticeable loss either. On the whole we are in fine shape . . . all thirteen of us living in one big room in the school and we have two stoves up and going full blast all the time. One is an oil stove and one wood-burning. We thought this up ourselves just in case one of them went on the blink. It is so cold here you think a lot of things.

Jean Kirnak
(1925–2010)
U.S. ARMY NURSE CORPS

Jean Kirnak grew up in eastern Montana and joined the Army Nurse Corps in 1948 to take advantage of a government-sponsored nurse training program. On November 14, 1950, she received orders to join nineteen doctors and sixteen other nurses at the 8076th MASH unit at Sunchon. She returned to the United States in August 1951 and was discharged a year later. She used her GI Bill to earn her bachelor of science in nursing at the University of Oregon Medical School. In 1994 she retired from nursing. She published personal essays about her war experiences, of which the excerpt below is one, in local newspapers. She died in 2010.

Kunuri

Kunuri, North Korea, is about twenty miles from the Yalu River at the Marchurian border and the Communist Chinese. The year was 1950 and I was a pre-op nurse in the 8076 MASH unit. . . . I had just joined the unit ten days earlier on November 15th in Sunchon, as replacements for two burned out nurses who were being sent back to Japan. They had been there since the war began on June 25th.

Our unit moved up from Sunchon to Kunuri, about twenty miles, the day before Thanksgiving in the bitter cold. Our living quarters were in an old, dilapidated hospital, my army cot next to a blood spattered wall. We tacked up army blankets over the broken windows. The weather was freezing cold and the oil heater in the middle of the room was quite inefficient.

On Thanksgiving would the menu be the usual canned pork or beef and gravy, canned vegetables, biscuits and fruit cocktail, we nurses wondered as we headed up the creaky hall, mess gear in hand, to stand in the long line for dinner.

To our surprise, sliced turkey, cranberries, sweet potatoes (all canned), dried mashed potatoes, gravy, biscuits, and red jello with raw apples were served. A surgeon carrying his dinner to the table stepped through the rotten floor and everything spilled.

After we washed our mess gear, Mary and I headed for the pre-op tent to start our twelve hour night shift at 7:00 p.m. Since we were expecting a quiet night, only fifty army cots were set up. We couldn't hear any small artillery and very little big artillery. But by nine o'clock litters were pouring in, wounded soldiers freezing cold and in shock quickly filled up the fifty cots. The ground outside was covered with more casualties on litters waiting while additional tents were quickly going up. An extra supply of blankets were needed to cover the hypothermic, shot-up soldiers on the icy ground. The little oil heaters in the tents weren't much help, even when they worked. We nurses wore heavy jackets over layers of warm clothes, but couldn't wear gloves on our cold hands.

Before the night was over, the fifty anticipated wounded turned out to be over six hundred stretcher casualties plus many more ambulatory patients. Every available doctor, nurse, and corpsman worked feverishly, crawling around on the tent floor, cutting off six or seven layers of sleeves and pant legs in order to take blood pressures and get blood transfusions started. There was no such thing as a type and crossmatch. Icy cold, type O positive, and sometimes negative, blood in glass containers, was given to everyone. Sometimes four transfusions at once were pumped into the shock patients. As soon as they had a pulse and blood pressure, off they went to the operating room, where the litter was the operating room table. The electric lights went out from time to time and the doctors had to use flashlights to complete an operation.

Wounded Chinese communist prisoners started showing up, and we knew that what had been a fear was now a reality. The Chinese had hit. Some soldiers reported that the Chinese had horse cavalry and were tooting bugles. Still we had no idea that things were so serious.

"This transfusion won't run. I'm sure it's in the vein. Will you try?" "No use. He's gone." This happened many times. By 5:00 a.m., our tanks were moving back, leaving us unprotected. I was too naive and too busy to be scared. *This is the U.S. Army. We don't lose battles*, I thought, *not against a little country like North Korea.*

At 7:00 a.m. I went off duty. I could hear the Colonel yelling our code on the inadequate telephone, "This is Red Hot Six. This is Red Hot Six," and more yelling about orders, but I was too exhausted to be alarmed. I broke the ice on some water in my mess cup and brushed my teeth, even put on my pajamas, and crawled into my freezing mummy bag, pulled blankets over my head and fell asleep. At 9:00 a.m., a nurse shook me and yelled excitedly, "Get dressed, pack up, and go back on duty so the day nurses can get packed. We're moving out."

The stench of gangrene greeted me as I walked into a room. Some American prisoners had been recaptured from the North Koreans. Their feet were badly frozen; black and gangrenous. They undoubtedly had to be amputated later. As each new bunch of casualties came in, I asked them where they had been hit. One group said, "We were ambushed between Kunuri and Sunchon," which meant we were nearly surrounded. We certainly couldn't escape the way we had arrived, but had to take a much longer route in order to get to Pyongyang.

Nurses usually rode in ambulances when we moved, but this time all the ambulances were needed for evacuating patients. In fact, some of the doctors, corpsmen and other staff had to stay behind until all the patients were evacuated. Bell helicopters and ambulances evacuated the patients to a small, nearby air strip where C-47s got all the patients out. Those who stayed behind to complete the evacuation barely escaped. They were drawing mortar and small arms fire, but luckily no one was injured.

We rode in the back of an army truck, our knees crowded against the generator which took up the center space. I kept my eyes on the mountainous horizon, thinking any minute the Chinese in their off-white quilted cotton uniforms would come swarming like ants to devour us. By 3:00 p.m. our convoy was on its way, but travel was very slow on the bumpy dirt roads. It seemed like we were always being delayed.

We stopped at the 8063 MASH for dinner. They were relieved that the rumors that we had been captured were false. Once during the night, our convoy got on the wrong road and was heading toward the front line. Sometimes we had to wait for other convoys with a higher priority to pass us on the narrow roads. The night was long and cold and we were uncomfortably cramped in the truck. We finally arrived at the 363rd Evacuation Hospital in Pyongyang at 3:00 a.m., where we were greeted by the chief nurse, Major Bradley.

"Are we happy to see you! We heard that everyone in the 8076 MASH had been taken prisoners. We can't wait to get out of here."

The 8063 MASH joined us the next day, and the evacuation hospital moved to South Korea. While we were at Pyongyang for a week, hundreds of casualties came through each day. Some men had gone berzerk [sic] and had to be restrained. I remember vividly the soldier with both hands blown off, another who had been shot through both kidneys and slowly died. The report "Everyone in our company was killed but us" was heard over and over again.

By the end of the week, the enemy was getting dangerously close. We were packed up, prepared to leave the next morning. All of the nurses, except me, went to sleep with their clothes on, even their combat boots.

"I wouldn't be able to sleep if I had to wear my clothes," I insisted.

About 4 a.m., I was awakened by the sound of small arms fire. It sounded like it was just outside the door. Quickly, I got dressed, although I was shaking so badly I could hardly lace up my boots. Even after I crawled back into my mummy bag, I continued to shake uncontrollably. I have never been so scared. A few hours later, we were heading south over a long bridge across the Nam River, while below us on the water, many Korean civilians were fleeing in boats (We heard that a short time later, the bridge we had used was bombed.)

Our convoy stopped at the Pyongyang air strip and dropped off the nurses who were evacuated by plane to Taegu, South Korea, where there was a large evacuation hospital. We arrived there at lunch time and sat down to eat in the mess hall, where we overhead the conversation at the next table.

"Isn't it terrible! All the nurses in the 8076 MASH were taken prisoner!"

"Are you sure? I heard that everyone was killed."

We introduced ourselves. We were very much alive. After a day or two, we rejoined our outfit, never again to return to North Korea. That was okay with me. I was in no hurry to go back.

Sarah Griffin Chapman
(1918–2010)
U.S. NAVY NURSE CORPS

Sarah Griffin Chapman, from Americus, Georgia, graduated from nursing school at West End Baptist Hospital in Birmingham, Alabama, in 1943. She joined the Navy in January 1944 and served in Oran. After World War II she was stationed in Bainbridge, Maryland, and in Guantánamo Bay, Cuba. An accident in Cuba led to her unique service during the Korean War. The following is transcribed from a telephone interview Chapman gave to Jan K. Herman, historian at the Bureau of Medicine and Surgery, on March 18, 2002.

One day I was out on a picnic with a group. We were walking along the edge of a cliff when I got too close to the edge and fell about 25 or 30 feet down into the water. I landed on top of coral. . . . The other people I was with on the picnic got some sticks and made a stretcher. When they reached me they floated me back to shore and got an ambulance. They put my left leg in a Thomas splint. I had fractured the tibia of the left leg. They didn't realize that the heel of my right foot was jammed up into the ankle. . . . So they put my left leg in a cast; nothing was done to the right foot. . . . I was semi-conscious for a few days; I don't remember too much. I recall waking up and screaming with pain in my left leg. When they cut the cast off I had wet gangrene from above the knee to the end of my foot. From then on the gangrene gradually went down to my toes. At first I lost the two middle toes—the second and third toe. I couldn't put any weight down on my foot. If I did, I'd get a blister on the big toe.

[Chapman was transferred to Bethesda Naval Hospital and on to Mare Island Naval Hospital on the West Coast, where she was placed under the care of Dr. Thomas Candy.]

When I got out there they decided that the best thing was to remove my limb below the knee—the left leg. . . . I had no problems and got along fine. In July I had a prosthesis and was walking on it and making good progress. Of course, they didn't let me go very fast. You had to take things gradually and go to physical therapy for exercise on your stump.

[Chapman was home awaiting orders to return to active duty when the Korean War began and the Navy needed to recruit medical personnel.]

Charles Asbell, who was in charge of the amputees under Dr. Candy, wrote me a letter suggesting that I write a letter to BUPERS. They still told me I couldn't come back into the Navy. But when they began getting all the amputees, I am assuming that Dr. Candy talked to [Rear Admiral] Swanson [the Surgeon General]. I got a letter from Swanson asking me if I would come back on active duty and work with the amputees. I wrote back immediately telling him that if he thought I would be of value to the Navy, I would be happy to come back. I then got my orders to return to active duty in October of 1950. [Her reply to Rear Admiral Swanson read:] "Since you think that I could render a valuable service to the Navy and to my country in rehabilitation of the amputees in the naval hospital, Oakland, California, I would be happy to volunteer for active duty for this assignment." And he said yes....

Dr. Candy wanted me because he liked how hard I worked to become a good walker.... So I worked with the amputees from October 1950 to January of '53.... I was very happy that they thought I was capable of doing something like that. I loved the Navy and I wanted to be a part of it....

We had a ward full of patients—forty-some patients. They were both below-the-knee, above-the-knee, and quadruples.... I told them that if they put their minds to it, they could walk again. I actually didn't do any nursing. I just worked with them and told them that if they worked hard they could accomplish what they wanted to and live a normal life again....

My days were very challenging, sometimes very disappointing and sometimes very rewarding. There were so many different personalities to work with each day. Some didn't want to walk and I had to be creative to get them to.... Once a week I went around with Dr. Candy.... We'd make rounds and Dr. Candy would talk to the patients. The patients would then come down to see me. I talked to them about working on their balance and strengthening their legs and muscles. I told them they would have pain but that they would just learn to live with it. I told them that if they walked properly and did the things they needed to do like balancing and building up their muscles in the remaining leg and arms, why they wouldn't have any problems. . . .

I remember the times we had and the problems we faced. I think about many of my patients and wonder what happened to them. Sometimes I remember specific patients. I'd talk to a patient who was despondent and refused to walk. I was determined that he was going to walk.

"I don't know why you want me to do this," he'd complain. "You don't know my pain. You have two legs and don't know how it is. You can't possibly know what I'm going through."

At that point, I'd reach down and knock on my prosthesis. That would generally set them straight. From then on, they had no more excuses.

Mildred Stumpe (Kennedy)
(1931–2003)
U.S. Marine Corps

After a short stint in college and work in a St. Louis real estate company, Mildred Stumpe joined the Marine Corps. Her three older brothers had served in the Army in World War II, and despite the common perception that women in the service did not have a good name, they thought military service would be good for their "spoiled" little sister. Stumpe served two and a half years of her three-year enlistment; she opted for a marriage discharge at the urging of her Marine husband when he took orders to Korea in 1952. She and her husband eventually settled in Connecticut and raised three children. She worked part-time in retail grocery for thirty years. In 2001 Mary Jo Binker interviewed her for the oral history program at the Women in Military Service for America Memorial Foundation.

> I kind of felt like I would never get out of the state of Missouri and I was an adventuresome person. I thought, well, this is one way to get out of Missouri. . . . I went to Parris Island. Then after Basic I went to supply school in North Carolina. . . . I had an easier time than

most people [in Basic]. I get along very well with people.... I met these two girls from Missouri [on the train to Parris Island] and we became very good friends. And of course they were going through the same thing in boot camp as I was so we kind of cried on each other's shoulders.

. . .

It was a new era in my life. I had no qualms about it. I knew I would make it.... And [I had] the right attitude.

. . .

When we first started we had men DIs. But then as we progressed more we had women.... About the only thing different between now and back then is now women fire actual weapons, which we didn't do. But your discipline—and, I remember, oh, God—this drill instructor was a very tall, thin man, and he used to ... we were stupid, let's face it. He would swear under his breath. In other words, he couldn't swear *at* us. But you could see his lips going through the SOBs and so forth.... In basic you were kept under such stern control that actually you didn't have a chance to ... you know, we were segregated. I remember I was there on Christmas. And I remember the big deal on Christmas Eve was marching to church, and actually seeing young males ... I don't think any of us got much out of church—we were too busy looking at the guys.

[Binker asks about black women. Mildred Stumpe Kennedy says they lived in an integrated barracks.]

We were all in the same boat. If someone became teary-eyed, she had a lot of shoulders to cry on. And we were all ... the same people.

[Binker asks about Stumpe's assignment to ordnance supply.]

At that point, anything was better than your basic training. And there were several of the friends that I had made, close friends, they were also assigned to North Carolina. So that was the good part. I was put into ordnance supply—like, a six-week course. And it was just so neat because you could go out with boys, you could look at boys. Especially when you're eighteen years old. And yet, you couldn't go very far because . . . being in North Carolina, none of the guys had cars. . . . It was kind of nice not to always have someone looking over your shoulder and telling you what to do. There were things such as dances, to where a busload of women Marines would go and there would be dancing, and at twelve o'clock they packed us up and took us back to the barracks.

[After supply school, Stumpe was assigned to Camp Pendleton.]

It's in southern California, not too far from San Diego. Near La Jolla. I loved it. . . . First of all, you didn't have as many people in the barracks. You had a little more privacy. And you actually had a nine-to-five job.

[Binker asks about Stumpe's responsibilities. She replies that her job in ordnance supply was locating weapons and placing orders for another department to ship them to Korea.]

What we were doing was, like, locating the weapons and putting an order in for them. And then it was sent to [another department] and they took care of notifying manufacturers. We did not do any of the actual shipping. What we did was to locate. And we had lists of everything in ordnance. Then someone else took over. [The requisitions] went from our department to another department.

We had a lot of fun. And I don't think . . . I guess I was in a good department. It was small. And I never felt any pressure. And it was just a great place to be. . . . I was the only woman Marine in there. There were civilians. And there were male Marines.

[Binker asks if she was treated well.]

Oh my goodness, yes. See, I guess back then we didn't know about things like that . . . but . . . no. There was never any harassment. . . . I felt that even though I was in uniform, I was treated as a woman.

[Binker asks if she was concerned about the war.]

No. Don't forget—we were eighteen, nineteen years old. . . . In fact, if you want to back up just a little. I first arrived in California when I was going to my job, the assignment, they sent a young Marine to pick me up in a Jeep [at the barracks] to take me to the office. And he was a nineteen-year-old. And we fell in love. . . . When I met him he was a corporal. He was from Connecticut. He'd been in a little longer.... He also worked in ordnance.... I kept telling him, "You don't fall in love this fast. You're lonely. You're away from home." But he kept at it, and we did not stop dating.

[She tells Binker that they did not need permission to marry.]

We went to see the priest at the Ranch House chapel in Camp Pendleton. And we had a little formal wedding. May 31st, 1952. But back then we got a leave together, a thirty-day leave. First we flew to Missouri. He met my family. We stayed there two weeks. Then we flew to Connecticut and I met his family and we stayed here two weeks and then went back to California. And it was cold, I would say maybe in like February, and then we decided to get married.

[Then] he got orders to Korea. He didn't want me to stay in the Marine Corps in California by myself. So we decided—back then, if you got married you could get out. So we decided I should get a discharge and go back to Missouri while he was in Korea.

[She says that she could have stayed on, and she was sad that she agreed to seek a discharge, because she didn't want to leave the Marine Corps. Binker asks if she thinks of herself as a pioneer.]

I always say that if I hadn't gotten married and stayed in the Marine Corps, I probably would have been commandant of the women Marines now.... I think we were the gateway to women going into the armed services, because back when I was a Marine there were only three platoons and one company.... It multiplied. They found out that, hey, having women in the service was pretty doggone good.

Because I was a Marine—I don't know if this is a novelty—I am held in such esteem, it's unbelievable. There was a gentleman [who] was in the Navy during the Korean War. He calls me his "hero." Isn't that amazing? Because I was a Marine. And he thinks I have so much stamina [despite my health problems]. It was my Marine Corps background that made me so motivated, that got me living as an ordinary human being again [after a serious illness].... In my mind, I figured it was from being a Marine.

I certainly enjoyed my time in the Marine Corps. Looking back, I wish I'd stayed in. I met some beautiful people, and it was quite an experience. I got out of Missouri!

8

The Vietnam War

"What the Hell Am I Doing Here?"

Lt. Bobbi Hovis, Navy Nurse Corps, walked out of the U.S. Navy Hospital in Saigon and realized that she was staring down the barrels of several guns emplaced by the Vietnamese Army (ARVN). Just a few weeks earlier, a crew including Hovis and four other Navy nurses spent four days in an abandoned five-story apartment on Tran Hung Dao, Saigon's main thoroughfare, setting up the first U.S. Navy hospital in Vietnam. A little after noon on November 1, 1963, they found themselves in the middle of a war.

Realizing that she could be caught in a crossfire between ARVN rebels and the National Police Force, Hovis dashed inside and up the stairs. When she heard a burst of gunfire, she went up to the fifth-floor balcony and saw the street below engulfed in a hailstorm of bullets. Pedestrians took cover in doorways, while the occupants of buildings popped out on balconies and rooftops to see what was happening. A male staff member joined Hovis. A bullet hit the balustrade wall directly in front of them. They dropped to the floor, crawled back inside, and took cover under a desk.

The shooting grew louder. Soon the sounds of machine gun and antiaircraft fire and the explosions of rockets fired from American-made T-28 fighter bombers filled the air. Staying low, Hovis and her colleagues watched the T-28 pilots open fire on the presidential palace, pull up, climb steeply, and then return. The sky clouded with smoke.

The day shift returned to quarters in an evening lull. By 8 p.m., tanks rumbled through the city. Shells exploded around the nurses' quarters; a 105-mm howitzer thumped on the city outskirts. Fuel farms at the Saigon River were burning. Hovis heard a whine and an explosion nearby: a shell had hit the building across the street.

The ARVN attacked the presidential palace at 3:30 a.m. that Saturday under a full moon. Tanks and armored personnel carriers jammed the streets; hundreds of troops marched slowly behind them in the moonlight. Flares illuminated the smoky sky. Soot and dust covered Hovis and her six companions, now trapped in their quarters. Cordite fumes burned their eyes. Their heads ached from the repeated explosions.

At six-thirty that morning, the gunfire stopped. The artillery fell silent. A white flag waved over the presidential palace compound. The seventeen-hour military coup had ended. President Ngo Dinh Diem tried to escape; he was captured later that day, tortured, and executed.

The war in Vietnam had begun.

By the beginning of the Vietnam War, both military women's policy and the attitude toward the women's components had stagnated or regressed. The women's components rejected any semblance of feminism. Policies aligned with stereotypical ideas of the 1950s about a woman's proper role in society. Most servicemen viewed the women's components as a ladies' auxiliary rather than a force multiplier. Recruiters and assignment officers considered physical appearance a critical attribute. Prospective women recruits posed for four photographs: front, side, back, and full-face. Physical training was intended to keep women "fit and trim" but not to improve their ability to serve in the field. Enlisted women and officers received instruction on grooming, hair styling, and application of makeup. Officers diverted the most attractive women, regardless of their technical expertise, into front-office clerical jobs or protocol. The directors of the women's components tolerated the double standard and even pushed servicewomen to maintain a "feminine" appearance, but they struggled behind the scenes for continued acceptance of women in the military and survival of the women's components. In short, women's military policy institutionalized segregation and discrimination.

A very small number of nurses and WACs served in Vietnam during the early days of the war. Two WACs arrived in December 1964 to train South Vietnamese Women's Armed Forces Corps servicewomen in Saigon.

Three hundred more military nurses trained in field skills such as camp site selection, tent setup, road marching, map and compass work, field sanitation, and disaster planning arrived in February 1966. By the end of the war, almost six thousand nurses and medical technicians had served in country. In addition to treating American and South Vietnamese wounded and enemy prisoners of war, they volunteered for public health missions in local communities. One nurse, Lt. Sharon Lane, ANC, died of enemy fire when a rocket hit her quarters. Six other Army nurses and one Air Force nurse also died in the line of duty.

Policies on the assignment of women were inconsistent. Nurses served under fire during the Tet Offensive in 1968 and routinely experienced more danger and inconvenience in the field than men assigned to headquarters commands in Saigon and on other major facilities. However, the Army refused women in the line assignment to Vietnam even when they volunteered. Only about five hundred WACs, fewer than forty women Marines, and a very small handful of Navy and Air Force women served in country. Almost all had volunteered to go. Exclusion from the combat zone reduced women's opportunities for promotion, especially in the Air Force, which combined men's and women's promotion lists. Women prohibited from serving in Vietnam received lower pay and fewer benefits: they were ineligible for hostile fire pay, cost of living allowances, tax exemptions, choice follow-on assignments and training, and accelerated promotion. Exclusion of women also forced men to carry the lion's share of the burden of one-year combat rotations.

Women returning from Vietnam, especially hospital staff, faced many of the same reintegration challenges as the men with whom they served. A 2015 Department of Veterans Affairs study of women veterans who served in Vietnam found that 20 percent experienced post-traumatic stress disorder: flashbacks and nightmares, survivor's guilt, medical trauma, and mixed feelings about saving the lives and treating the wounds of the enemy. Some experienced sexual harassment and assault. In addition, upon their return, society did not recognize them as veterans because of their sex. To this day, many women who served in Vietnam or during the Vietnam era discuss their military experience only reluctantly. Or they remain silent.

In the 1980s women veterans of Vietnam began to publish. Thirteen years after her Vietnam tour, Army nurse Lynda Van Devanter published a memoir of her service. She also edited a collection of poems from other military nurses, civilian women who volunteered in Vietnam or worked there with international relief agencies, and Vietnamese women. Former nurse Elizabeth Ann Scarborough's novel *The Healer's War*, set in Vietnam, won the 1989 Nebula Award. In 2015 Vietnam veteran Donna Lowery published a collection of reminiscences from women who served in the line in Vietnam.

Lynda Van Devanter
(1947–2002)
U.S. ARMY NURSE CORPS

Lynda Van Devanter (Buckley), from Arlington, Virginia, joined the Army in 1969 and served a year in Vietnam as a surgical nurse. After returning from Vietnam, she continued her nursing career despite suffering from post-traumatic stress. She eventually founded the Women's Project of the Vietnam Veterans of America, served as its executive director from 1979 to 1984, and testified before Congress and other agencies on behalf of women Vietnam veterans. Her 1983 memoir inspired the 1988–91 television series *China Beach* and ignited a backlash from military nurses who refused to corroborate her experiences. Van Devanter died in 2002 at the age of fifty-five from a systemic collagen vascular disease that was attributed to chemical exposure to Agent Orange in Vietnam. The following are excerpts from her 1983 memoir *Home before Morning: The Story of an Army Nurse in Vietnam*.

It was a few days before my hump day, the exact middle of my tour. . . . I was lost in a heavy sleep under my bed when the phone started ringing. The sound was more impossible to ignore than the rockets that had driven me there a couple of hours before. Still half asleep, I listened to the words: "More casualties, Van. We need you in surgery." . . .

I . . . reported to the head nurse for my assignment. Her short red hair was wild, the front of her scrub dress blood-stained. A mask dangled from her neck. "There's a bad one in the neuro room," she said. "I need you to pump blood in there."

The neuro room was one of the places I usually tried to avoid. Head wounds were so messy and this one would undoubtedly be bad. But even knowing that, I was totally unprepared for the sight that awaited me when I stepped through the entrance.

Leading to the operating table was the largest trail of blood I had ever seen. I tried to walk quickly through it but slipped. When I regained my balance, my eyes were drawn to the gurney, where several people were transferring the wounded soldier from the green litter to the table. Three intravenous lines ran from bags of blood to his body, one in his jugular vein and one in each arm. The lower portion of his jaw, teeth exposed, dangled from what was left of his face. It dragged along the canvas litter and then swung in the air as he was moved from the gurney to the table. His tongue hung hideously to the side with the rest of the bloody meat and exposed bone. When he was on the table, Mack Shaffner, the facial surgeon, dropped the lower jaw back into place. . . .

[Van Devanter assists in an emergency tracheotomy, then helps the facial surgeon clamp off bleeding arteries. She hangs a fourth bag of blood, and then begins circling the wounded soldier, replacing bags of blood and handing the surgeon instruments and supplies.]

In the middle of the confusion, the neurosurgeon . . . came into the room. He looked at the soldier on the table and shook his head. His face was red. "Who the fuck woke me up for this gork?"

"The brain doesn't look too damaged," Mack answered.

"You're wasting your time."

"We can fix him," Mack insisted. "Just give me a chance."

"Bullshit," the neuro guy answered. "That sucker's going to die and there's not a fucking thing you can do." . . .

When the circulating nurse arrived, my sole job became pumping blood, while Mack fought against the odds. After a while, I turned it into a routine: Start at the neck, take down the empty bag of blood, slip a new one into the pressure cuff, pump up the cuff, rehang it, and check the temperature in the blood warmer. Then go to the left arm and repeat the process. Next the left leg and finally the right arm. Then start back at the neck and repeat the entire sequence. It took about five minutes to complete the steps at each site, about twenty minutes to make a round of him.

As Mack and the scrub tech clamped and cauterized the blood vessels, little puffs of smoke rose from what was once the soldier's face. The smell of burning flesh filled the room.

Following every second or third time around the soldier, I changed the IV tubing because the blood filters were getting thick with clots. Since we only had two blood warmers, I had to run the other lines through buckets of warm water to raise the temperature. When the buckets started to cool, I changed the water. It was all just another simple job where I could turn off my mind and try to forget that we were working on a person.

But this one was different. The young soldier wasn't about to let me forget.

During one of my circuits around the table, I accidentally kicked his clothes to the side. A snapshot fell from the torn pocket of his fatigue shirt. The picture was of a young couple—him and his girlfriend, I guessed—standing on the lawn in front of a two-story house, perhaps belonging to her parents. Straight, blond, and tall, he wore the tuxedo with a mixture of pride and discomfort, the look of a boy who was going to finish the night with his black tie in his pocket, his shirt open at the neck, and his cummerbund lying on the floor next to the seat. She, too, was tall, and her long brown hair was mostly on top of her head, with a few well-placed curls hanging down in front of her ears. A corsage of gardenias was on her wrist. Her long pastel gown looked like something she had already worn as a bridesmaid in a cousin's wedding, and it fit her in a way that showed she was quickly developing from a girl into a woman. But the thing that made the picture special was how they were looking at each other.

I could see, in their faces, the love he felt for her, and she for him, a first love that had evolved from hours of walking together and talking about dreams, from passing notes to each other in history class, from riding together in his car with her sitting in the middle of the front seat so they could be closer.

On the back of the picture was writing, the ink partly blurred from sweat: "Gene and Katie, May 1968."

I had to fight the tears as I looked from the picture to the helpless boy on the table, now a mass of blood vessels and skin, so macerated that nothing could hold them together. *Gene and Katie, May 1968.* I had always held the notion that, given enough time, anything could be stopped from bleeding. If you kept at it, eventually you would get every last vessel. I was about to learn a hard lesson.

I pumped 120 units of blood into that young man, yet as fast as I pumped it in, he pumped it out. After hours of work, Mack realized that it was futile. The boy had received so much bank blood that it would no longer clot. Now, he was oozing from everywhere. Slowly, Mack wrapped the boy's head in layers of pressure dressings and sent him to post-op ICU to die.

Gene and Katie, May 1968. While I cleaned up the room I kept telling myself that a miracle could happen. He could stop bleeding. He could be all right. *Please, God, help him.* I moved through the room as if in a daze, picking up blood-soaked linens, putting them into a hamper, trying to keep myself busy. Then I saw the photograph again. It was still on top of the torn, bloody fatigue shirt. A few drops of blood were beaded on the edge of the print. I wiped them off and stared.

This wasn't merely another casualty, another piece of meat to throw on the table and try to sew back together again. He had been real. *Gene.* Someone who had gone to the prom in 1968 with his girlfriend, *Katie.* He was a person who could love and think and plan and dream. Now he was lost to himself, to her, and to their future.

[After she finishes cleanup, she goes to post-op to see Gene.]

His bandages had become saturated with blood several times over and the nurses had reinforced them with more rolls of gauze, mostly to cover the mess. Now, his head seemed grotesquely large under the swath of white. The red stains were again seeping through. I held his hand and asked if he was in pain. In answer he squeezed my hand weakly. I asked him if he wanted some pain medication, and he squeezed my hand again. All the ICU patients had morphine ordered for pain, and I asked one of the nurses to give Gene ten milligrams intravenously, knowing that, while it would relieve his pain, it would also make him die faster. I didn't care at that point; I just wanted him to slip away quickly and easily.

The drug went to work immediately. As his respiration slowed and his grip became weaker, I imagined how it would be back in his hometown. Some nameless sergeant would drive an Army-green sedan to the house where Gene's parents lived. The sergeant would stand erect in his dress uniform, with his gold buttons glinting in the morning sun and bright ribbons over his left breast pocket. Perhaps a neighbor would see him walking past a tree in the front yard, one that Gene used to climb before the war; perhaps a little boy would ride his bicycle along the sidewalk and stop near the house to watch the impressive stranger stride confidently up the stairs and to the door. And when the mother and father answered the knock, no one would have to say a word. They would both know what had happened from the look on the sergeant's face.

And Katie? She would probably find out over the phone.

I ran my finger along the edge of the picture before putting it into the envelope with his other possessions. Then I walked outside, sat on the grassy hill next to post-op, and put my head in my hands.

I wouldn't cry, I told myself. I had to be tough.

But I knew a profound change had already come over me. With the death of Gene, and with the deaths of so many others, I had lost an important part of myself. The Lynda I had known before the war was gone forever.

Angel Pilato
(1942–)
U.S. Air Force

Angel Pilato, the first woman Air Force officer assigned to manage an officers' club, served more than five years on active duty in the United States, Europe, and Thailand. After her tour in Southeast Asia, she transitioned to the Air Force Reserves as a training specialist. She retired as a lieutenant colonel and earned a doctorate degree from Oregon State University. She has held management positions at a Fortune 500 company, a Top Ten university, and a nonprofit organization. A Rotarian, private pilot, Paul Harris Fellow, and member of the Veterans of Foreign Wars, she serves on the Boots to Shoes Board. She lives in Oregon. The following is taken from her memoir, *Angel's Truck Stop: A Woman's Love, Laughter, and Loss during the Vietnam War.*

[On the first day of her assignment to Udorn Air Force Base in Thailand, in 1971, the outgoing officer, Captain Hightower, gives Pilato a tour of the Officers' Club, where a topless Thai dancer is performing in the bar.]

As we walked through the lobby to the main dining room, Hightower stopped and pointed to the plaque on the wall. "This is our Honor Roll plaque. Anytime someone gets shot down, we add a brass name plate with the guy's name, rank, the date he was shot down, and whether or not he's KIA or MIA. Pip [a Thai club employee] knows where to get them made," he said in a detached tone, like it was just another mundane part of his job. It struck me that all a guy got for losing his life was a small bronze nameplate on a plaque in the lobby of an Officers' Club, outside a bar with a topless go-go dancer.

We sat down to lunch, and the waitress hurried over to take the boss' order. Our conversation continued. "We've got about eight hundred and fifty club members, and only about three dozen of them are American women. Most of them are nurses, a few teachers from the Air America compound, some civilian secretaries, and the rest are support officers. It's going to be interesting having a woman running the Officers' Club."

"Oh, why's that?" I said, trying to be nonchalant and not wanting to show I was annoyed.

"The guys are worried you'll try to change things," Hightower replied.

"What things?" I wondered why he was bringing this up.

"They're afraid you'll cut out all their fun stuff. You know how these fighter jocks like their amusement, and they want a place to let off steam. After all, there's a war on. They just don't want anyone messing things up."

"They needn't worry," I retorted. "I won't plant any flowers in the urinals."

Before I ever set foot on the base, rumors had spread that a woman was replacing Captain Hightower, the wunderkind club officer. I found out later that the Base Commander had extended Hightower's tour and tried to get me reassigned to another base. Maybe that was why Colonel Sifford had met me and asked me to come to Udorn. These guys probably thought I'd be a prudish, stiff-faced, unreasonable moralist who was ugly to boot. They were conjuring up tales that I'd make the bar waitresses wear long skirts, put a stop to the topless go-go girls, or cringe at them saying the "F" word.

Hightower laughed, "Well, the Air Force sure is changing. It hasn't been the same since they lifted the ban on women officers being allowed in the O-Club stag bars."

"Yeah, who knows what they'll do next? They'll be letting women in the Academies and allowing them to fly airplanes," I said sarcastically.

Hightower replied, "Don't know if we'll see it in our time." Then quickly added, "Frankly, I think women should be allowed to do any job they're qualified for."

Hightower had put me to the test on the very first day. At that moment, I decided exactly how I'd handle this assignment. I wasn't going to play into any of their preconceived notions of how a woman might run an Officers' Club. I knew I could run the club as well as any guy, and I sure as hell was no prude. All those repressive rules I'd learned in my thirteen years of Catholic education were not going to stand in my way. No, that was not part of my life any more. I'd broken away from all that guilt and trauma. I was free to do as I pleased without anyone or anything tugging at my conscience. After all, a stripper was just a stripper. It was no big deal. Besides, my job was to be in charge of morale, not morals.

[Pilato, the first female club officer, is never well received by any commander at any assignment until she has proven herself more than capable of running an officers' club. Her performance evaluations reflect a pattern of low-to-high ratings that will prevent her from being selected for promotion. Although she has decided to resign her commission after the Udorn assignment, she's embarrassed when the poor ratings are brought to her attention by the newest commander, Lieutenant Colonel McHale, with whom she is romantically linked.]

I desperately tried to get rid of the lump in my throat, but I couldn't seem to swallow. However, I did manage to hold it together. . . .

"How could that asinine boss of yours, Major Anastasio, ever give you an eight and a two? Good God, an eight and a two are the kiss of death for getting a promotion. Why didn't you use your ace and tell us about this? You knew Gabriel and I would have never signed off on this OER [Officer Effectiveness Report]."

I was quickly getting the picture. . . . To get promoted, an officer needed to get all nines, or what they called a "firewall OER," which meant xs all the way down the right side of the page. Humiliated and embarrassed, I realized I was probably the only officer in the entire Air Force that didn't know how the "real" system worked. McHale now knew how dumb I was.

Finally, I found my voice and said reluctantly, "I didn't know how it worked. Besides, I didn't wanna take advantage of you or ask for any special favors." Why would a woman ask for what she wanted or speak up for herself? If she did, she would be labeled as aggressive and unfeminine, a braggart with a poor upbringing.

"For God's sake, Angel, you wouldn't be taking advantage of anybody, you'd be getting what you deserved, which is an outstanding OER. Well, damn it!"

Now, even if I wanted to withdraw my resignation papers, it would be impossible. The joke was on me. Instead of me deciding to leave the Air Force on my own, "x's" on a sheet of paper had decided it for me. It was totally ludicrous. I couldn't believe how naïve I'd been.

The final zinger came when the Wing Commander entered the office. Any self-esteem I might have had left was about to evaporate like water spilled on hot pavement.

[McHale hands a sheet of paper with the ratings to Gabriel.]

"Charlie, what would you think of an officer who had OER ratings like these?"

"God, I sure hope this guy isn't assigned to us!"

That did it—one last punch in the stomach—it was a TKO. I'd never be able to face these guys again.

"Well, these ratings are hers," [McHale] said, as he looked right at me.

When Colonel Gabriel realized he'd just "stepped in it," he winced and quickly searched for something to remedy his faux pas. "Angel, I can't imagine anybody giving you OERs like these when you've got such great looking legs!" he quipped in his North Carolina drawl.

At the time, his statement didn't offend me. Even today, after years of sensitivity training about comments that might be construed as sexist, I still don't consider what he said offensive. He was doing his darnedest to say something to make it up to me, and as far as I was concerned, he did the best he could. Besides, I liked him.

LouAnne Johnson
(n.d.–)
U.S. Navy and Marine Corps

Pennsylvania native LouAnne Johnson enlisted in the U.S. Navy in 1971 and served nine years on active duty, achieving the rank of petty officer first class in the Navy and, later, second lieutenant in the Marine Corps. She earned the Navy Commendation Medal and Air Force Achievement Award for her work as a journalist/radio-TV broadcaster. After leaving the service, she earned a doctorate in educational leadership and became a high school teacher. She has written ten books; *Dangerous Minds*, an account of her experience teaching at-risk teens in Palo Alto, California, became a *New York Times* bestseller and a 1995 film starring Michelle Pfeiffer. The excerpts below are taken from her 1986 memoir *Making Waves: A Woman in This Man's Navy*.

[Arriving at her first duty station, Johnson conducts a barracks check-in with the assistance of two first class petty officers—one male, the barracks master-at-arms (Hawkins), and one female ("Ski").]

A tall girl with curly red hair stood at the head of the line in front of the check-in desk. She had three stripes and an eagle on her left sleeve and, from the way she ignored the comments of the men hanging around the lobby, I guessed that she'd been in the Navy for a while. [Petty Officer] Hawkins handed her a stack of envelopes and she walked away from the desk, sorting through her mail. As she passed the crowd of guys, one of them reached out and grabbed her butt. Without looking up, she brushed his hand off as though it were a pesky fly.

"Your mother is a sow, Felton," she said over her shoulder as she nonchalantly walked up the stairs. . . . I wanted to ask her how she learned to handle men so well. . . .

[Hawkins] glanced at my orders, then snorted and hollered, "Lookee here, fellas, we got us a virgin sailor girl checkin' in. This is her first duty station. Which one of you wants to volunteer to be her new roommate so's you can break her in right?"

He didn't wait for an answer before he turned back to me and said, "Don't bother actin' indignant, honey. I know you wouldn't of joined the Navy if you was really a lady. Ladies stay at home with their husbands or their mamas. The girls with hot pants join the Navy so's they can get some of that good US Department of the Navy grade-A meat. I run a tight ship here, so don't let me catch you screwin' around in my barracks."

I was too shocked to say anything, so I just stood there and stared at him as he sniffed, hitched up his pants, and belched.

"This is a man's Navy, sweetheart, and women only have three positions where they really belong—on their backs, on their bellies, and on their way out the door."

This wasn't the Navy I'd expected. I'd planned to march in, salute sharply, and be welcomed aboard by my commanding officer. Then I'd begin writing wonderful press releases and making plans to travel to exotic ports. My chin started to quiver and I fought to keep from crying.

"Hawkins, you asshole! Why do you have to harass all the new women?" The girl I had seen earlier had come to my rescue. Nearly six feet tall, she stood looking down at Hawkins, with her hands on her hips, her eyes blazing. The fire-colored hair tumbling wildly around her shoulders only made her seem more fierce.

"You're the sorriest excuse for a petty officer that I've ever seen," she snapped. "If your brother-in-law wasn't an admiral, you'd be out of here in a flash. And you have a lot of nerve talking about women lying on their bellies." She poked her finger into the soft flesh that swelled above Hawkins's belt. "You're just jealous because you couldn't lie on your fat belly to save your soul, you slob."

Hawkins glared at her for a minute, obviously trying to think of a retort. Then, noticing her hair, he said, "You ain't allowed to wear your hair down in uniform, Miss Smarty Pants Petty Officer."

"For your information," she said, "I was combing my hair when I heard you down here making an ass of yourself again, Hawkins." She grabbed my check-in sheet out of Hawkins's hand and turned to me. "Come on, honey. I can tell you're gonna need some help getting used to this place. My name's Ski. Actually, it's Ursula Marie Dubrokowski, but you can see why no one calls me that. Most of us call each other by our last names, just like in basic training."

[Johnson's experience in the public affairs office in the Philippines is no better.]

Commander Willenbrau [her commanding officer] was making his own plans to celebrate my promotion, but it wasn't a fiesta. Instead, he told me I'd have to wait for a few months before I got to be the anchor person on the news because he had an exciting new project for me. My assignment was to develop a women's feature television program. The new project kept me busy, researching stories, writing scripts, designing the set, producing the introduction, taking photos for slides to be used on the show. I designed and helped build the set, then took my place in front of the camera, welcoming the audience to "Woman's World." Each show had a different theme—women in science, women in medicine, women in sports. The co said the shows were good, but he didn't schedule them for immediate broadcast. He said he wanted to have a whole series taped before we started showing them.

Kruger [a petty officer she worked with] wasn't as naive as I was. He pointed out the fact that some of the junior men were being assigned to the anchor spots while I was busy writing stories offering advice to women on career advancement, education, and professional opportunities. I had followed the same job progression as everyone else on the staff, but men with much less experience and training were moving ahead of me.

"It's no skin off my teeth," Kruger said, "it's just the principle." He bit off the end of a cigar and spat the tobacco off the end of his tongue. "I figure you pay your dues, you ought to get what's coming to you, man or woman, instead of wasting your time on some program that will never be aired."

I looked up from the script I was reading. "What do you mean, never be aired?" I asked Kruger. "I just spent six months of hard work on 'Woman's World.' The CO is going to schedule them after I have a whole series on tape." Kruger shook his head slowly as I spoke.

"Don't quote me, but I figure it this way," he said. "Commander Willenbrau isn't wild about broads in the Navy, so he figures that it'll catch up with him one of these days. When it does, he'll whip out these programs and demonstrate his unbiased support of women. I don't like that one bit. It's too sneaky. I prefer to know who my enemies are right up front."

Kruger's support surprised me. He had always been pleasant to me, but I hadn't realized that I had a friend behind those smelly cigars.

[Kruger recommends that Johnson talk to the CO, who avoids her until she receives her performance evaluation.]

The CO had described my performance as mediocre, my attitude as uncooperative, and my potential for further advancement as poor. I couldn't believe it. It had to be a mistake, especially after all the extra work I'd been doing. I knocked on Commander Willenbrau's door and walked in before his secretary had a chance to stop me. The CO didn't look a bit surprised. He had been expecting me.

"This isn't right," I said, shaking the report. "It is not a fair evaluation of my performance. I won't sign it."

The CO pursed his lips and clasped his hands under his chin. "It doesn't matter if you sign it or not," he said. "It will just go into your record, noted as unsigned and protested by you."

"But it isn't accurate," I argued. "I've done a good job here. How can you say that I'm a below-average performer?"

"That's the way I see it," he said, "as your commanding officer."

"What about all the extra college classes I've been taking in my free time?" I asked. "And what about the new women's program?"

"Yes, you've spent a lot of time on that extra assignment. Of course, it wasn't an official assignment. Nothing in writing. Maybe you've spent too much time on it and that's why your work suffers occasionally."

"What do you mean, my work suffers?" It took all my control not to shout. "I just got promoted to second-class petty officer! Stratter signed off all my required practical factors. You know he wouldn't sign them off if I couldn't do them." I paused for a minute, but the CO was silent, so I continued. "I've been here almost two years. It's my turn to move into the anchor spot. You know I'm a good broadcaster."

"I don't care if you're the best broadcaster I have, you're not going to anchor a newscast."

"But why not?" I insisted. "Haven't I done a good job on the weather?"

"Yes," the CO nodded. . . . "Weather isn't real news."

"I do spot news, too. When I tape my women's program, I only need one take. The engineers love me—they call me 'One-Take Johnson.' Lots of the guys stutter and stammer and need ten takes to do one little sixty-second spot."

"Feature programs aren't real news either," the CO said.

"So what are you gonna do with all those programs I've been taping for the past six months?" I asked. "Aren't you going to air them?"

"That's up to the program manager," the CO said. Kruger was right. Commander Willenbrau was just wasting my time, keeping me busy on projects that would stay on the shelf in the film library.

"Those shows are good," I said. "You know they are."

"You're still not going to anchor the news," the CO repeated.

"Why?"...

"Because I don't believe women have the credibility as announcers to anchor the news. No one will believe you."

"Let me try and see."

"No."

"*Why?*"

The CO realized I wasn't going to give up. He cleared his throat. "Because I don't think women belong in the Navy, that's why." Commander Willenbrau's voice was so low, I could barely hear him. He finished rearranging his pens and then lined up all the papers on his desk. He drummed his fingertips on the desktop for a second, then stood up and walked over to look out the window. "I used to be an enlisted sailor and the women got the shore billets," he said, with his back to me. "I swore that when I became an officer, women weren't going to do men's jobs in my command." When he said that, I realized I was not dealing with a rational man. I tried, desperately, to think of another argument.

"It's against Navy policy to discriminate against women," I said, without conviction, sensing his answer in advance.

"You can't prove it's discrimination." The CO looked up at me, but he didn't smile. He wasn't enjoying his power, just abusing it. "Your performance appraisal is mediocre. In that case, I'm forced to put a junior man ahead of you."

There's a point at which bravery becomes stupidity. I knew it would be stupid to try to fight the CO. An overseas commanding officer has even more power than he would in the States. I could write all the appeals and arguments I wanted to; he would just say I was acting like a typical bitchy broad and the appeals board, men just like him, would believe him.

Suddenly, I was tired, too tired to fight anymore, tired of working so hard for no reward, tired of rain and lizards and roaches and cold showers and not being able to call my mom on Sunday afternoons and—most of all—tired of being told that women couldn't this and women couldn't that.

[Johnson negotiates with her commanding officer: he improves her performance appraisal in exchange for her "voluntary" request to return stateside.]

"I'm glad you're not going to be silly about this. The last woman we had onboard here wasn't as cooperative as you are."

"What happened to her?"

"She's gathering weather reports on Adak Island."

"Adak is off the coast of Alaska, isn't it?" I shuddered just thinking of the frigid weather reports she must be collecting. The CO nodded.

"I see," I said quietly.

"Yes, I'm sure you do."

Lee Wilson
(1947–)
U.S. ARMY

Lee Wilson grew up in Las Vegas about forty-five miles from Area 51, where her mother worked for a time. In an oral history that she provided interviewer Therese Strohmer in 2010 for the University of North Carolina at Greensboro Women Veterans Oral History collection, she describes the forces that shaped her interest in military service, her reasons for joining the Army, and her decision to volunteer for orders to Vietnam.

[Wilson's first assignment after basic training in Alabama was supply school at Fort Jackson, South Carolina. However, she was soon assigned "boring" clerical duties that involved separation packages for soldiers on their way out of the Army. She found the humidity unbearable and the work less than exciting, so she started considering Vietnam as a way out of South Carolina.]

One of the girls apparently had gone to Vietnam on the first wave. I met her when I first got there at Fort Jackson, and then she departed and sent a postcard, or something, saying, "Hey, they really need more women over here." So I applied for that. One of my roommates worked where the orders and whatnot come in from headquarters. She said, "Lee, you've got two orders here."

I said, "What do you mean?" I says, "I just put in for Vietnam."

She said, "Yeah, but you also have been ordered to the Pentagon."

I said, "Oh."

She said, "Would you like me to lose one?"

I said, "Yeah, lose the Pentagon." I didn't want to go to the Pentagon. [Chuckle] I didn't know what Vietnam was. There was very few soldiers had been coming back—but very, very few. I told her I wanted her to lose the one for the Pentagon, because I couldn't afford civilian clothes, and you would have to have civilian clothes a lot more than any place else. So I put in for Vietnam and they approved it."

[Wilson explains that she landed at Bien Hoa Air Base, about twenty-five miles south of Saigon, during the first night of the Tet Offensive.]

Tet of '68, the major battle, nobody mentioned anything about it. I don't remember anybody saying anything about when we took off. Until we got close to Vietnam [and] they said, "Close your windows." And because it was—what was it—early morning?—I think it was early morning when we were arriving. So it was . . . right before the sun come up. They said, "Close your windows."

I asked one of the guys, "Why are we closing our windows?" And he didn't know. We pulled the shades down. And they finally told us that we were under fire. The base was under attack, but we were coming in and shouldn't have any problem. And I said, "Oh, this is good." Of course, I was in my cord uniform with high heels, short skirt—wrinkled.

And they said, "When you get off of the aircraft run for the bunkers."

And I looked again at this poor guy next to me and said, "What's a bunker?" Because, our training in South Carolina for Vietnam was how to get into a hole in the ground, simulated fires going off. And when I jumped in the hole it was covered with ice. So other than that it's the amount of training we got for Vietnam. But when we landed everybody jumped off, and the guy next to me—I never did know his name—he grabbed my hand and drug me to a bunker. We came out a little bit later. You could hear—it was slowly clearing out because it was getting daylight. When daylight comes they kind of—the bad guys, kind of, back off.

[Wilson explains that women in Vietnam weren't allowed to carry weapons, and this bothered her.]

So eventually down the line I ended up working at engineer head-quarters, and one of my bosses was a big skeet shooter. In fact, the general of the engineers was a big skeet shooter, and he had found out that I liked to shoot skeet. He'd come talk to me. He said, "Lee, what would you think of having a skeet range?" That's where I also got hold of a sawed-off shotgun, because sometimes I'd go into Saigon—not by myself—I'd talk somebody in the company, or in the office, that was having to go into Saigon to take me along—just to get out of the office. And so, I'd drive along and then we'd stop by and I'd pick my shotgun up just to feel a little more comfortable.

[The shotgun would help to save her life.]

A guy I was dating . . . was going in for something, and I sweet talked him into taking me along. We were ambushed. Luckily it wasn't a big, big ambush—in other words they didn't use rocket grenades or anything like that—just rifles. We just jumped out and got on the right side of the jeep and used that for cover. I think we ended up in a ditch, and just started firing back. I don't know if I hit anybody— shotgun doesn't have that good of a range—

At the time you're not nervous. You're in survival mode at the minute. You kind of just say, "They're not going to get me." You just kind of go with the flow and most of the time the people I was with knew exactly what to do. The guys that were shooting at us were injured, because there was another jeep behind us and they had—what do you call it—they had a mounted machine gun. Because they were—I don't know how many jeeps in the convoy—it wasn't really a convoy, but it—the machine gun in the jeep behind us got them. It was scary. Like I said, at the moment, other than you're trying to get your face down in the dirt—you're also trying to survive. The guys would always put themselves in danger for me. And that—that's why I think that women don't belong in direct combat, because guys are putting their lives for mine. Del had grabbed me and pulled me—you know behind the tires or something like that. A couple of times—other places—the guys would put me in front them—or push me out the way. That's one of the main reasons that I disagree with women in direct combat. And I've had some arguments with women. They say,

"Oh, but we deserve to be able to do that." I say, "Yeah. You go out there do it in real life and do it and tell me." You are not—it's just the way that we're brought up. I don't care how they do it or change things. The man will always try to protect you. Even if you don't want him to, he will try to protect you. So I knew—I mean once I got behind a tire I knew what to do, but standing there like a dumbo—we don't have the training even now—with the training they have—a guy will put his life out in front of you. Yeah, it was scary, but I survived."

[Wilson talks about the camaraderie among her peers.]

We were the rebellious crew, because when they had sirens go off— you were supposed to run downstairs and get in a bunker. But before you ran you had to put your uniform on—we never did [chuckles]. We didn't—Finally, the first sergeant got on us enough [to] where we finally did carry our helmet down there. That was kind of silly. When you were inside of a bunker, why would you wear a helmet? After we would watch her for a while—When she'd go to sleep we'd go outside, because it was too stuffy in the bunker. And you could tell when something was coming close to you. Like I said, you could hear it. One night the finance company near her barracks and the mailroom took direct hits. And we got shrapnel.

When I first started [in Vietnam], it was just typing everything, but eventually I wormed my way into—our sergeant major, who was really—we had a colonel, but the sergeant major really ran the office—I became his left hand girl [chuckles], and I learned a lot. He taught me how to do things that most women weren't supposed to be doing. Women were only really supposed to type. You know, we weren't smart enough to do anything else. Serious—I'm serious! So he had let me get in on—I don't even know if we have viewgraphs anymore. He let me get on making those for some of the projects. We had our engineer projects that we'd take down to General—what's his name—I've forgot the general's name. He would approve them. A viewgraph is like a plastic sheet and you—not paint it, but you mark it so that when you put it on a projector like thing, it would go up on a big board. I don't know why. We made these for briefings. We were engineers and we handled the counting of rubber trees, certain water purification equipment—a lot of weird stuff. It seemed like every little engineer group had little things that needed to be acquired, and we would acquire them for them. And like water purification was a big thing out in the field. So we would have to go here and find a piece of this and that, you know, like a supply depot almost. So we had to get all the—the work finding the stuff. And the sergeant major was teaching me, as I was going along, all these different skills. We had—we were in charge of counting rubber trees, because we had to pay the French for each rubber tree that was shot. So I got in on that detail because I could go up in a helicopter and that was fun. Then we had bridges that were damaged or needed to be built. We had to go out and do blueprints—mostly from the air—of what needed to be done; and then we would take it back, and almost break it down by photograph of what needed to be required to do it.

[Wilson explains that she had a foot, so to speak, in two camps. During the day, she worked for the sergeant major and with engineers; but she was also part of the female detachment and under the supervisory control of female company commander, who wanted women to conform fully to regulations, even if those regulations denied a great number of opportunities. Women, for example, were not allowed to fly in helicopters.]

I didn't tell them. [She laughs.] The sergeant major and the colonel knew—he knew. But women—we were—Let's see, how do you explain it? The WAC detachment had our living and feeding—[that] was their priority. Like in the states, the WAC detachment—whatever they call it now—that was their thing, but they weren't really my boss. My boss was where I worked, but I was attached to the WAC detachment. And so we figured, "Hey, you know, they don't need to know." The sergeant major and the colonel, they all knew what we were supposed to do and what we weren't. So if I were to ever get into trouble they would have stepped up and said "Excuse me, we're the boss." Because sometimes we worked—I got out of a lot of details because we worked like six and a half—sometimes seven days a week—like twelve to sixteen hours, longer sometimes. So we were busy. When they wanted something done, you know, I always volunteered. They said, "Hey, you don't know how to do that!"

"Yeah, I'll learn." Anything like that—but it was just so interesting. And again that's—you know—We would go up in choppers and I'd take photographs—classified photographs—and that would give us what needed to be done on the ground. I think [the men] saw that we could do more—my bosses did. I don't think the company commander of the WACs there [did]. That's how women were treated back then. We were only supposed to do these certain things. A lot of—most of MOSs [Military Occupation Specialties] were not open to us. And I think that's—I'm positive that those of us that were in Vietnam opened the door to a lot that's opened up now for the women. It's like the women in World War II—the nurses—they were sent to combat, and that opened the door for all the nurses with the enlisted women back then—there were very few of them—and the ones that were, were doing office duties.

But in Vietnam—like in Europe they were stationed in London, or someplace like that—but in Vietnam there wasn't a safe place to hide. So a lot of us did things that proved and opened the doors for the women nowadays that have—I get tickled when I see women helicopter [pilots] and things like that. I still don't like them in direct combat, you know, there's so many doors open to them now; whereas we had very few doors open. I think over there [the men] were more open because they realized that, "You know, hey, these girls over here, they're pretty smart." And most of us were young, and I think that back then I was young and our CO [commanding officer] and company commander and the supply sergeants—they were old. They had to be at least thirty. [She chuckles.] So you know we saw them as the old ladies. But I really think that everybody's eyes were opened back then—the men especially.

Barbara J. Dulinsky
(1928–1995)
U.S. MARINE CORPS

Barbara Dulinsky was the first of eight female officers and twenty-eight enlisted women Marines to serve in Vietnam. Assigned as the Top Secret Control Officer for the Military Assistance Command Vietnam (MACV) Headquarters from March 1967 to March 1968, she supervised enlisted personnel, processed correspondence, and maintained custody of more than five thousand classified documents. She retired as a sergeant major. The excerpts below are taken from her unpublished memoir, held in the Archives and Special Collections branch of the Library of the Marine Corps.

The first question most generally asked about my tour in Vietnam, was it voluntary? Well, yes and no. In February 1967, I was completing a tour as First Sergeant of Recruit Company, Woman Recruit Training Battalion, Marine Corps Recruit Depot, Parris Island, South Carolina. As anyone who has served in a Recruit Training Command, when your tour is completed, you're ready to go, but not necessarily to Vietnam. . . . [I said when a major from Marine Corps Headquarters asked if I "was interested in going to Saigon":] "Major, you've got to be out of your mind, I'm a devout coward." . . . Also, at this time, the news medias were filled with Viet Cong terrorist activities in Saigon, blowing up BOQs, theaters, and anything that had American advisors and/or families in them. I just felt anyone volunteering for such duty had to be partially demented or lacking a full sea bag. I gave a negative response to a couple of more telephone calls from [Marine Corps Headquarters].

[Director of Women Marines Col. Barbara Bishop coaxed Dulinsky to "volunteer" for the assignment.]

Prior to my departure from Parris Island, in my checking out process, I inquired as to what the uniform of the day would be upon reporting to Travis [Air Force Base]. With all the air of knowledgeable authority that only a company clerk can convey (I should know, I certainly practiced it on many a poor soul) I was told, "Winters, of course, that's your departing uniform of the day." My intuition told me this was dumb. . . . [Dulinsky dutifully changed into her winter wool uniform at Travis AFB. By the time she reached the Philippines, she said, the uniform had turned into "a walking wool steam bath." The commercial airliner on which she flew, in contradiction of policy, landed during the dark on February 18, 1967—under fire.]

●●●

After all the literature I had read concerning personal conduct while in Vietnam, on that night I was to learn that there were exceptions to the rule of courtesy.

The convoy, led by two gun jeeps, ran helter-skelter through a Vietnamese hamlet, scattering people, dogs, vendors, stray chickens, and everything in sight. . . .

Above the din of the bus driver running through the shifting of gears and the commotion from without, I managed to ask the driver why. "It doesn't give Charlie a chance to throw a grenade under us," was his reply. *Oh*, I thought, *isn't that just peachy-keen*.

●●●

My life as a Marine had never been too far from an iron, so I naturally had taken one with me. Needless to say there was no laundry room in the hooch I was in, so my suitcase (God bless Samsonite) with towel over the top became one of the best portable ironing boards I've ever used. Getting a summer uniform ready for the following day was my first priority. It was a struggle getting the one-piece Dacron uniform pressed to my specifications, but my cover was a real bear. Fortunately, I had a can of "Fabric Finish" with me that made the task less painful. . . .

Once the bus passed over the Saigon River bridge into the city of Saigon it was unbelievable. The din of honking Renault taxi cabs (if you ever want to see the height of ridiculous, see a six-foot GI crammed into the back seat of a Renault cab), motorized pedi-cabs, one trillion motorcycles, bicycles, and a swarming multitude of humanity all going in different directions. . . . The stench of fish heads and rice penetrated the air and combined with exhaust from the vehicles created a horrible stench. I don't believe that anyone could dream up a torture worse than being caught in a bus, in downtown Cholon, behind a garbage truck. This too became an adjustment that was just accepted and you just became part of it. . . .

[On the following day], I was taken to my duty assignment as Top Secret Control Officer/Custodian of Classified Documents. . . . Colonel Adrian St. John, U. S. Army, was the CO of the center.

If I had an ice pick, it would have made it easier to have chipped away the ice after my interview with Colonel St. John. A dynamic individual, but it was obvious that "no woman" could fill the billet, not in his eyes at least. There began my first real challenge.

Women Marines have but one man to thank for getting the job that they were originally sent to Vietnam to do, and that was Brigadier General John R. Chassion, USMC. Fortunately, he was the director of the Combat Operations Center and senior Marine officer in MACV.

I found out later from two of my operations NCOs that when Colonel St. John found out he was getting a woman replacement for GySgt Blanton, he had a fit. He and the XO made several trips to see the general. But General Chassion insisted that I was to be given a chance. Captain Jones was also to be placed in a public information job at MACV, but again General Chassion put the nix on that and she too assumed her assignment as OIC, Marine Liaison Section when she arrived in country in July of 1967.

• • •

On certification of my clearance, I then started standing evening watches along with other Operations personnel. An incident occurred that was to change the attitude of my CO and XO.

It was when I stood my first security watch that ended at 2000. There were still operations officers working in the Plans section along with Colonel St. John. I am sure to this day that I had cleared my desk of all classified material before I secured to go to dinner.

Later in the evening when Colonel St. John was about to close the vault, he glanced down to see a Top Secret document laying in my bottom basket. Since I was the only one who had the combination and Colonel St. John would not have gone down to the War Room to get the combination . . . I was off to a flying start.

The next morning, one of my Ops sergeants warned me of what had occurred, so I awaited my summons. Instead, the XO called myself and all of Ops sergeants and clerks together and started chewing everyone out. That bothered me, since it was my watch and I was responsible. I interrupted the colonel and identified my responsibility for the securing of documents and didn't think the others should share this reprimand. His whole attitude changed, and it became a security reminder, rather than a chewing out. With that, I developed the respect of both the CO and XO and the lofty of my Operations sergeants and clerks. Apparently, it was a shock to the Army that anyone would accept their responsibility.

• • •

Of some of the close calls I had, I guess the most terrifying was the Tet Offensive, February 1968. I and many others who were billeted in Saigon proper had our first taste of real war.

The Tet Offensive opened with a big bang. I had the early watch and had arrived down in the lobby of our BEQ to find it in darkness and sentries lying prone on the deck with lights out and weapons poked through the iron grating towards the street. Some of the male personnel from our BEQ with weapons (of undetermined origin) were lying alongside the two sentries. . . .

A Navy chief . . . arrived in the lobby shortly after me.

There was a shortwave radio in the lobby . . . that was squawking and squeaking voices of other Security Forces telling also of their plight and asking for reinforcement.

In this case, the best part of valor was to make a hasty retreat to the eighth floor for a cup of coffee and to try to find out what was happening.

We were to learn that five VC had tried to lay a satchel charge up against our BEQ and the alert sentry dropped one of them and the others took off at high port. Those who were in the lobby awaiting earlier transportation found not weapon one in the BEQ armory, so went to their rooms and assembled some "souvenirs." So until proper security reinforcements arrived, security was based on Yankee ingenuity.

My three-day confinement to the BEQ was to commence with a panoramic view of the war from a hotel window.

As we arrived at the eighth floor, we grabbed a cup of coffee, stopped to listen to the Armed Forces Radio Station from a portable radio that some kind soul had sense enough to bring with him, and it was to be our last bit of "official" news for three days.

The announcer had just related the news that the VC had satchel-charged the wall of the American Embassy Saigon, and Eighth Air Cavalry helicopters had moved in for support and to remove the Embassy guard from the roof. . . . So the chief and I stepped over to the windows that faced toward the Embassy and as dawn was breaking, watched the opening of the Tet Offensive.

Intelligence had known that there was a buildup of enemy activity, but they had underestimated their strength.

From our bird's-eye view, we watched the Marine embassy guard being airlifted off the Embassy rooftop. . . . I remember the helpless feeling of not being able to respond in some way. Also I remember trying to control the fear in the pit of my stomach, the feeling of inadequacy was overwhelming.

Radio Armed Forces warned all personnel to remain in their quarters, and units and personnel would be informed by radio or messenger when they were to report to their units.

After watching armored vehicles and jeeps rushing around in the streets below and listening to all sorts of speculation, I retired to my second floor to get away from the hubbub. I slipped out of my uniform and tried to relax. It was next to impossible. Firecrackers are part of the Tet holiday, and either because of ignorance of what was going on, or indifference, the Saigon celebrants continued to set the crackers off. In a narrow street or alley they had the effect of gunfire. After a couple of hours of struggling to rest, I gave up, took a shower to get rid of the odor of fear, climbed into some shorts and went back up to the mess.

I think through this ordeal, the most difficult thing was not knowing how close friends that were located at other BOQs or BEQs spread throughout Saigon and Cholon were doing. . . . Captain Jones got out to BEQs as soon as she could to check on the women Marines.

When I arrived back at the mess, some of those who had been at their sections at the execution of the Tet Offensive were beginning to return. They were to be our only source of information for three days. Those who had been wounded and could walk were returned to their quarters. The 17th Army Field Hospital was a half block down the street from us and by leaning out the window, you could watch helicopter ambulances delivering the wounded by stretchers. . . .

By glancing straight ahead, once could see the South Vietnamese Air Force laying bombs down on Cholong with their T-28s trying to shake the Viet Cong loose from their hold there. Through these three days it all seemed like a bad dream. My original response to Major Hilgart with regards to this assignment was to come roaring back to my thoughts more than once. I think everyone was anxious to get back to their unit, do anything but be idle.

• • •

The Vietnamese [housekeeping staff] were restricted from entering any American facilities until new security checks were made, but allowed to have Vietnamese galley help from 0700 to 1400 so that left the dinner meal up to management. So Army, Air Force, and Marine women took on volunteer mess duty on their own and helped secure the galley each evening. (At this time there were no enlisted Navy women assigned to Vietnam.)

I learned to do Vietnamese style laundry during the first few days of Tet. With a scrub brush and soap in the bottom of my shower stall and stringing my uniforms and unmentionables out the window, over an alley on a wire rope to dry. I had gotten hold of an ironing board some months back, and . . . I was able to keep my uniforms from looking like battle fatigues.

With Tet, even office pinkies went into the battle dress of the utility uniform. Good sanitation was a must if you were to maintain good health while there. When time and location permitted, I would shower anywhere from three or four times a day.

• • •

One of the first things that happened when all the women personnel got back to MACV was to be taken along with Air Force personnel to Koepler Compound to be issued lightweight jungle utilities with combat boots. My women Marine green utilities, had four sets, were ideal. We were the only branch of the women's services who had practical utilities and were in the process of changing over to the nonfunctional navy blue outfit.

[Most of the women Marines had been granted seven days' leave to attend the twenty-fifth anniversary celebration of the creation of the women Marines in Okinawa. Because the Tet Offensive was in its second week, the leave was canceled.]

Lieutenant Wiley (USN) did the next best thing. She had a cake baked and decorated and published a citation. Although considering we were into our second week of Tet, everyone appeared fairly fresh and enjoying this special occasion. The male Marines went out of their way to ensure that we had our celebration, no matter what. They were fantastic.

• • •

I don't think I'll ever forget when the VC tried out their first rockets on the MACV Headquarters. It was around 2330, Staff Sergeant Brown had just given me the quickest familiarization of a M-16 rifle in military history and he went topside to sleep. It was at this time that I was glad I had fired different weapons with Marine Corps Rifle and Pistols Clubs in some of my past tours. So I was not afraid of the M-16. In fact had my own T/O weapon, a .38-caliber pistol that went with my job as top secret control officer.

We had sat from evening chow to this time inventorying. I had been getting SITREPs and spot reports across my desk all night. We knew in advance things were getting hairy. All night long, Army cannon had been laying down H&I fire, but we worked right along with the assurance that the troops in the field were keeping the wolf away from the door. It just sounded like a nice security blanket.

I had a cot in my vault, while the action officers bedded down in cots beside their desks in their offices. I had pulled off my boots, pulled my poncho liner over me and had settled the weary body onto my canvas stretched mattress.

I don't believe it was five minutes when [there was] this overwhelming light, preceded by this horrible scream of noise that ended with a devastating explosion. The fear I felt upon this rude awakening I could never fully put into words. The few seconds I had before the next round landed was spent controlling the panic inside me.

Lights for our office were turned off at a breaker panel clear at the end of the inner hall passageway and we were in complete darkness. The next round went off while I was regaining composure, but it provided the light I needed to stumble towards the inner courtyard windows. Master Sergeant Griesmier, USA (admin chief) had pushed his cot out of the way and helped me scurry over the window ledge and he followed, with our boots and weapons in hand, raced towards our assigned bunker, when another rocket came sailing overhead that caused us to bury ourselves in the ground. It took a couple of seconds to see again after the blinding light created by this monster, but took off again and made it to the bunker. . . .

Vietnamese laborers had built the bunkers and . . . were much smaller in stature than Americans. As I dived through the entrance of the bunker, even in a crouched position, crash! I hit an overhead cross beam that lit up my head with stars that were far brighter than the glare of the rockets from without.

Stunned, but not hurt, I crawled into the bunker with Dave right behind me. We caught our breaths and wondered where in the blue-eyed world everyone else was. We crawled to the entranceway on our stomachs and looked back to our office. The lights were on now, and we watched operations officers scrambling to secure their classified documents. I had been after them to secure their documents prior to retiring, but it was a losing battle. Unfortunately that night they learned their lesson the hard way and I never again had to remind them of security. Making an enlisted top secret control officer put one in an awkward position. Fortunately, I only had one or two who had ever given me a difficult time. After that unnecessary exercise, the rest of COC-1 and the War Room personnel joined Dave and [me] in the bunker. About two more rounds went over. We sat quietly leaning against the bunker wall. Some strange things crowded my thoughts during this time. The first thing was wondering "What the hell am I doing here?" I thought of very private things I hadn't thought about in years. Went back to early childhood happenings, and shockingly, was glad my mom wasn't alive so that she wouldn't have to worry about my being here.

I can assure you that there was no John Wayne movie bravado in the bunker that night. Everyone sat in silence and I'm sure they had thoughts similar to mine.

When the all clear came, we climbed back through the window. The Deputy J3 was waiting in our shop and as I crawled back in he asked [how I was].

"Sir, I've discovered I'm a devout coward."

His reply: "Top, you were not alone—so was every man sharing the bunker with you."

By now, complete and total exhaustion took over, and Charlie be damned, with my M-16 beside me, I climbed onto my cot and crashed!

Captain Jones called the next morning, since she knew I was inventorying at night and she had heard MACV had gotten some incoming. Besides a big knot on my head and being tired, I was fine.

Charlie was to continue his harassment, but since he never made any direct hits on our Headquarters, we got in the habit of when he would start his midnight fireworks, we'd just go into the vault, pulling open the top drawer of the safes and sitting under them until the all clear came. Although the Army engineers came in and rebuilt the bunkers to American size, they never could have withstood a direct rocket hit, plus Vietnamese workers had taken to cooking their noonday lunch of fish and rice in them, plus being used as a place to relieve themselves. As a result safes became a far better place to wait out the VC nightly intrusions.

[She goes on to describe getting exercise from a mile hike to an Army Olympic-size canvas swimming pool and from a noontime swim.]

Although I had never been that much of a swimmer, I soon became one and it was what I needed to get the exercise and to stay mentally relaxed to get me through twelve to fourteen hour days.

The day before the Tet Offensive, I had taken a flight on Air America with Captain Jones to Na Bhe at the invitation of some American security forces there. It was crazy, lying on this beautiful beach drinking beer and soda pop, eating a picnic lunch and watching helicopters keeping the Viet Cong away from the local fishermen who were spreading their fishing nets along the shallow waters about a mile across the bay from us. I wondered if I was becoming so calloused that I could no longer be concerned with the plight of the poor fishermen who were scrambling for their lives.

[She describes the loss of a friend in a mortar attack on Tan Son Nhut Air Base two weeks before his departure date, and how precious life was becoming. A bit later than she'd expected, she returned to San Francisco. She describes how beautiful the city seems.]

I really believe at that time I truly appreciated the United States.... Dr. King had just been shot and Kansas City, my new duty station, had just undergone rioting as the result of his murder. No matter what, we were so [much] better off from where I had been, I knew I could cope. My only real fears were for the dear friends I had left behind. I had survived and so now my thoughts were with them.

Would I ever do it again? I'm sure I would. Always a new challenge—something different. (I think.)

9

Gender Wars

"Hounded and Hunted"

Navy helo pilot Paula Coughlin left the pool patio on the third floor of the Hilton Hotel in Las Vegas, stepped through the doors near the main passenger elevators, and started down the hallway toward the squadron administrative suites—rooms rented by squadrons of naval aviators attending the 1991 Tailhook Conference.

The narrow hallway reeked of alcohol, vomit, and urine that Saturday night in September. Loud, rowdy naval and Marine pilots and flight officers lined the sides of the hallway. Men leaned on both walls; two in the center had their backs to Coughlin. She tried to pass on the right, and one of the men deliberately hip-checked her. She excused herself. Someone shouted, "Admiral's aide!"

Suddenly, someone behind her grabbed her buttocks with such force that she was lifted off the ground and pushed forward a step. She turned and yelled, "What the fuck do you think you're doing?"

The men in the group began grabbing her breasts and buttocks. They pushed her down the passageway. One man put his hand inside her tank top and bra and fondled her breasts. She dropped into a crouch and tried to pry the man's hands off, then bit his left forearm—hard enough, she hoped, to draw blood.

One man started to walk away. She reached out, tapped his right hip, and asked if she could get in front of him. He stopped, turned to face her, put one hand on each of her breasts, and smiled.

Coughlin broke free and ran into an open door into an empty

administrative suite. She sat alone in the dark and tried to process what had just happened.

She had encountered the "gantlet," a Tailhook Convention tradition.

The next morning, Coughlin reported the assault to her supervisor, Rear Adm. Jack Snyder, commander of the Patuxent River Naval Air Test Center. He replied, "That's what you get when you go to a hotel party with a bunch of drunk aviators."

The following June, frustrated by senior officers' unwillingness to address her complaint, Coughlin took the aviators' behavior to the media. Assistant Secretary of the Navy Barbara Pope refused to accept the results of a Naval Investigative Service investigation that minimized the scope and number of the assaults and blamed most of the lewd behavior on enlisted men. A subsequent investigation by the Department of Defense Inspector General's office found that aviators had assaulted eighty-three women and seven men; that they—and civilian women—had participated in public sex acts; and that they had engaged in indecent assault, indecent exposure, conduct unbecoming an officer, and failure to act in a proper leadership capacity. Ultimately the scandal ruined or damaged the careers of fourteen admirals and three hundred aviators. The Navy grounded Coughlin and questioned her psychological state. Her male colleagues shunned or harassed her. Most Navy women chose not to express support for her publicly, fearing that they would be tarred with the same brush. In February 1994 Coughlin resigned her commission. The scandal delayed officer promotions for several years afterward, lowered morale for both men and women, and changed the Navy's approach to sexual harassment.

In the aftermath of the social and political upheaval caused by the Vietnam War, the services realized that America's armed forces could no longer rely on involuntary conscription. In 1969 President Nixon charged the Gates Commission to advise him on the creation of an all-volunteer force, and he announced an end to conscription on January 1, 1973. By accident rather than by design, establishment of an all-volunteer force that relied on women's participation coincided with a national movement to improve women's legal and economic equality; changes in women's military status were driven not by a desire to impose equality or by abstract notions of "political correctness," but by the armed forces' reluctant recognition that they would need to recruit and retain women in order to meet personnel goals for an all-volunteer force and their desire to avoid outside interference in military personnel policy. Military women's own desire to change policies that they recognized as discriminatory, and their willingness to challenge policies in court, contributed to the changes as well.

In 1972 a Department of Defense All-Volunteer Force task force identified policies that restricted the use of women in support of personnel recruiting and retention goals. These included higher enlistment standards for women, policies denying enlistment of married women and those with dependents, and restrictions on the number of occupations open to women. The integration of women sped up exponentially.

The first changes took place in assignment and promotion policy. The first women were promoted to general/flag officer rank in 1967; the 2 percent cap on women's participation was lifted in 1973. Promotion lists were integrated, though combat exclusion laws that restricted women's assignment continued to make them less desirable for promotion in senior ranks despite service efforts to create "equivalent" career pathways. The separate women's components were disbanded: the WAVES in 1972, the WAF in 1976, and the WAC—which had to be disestablished by Congress—in 1978.

To meet personnel requirements, the services had to change accession policies. The Air Force opened ROTC to women on a test basis in 1969; the Army and Navy followed suit in 1972. The Navy's first coed class at Officer Candidate School in Newport, Rhode Island, graduated in 1973. In 1975 Congress ordered service academies to admit women in the fall of 1976. Many men resented women's intrusion into the hallowed halls of the service academies; press interest complicated the situation for women, and accusations flew that standards were being lowered. But 229 women graduated from the service academies in 1980: 98 from the

Air Force Academy, 62 from West Point, 55 from the Naval Academy, and 14 from the Coast Guard Academy.

An expansion in occupational specialties open to women was necessary. Over the coming decades, the Army classified occupational specialties first as "support," then reclassified them as "combat," and then classified them yet again as "support."

The Coast Guard and Navy began integrating more women into service at sea. Navy nurses had long been assigned to hospital ships; in October 1972 USS *Sanctuary* sailed with a mixed-gender ship's company that included fifty-three enlisted women and twenty women officers, some assigned to deck, supply, operations, and administrative (but not engineering) departments as well as to the hospital. The commanding officer reported that women performed every shipboard task with equal "ease, expertise, and dedication" as men, including on general quarters repair parties and on emergency teams. Law continued to restrict Navy women—but not their civilian counterparts—from assignment to naval vessels and transportation on them; women Navy pilots could not land on carriers, though Army and Air Force women were not restricted; and women in officer accession programs could not obtain mandatory sea duty training. Enlisted women could be assigned to seagoing ratings but could only be assigned ashore, which disrupted the sea/shore rotation cycle for men.

The Coast Guard assigned women to two cutters, *Morganthau* and *Gallatin*, in 1977; that same year, Beverly Kelley took command of the cutter *Cape Newagen*. The Navy then requested congressional authority to assign women to naval auxiliary vessels, tenders, repair ships, and rescue ships. In 1978 four Navy women brought a class-action discrimination lawsuit (*Owens v. Brown*) challenging the assignment policy, noting that civilian women could be assigned to naval vessels but military women could not. The court ruled that the assignment policy unconstitutionally denied Navy women equal protection of the law, but left up to the Navy the decision on how to proceed. In 1978 President Jimmy Carter signed PL 95-485, which prohibited women from permanent assignment to combatant vessels and from temporary assignment for a period exceeding 180 days. The first Navy women—55 officers and 375 enlisted women—reported for duty at sea on auxiliary vessels in 1978.

Integration of the military aviation community also expanded on a small scale. The Navy began accepting women for flight training in 1973, the Army in 1974, the Coast Guard in 1975, and the Air Force in 1976. These women understood that while their missions were designated "combat support," they could still find themselves flying in a combat situation and exposed to enemy fire. Numbers of women aviators remained low through the early 1990s. The Air Force also began considering integration of ICBM crews late in the 1970s; the greatest opposition came from officers' wives, who objected to their husbands standing duty overnight with women.

Family policy provoked the most emotional disputes in the 1970s, not least because some of the changes played out in the courts instead of the service personnel offices. Military family policy developed after World War II reflected prevailing social expectations of women's primary role as wife and mother, the assumption that military and family duties were inherently incompatible, and the idea that women should prioritize family responsibilities over military duties whenever the two conflicted.

The first policy changed was one that discriminated against men—the option for women to seek early discharge on the basis of marriage. The ban on enlistment of married women was revoked. The requirement for services to separate married couples gave way to prioritizing spouse co-location, subject to the needs of the service. In 1970 1st Lt. Sharron Frontiero filed a class-action equal protection suit in federal court challenging sex discrimination in family dependent entitlements; the court concurred.

As early as 1949, the chief of the Bureau of Medicine and Surgery had suggested that women with families should be allowed to continue serving, noting that pregnancy was a "normal biological phenomenon" for the military age group. But Executive Order 10240 of 1951 permitted the armed forces to terminate the service of any woman who became a parent, stepparent, or custodial parent of a minor child. Although the order was permissive, the services interpreted it as mandatory and granted few waivers. Men who were widowed or granted custody after divorce, however, were retained. Repeated attempts to challenge the double standard in court failed, but in June 1974 the Department of Defense ordered that separation of mothers would be voluntary. Service pushback against retention of mothers continued through the early 1990s. A woman Marine, ordered to participate in a full physical fitness test in her eighth month of pregnancy, went into labor the following day; her doctor extended her hospital stay "to keep your commanding officer from killing you." Men frequently subjected women to complaints about the so-called nine-month flu and special treatment (policies limiting activity in the second and third trimesters of pregnancy, and maternity leave). Men accused them of deliberately getting pregnant to avoid deployments or unpleasant duty; while this certainly occurred, it was hardly the norm.

A perception that gender integration in the military was a creation of social activists who supported passage of the Equal Rights Amendment (ERA) at the expense of readiness amplified resistance to women's integration. Congress intended that physically and mentally qualified women should be subject to Selective Service registration, and they included the requirement in the unamended ERA bill passed on March 22, 1972. This provision contributed to states' decisions not to ratify the amendment.

Hearings in the House Armed Services Committee on the repeal of combat exclusion laws in 1980 reinforced the perception that women's integration was a social experiment. Congresswoman Marjorie Holt noted that "Capitol Hill and the media gained the impression that the proposal [to rescind combat exclusion laws] was being pushed by civilian feminists within the administration who, rightly or wrongly, were perceived as being more concerned with women's rights and 'social experimentation' than with legitimate personnel requirements or the needs of national defense." That perception continues among many today.

The increase in the number of women serving in the armed forces and changes in personnel policies to encourage recruiting and retention of women inevitably stoked tension between women and men. When the numbers of women serving were lower and women were inclined to accept discrimination and harassment as the norm, little was made of discriminatory policies and crimes prejudicial to morale and even deeply damaging, such as sexual assault and rape.

The 2013 documentary film *The Invisible War* brought renewed attention to the problem of sexual assault in the military. Partly in response, Sen. Kirsten Gillibrand (D-New York) proposed legislation to remove the decision to prosecute serious military crimes out of the chain of command. Under the proposed law, an independent cadre of military prosecutors would handle sexual violence allegations. Serious military crimes and all crimes punishable under Article 15 of the Uniform Code of Military Justice would remain with the chain of command. Debate on the bill has continued through two sessions of Congress with no resolution to date. Recent press reporting has focused on chain of command retaliation against victims who report assault and rape—including the practice of labeling victims with a personality disorder diagnosis and separating them administratively or under other than honorable conditions (so-called "bad paper" discharges).

The incidents described in this chapter do not represent the experiences of every woman who has served in the armed forces. Nor is it possible in a work of this scope to give examples of every group of women that has faced discrimination in the military, or to do justice to the intersections of race, gender, and sexual orientation that further complicate the picture. Individual women also react differently to harassment and discrimination. However, for those who have experienced these issues, the ramifications can be serious and lifelong. Resolution is difficult. The effects of gender discrimination and gender-based violence are now understood to contribute significantly to the incidence of substance abuse, trauma-related disorders, and homelessness in the women veteran population. The experience of military women in America cannot be fully understood without an appreciation of stories of discrimination, harassment, and sexual assault—stories that were once, and are still too often, silenced.

LouAnne Johnson

(n.d.–)

U.S. Navy and Marine Corps

We first introduced Vietnam-era veteran LouAnne Johnson in chapter 8. Accounts of gender-based harassment appear in the writing of women veterans who served in almost every era, but Johnson's depiction stands out for its candor. Harassment begins for many women in accession training. Military women respond to verbal harassment in different ways: some ignore it, some file complaints with their chain of command, and some fight fire with fire. This excerpt is taken from Johnson's memoir *Making Waves: A Woman in This Man's Navy*.

I wasn't feeling very friendly.... Everywhere we had gone that day, the men screamed and whistled and hollered at us. But, if we even *looked* at them in response, we got demerits. It wasn't ladylike to respond to vulgar overtures, we were told. Men didn't exist as far as female recruits were concerned. In fact, they were referred to as "trees" by our cc.

"We don't talk to trees," she would remind us.

The men in one company managed to find out the name of a particularly pretty girl in our company....

"Hey, Morgan!" a male recruit had yelled as we marched by that afternoon. Morgan automatically turned her head to look at him. Within seconds, a petty officer handed Morgan a report chit and she had to spend her rest hour that evening standing at attention in the middle of the sidewalk in front of the barracks, wearing a sign that said "I'm Stupid. I Talk to Trees." After that humiliation, she got five demerits. Twenty demerits meant a girl got recycled to a new recruit company.... Morgan was a popular girl, so our whole company was mad at men in general.

That evening, the same company of men entered the chow hall just ahead of us. We had to stand beside their tables as we waited for our turn to be served. They undressed us with their eyes, which was bad enough, but they also made comments about every nasty thought that entered their dirty little minds.

"Look at the tits on that one!"

"Mmm. Mmm. How'd you like to eat that candy, boys?"

"That's why I joined the Navy—to ride those Waves!"

I could see the red face of the girl in front of me and I knew my own face was blushing just as hard, but we were forbidden to respond to the taunts. It wouldn't be ladylike. By the time we sat down to eat, I was completely humiliated, but inspiration struck. I whispered to the girl next to me to stare at the men's crotches as they filed past on their way out of the door. She passed the word down the line and soon we all sat, staring wide-eyed and innocent, at their crotches. It was hilarious. At first, the boys grinned, but when we didn't say a word or move our eyes from their private equipment, they started fidgeting and blushing, checking their zippers to see if they were down. We kept staring. They began dancing around, trying to stand so their backs were toward us. Their CC finally gave them the order to move out and started yelling that this one or that one was going to get demerits for fidgeting in line because he had been watching them.

They protested loudly, as our company was called to attention and mustered to leave. As we started to march off, I heard their CC yelling at our CC, "Hey, hold it! My men say your ladies were hassling them in the chow hall!"

Carol Barkalow

(1958–)

U.S. ARMY

Carol Barkalow, from New Jersey, was one of the first 118 women to attend the U.S. Military Academy at West Point. She graduated in 1980 as a second lieutenant in Air Defense Artillery. Three years later, she transferred to Transportation Corps and, among numerous positions, served as a division transportation officer with the Twenty-Fourth Infantry Division during Operation Desert Storm. In 2002 Lieutenant Colonel Barkalow retired after twenty-two years of service. Her awards and decorations include the Defense Superior Service Medal, the Bronze Star, the Army Meritorious Service Medal, the Joint Service Commendation Medal, Army Commendation Medal, National Defense Service Medal, the Armed Forces Expeditionary Medal, the NATO Medal, and the Parachutist Badge. The following are excerpts from her 1990 memoir *In the Men's House.*

According to the logic of the Fourth Class System, hazing was a necessary crucible for bringing would-be West Pointers up to speed. In its ideal form, hazing was specifically related to performing tasks, memorizing required information, and, most important, learning the time-management and self-disciplinary skills that would enable a potential officer to function in a high-stress military environment. Harassment was meant to be aimed only at those individuals who were not seen as meeting the "standard"—but never directed at their gender, religion or race. If misapplied, however, the Fourth Class System could be twisted into very cruel contortions. As with any draconian system entrusted to human hands, misapplications were inevitable.

Women, in particular, became a target group for special hazing, though certainly men were not exempt. The difference was, men had to prove themselves weak before they became subject to this kind of harassment; women had to prove themselves strong before they were spared it.

In one company, I'm told, the men had formed a secret committee that would target one female cadet a month and harass her until she quit, or just make her miserable while she was trying to stick it out....

Hazing was constant, emotional, mental. It was like a form of terrorism, because we never knew when it was coming and where it was coming from, whether the upperclassman walking behind us would leave us in peace or start making foul remarks about our mothers. The worst part of it was, we were completely defenseless, and there was nowhere to turn for recourse. We realized very quickly that we had to make it on our own.

"Turn and face the wall," an upperclassman would tell a female new cadet. "You're ugly."

Even the simplest social exchange could become an occasion for contempt. If a female new cadet passed an upperclassman in the hall and said, "Good morning, Sir," she might be greeted in return with cool civility. Then again, she might hear back, "Good morning, bitch." Or, "It was a good morning until you got here, whore."

One disgruntled fellow snuck into the women's locker room one night and discovered an anonymous way to express his feelings on the subject of women at the Academy. The next morning, my classmate found her bathing suit sticky with his opinion.

. . .

A woman at West Point was judged not only for the inescapable fact of her sexuality but for how she projected it, and always according to what was deemed appropriate—however arbitrarily—by men. We seemed to be continually stuck in a tiresome stereotype—if we were not socializing heavily with male cadets, then it meant we must be lesbians. If we *were* socializing heavily with male cadets, then it meant we must be whores. The rumor mill at the Academy turned so thoroughly and well, that the slightest innuendo about a female cadet took only minutes to traverse the entire Corps.

. . .

Press Day, Lake Frederick. The Academy had refused to allow any media to film us during our training because they had wanted us to concentrate on the training itself. So they set aside a Press Day when anybody who was anybody could come. And they certainly did—cameras, reporters, the whole nine yards. The entire day was designated for interviews. The scene reminded me of people flocking to a Macy's sale right after Christmas. There were camera crews *running!* And where did they run to? The women, of course. And did it sit well with the guys? Hell no.

Every reporter brought the same bag of questions:

"Why did you come to West Point?"

"How are you adapting?"

"How does it feel to be here with all these men?"

"Are you being discriminated against?"

Our answers would be equally pat:

"I wanted to be an officer, and this was the best place to go."

"We're not being discriminated against; some guys don't like us being here, but we expected that."

But my favorite question was, "Do you feel that you've lost your femininity?" As though femininity were an umbrella, or a hat. Some of the women said, when they wanted to feel more feminine, they'd put on makeup or a skirt. For me, femininity was not a matter of how I looked or what I wore, but how I felt that counted. Because no one could take that from me.

Soon, nearly everything we did came under scrutiny. Outside West Point, the press attention was overwhelming. Inside, it became an excuse for further divisiveness. When my classmate Fran Boyd was once quoted in the newspapers, men she didn't even know would come up to her and say, "You're Cadet Boyd, and you said such and such in the *New York Times*, and I don't agree." Officers would not return her salutes. Upperclassmen spat insults at her. Much of the backlash against the media attention was sour grapes on the men's part, but this time we understood their resentment—some women even felt it was justified. The possibility of coming to West Point had always existed for these guys. Many of them had been looking forward to it since they were kids. They had worked hard to get there. Yet the only thing people wanted to hear about was what the women were up to. And there wasn't a damn thing we could do about it.

The Public Affairs Office would refer reporters to women who were doing well at the Academy and would present a positive image. A few were outspoken—they'd comment frankly on the guys' immature behavior and how they felt we were being mistreated, statements for which all of us were held responsible. Some of us turned ourselves inside out trying to distance ourselves from this remarks, to prove that *we* weren't the ones who were deliberately trying to stand out. We'd sit around with our male classmates and bad-mouth those women, not to mention the press.

• • •

With the arrival of the new Fourth Class in the summer of 1977, the women of my class were confronted with the task of administering what little authority we had over a younger version of ourselves. I, for one, tried to make it my policy to use hazing as a means to correct plebes, not to harass them. Most of my female classmates behaved in similar fashion, but there were dissenting opinions. Others, once free

of the shackles of the Fourth Class System, flatly refused to participate in hazing of any kind. In another group there were some very
enthusiastic female participants, a number of whom went overboard
harassing younger women—ordering them to do rapid-fire changes
of uniform, summoning them into their rooms for questioning like
Grand Inquisitors, grilling them relentlessly on their memorization
of trivia. A few of these women claimed they needed to be demonstra-
bly tougher on female plebes so no one could accuse them of showing favoritism. I believe these women suspected—and rightly so—that
our newly acquired upperclass status did not unanimously assure our
position within the Corps. Even as the ranks of women cadets gradually swelled from one glassful to two, many of us remained in separate camps. At best, we observed each other from a distance—across
a divide of diffidence, misunderstanding, and fear.

From the beginning, there was a wedge between our class and those
who came later. Some of the younger women seemed to regard us
with awe, because they knew we had broken the ice and made their
lives a little easier. At the same time, we were still the Amazons, the
guinea pig class, the weirdos. The new girls coming in fresh off the
street didn't see themselves that way. They were not icebreakers, they
were part of a "normal" class. They felt that they belonged. . . .

"My classmates and I still feel that the men and women from our
class bonded together well, that there was not a lot of hostility between
us," [said member of the Class of '81 Traci Reid]. "But we felt, and I
know *I* always felt, that the class of '80 men disliked their women. And
the feedback we were getting from the Academy seemed to confirm
that. In lectures or in surveys, all the statistics seemed to point to the
women in our class as being better than the class of '80. So there may
have been something close to resentment between the two classes of
women. The upperclassmen, especially, were trying to get us to hate
our predecessors. But, of course, we didn't hate them. We just said,
'Fine. We'll take all their hard lessons learned.'"

• • •

It was fairly easy to anticipate that in the early years of women's integration at West Point, contact with female officers was going to be

hard to come by. To fill the gap, a new position was created within West Point's chain of command. Before our arrival, four women were brought in by the Academy to be SATOs—Special Assistants to Tactical Officers. The SATOs were intended as role models for women cadets and advisors to the male tactical officers on "women's issues." However, no doubt because of their auxiliary status, the SATOs were relatively ineffective. Once Beast Barracks was over, it was recommended that their positions not be reinstated. Instead, it was magnanimously suggested that women be made full-fledged tactical officers. And so they were—all two of them.

There were other female officers on post, but just a scattered handful. Colonel Mildred Hedberg (now a retired general) was chief of staff of the U.S. Corps of Cadets when we were at the Academy, but we saw her only at official functions. We knew Colonel Hedberg had begun her military career in the pre-integrated Army—in the Women's Army Corps—and we wondered sometimes how her early experiences compared with ours as cadets. Unfortunately, she was too high-ranking and remote for her presence to have any impact on our daily lives. . . .

Lieutenant Kim Rorbaugh was one of the few military females at West Point I knew personally. A hard-core Army officer, she was five feet seven and muscular, with freckles and strawberry blond hair. Lieutenant Rorbaugh had a dog named Smaj, which was short for sergeant major. That's how gung-ho Army she was. We rarely, if ever, got to see her human side. West Point officers often remained aloof from cadets, but this was particularly true of women officers—especially with regard to women cadets—to avoid accusations of showing favoritism, or, even worse, charges of fraternization. There was more than a touch of paranoia about such charges at the Academy. At practically every moment you had to stop and check your behavior—was it correct? Given half a chance, almost anything could, and would, be taken for impropriety.

Although it never occurred to many of us until much later, the most disturbing thing about all this was that we really needed contact with women officers. We needed their experience, their advice and their example. We needed to be able to talk to them without suspicion or fear. We needed to be brought up the way men at the Academy had been brought up by their own for almost two hundred years.

• • •

Within the cadets' inner circle existed a system of enforcement—we'd sense who would survive and who would not. Those who were weak would be hounded and hunted, pushed to the limit to see how much they could stand before they broke down and quit. Among the women, the drive toward perfection was consuming, not only for oneself, but for everyone. . . . The tiniest infraction by one woman reflected on us all. It would spur any number of men to comment, "Look at that one. I told you females don't belong here." Flawed men were glossed over as exceptions. So were stellar women. In the minds of these men, one "bad" woman would obliterate twenty "good" ones. Yet, as talents emerged, they inscribed their own futures. A woman who could make the runs, who could pitch a tent, who could fire a rifle well, who didn't snivel or cry, this woman would earn friendship and support. But if a woman was incompetent we would destroy her—even quicker than the men would—because she threatened all of us.

Some women felt that the most compassionate thing we could do for a female who couldn't cut it at West Point was to help her to leave. Not to "help" her in a negative way, but to say, "Look, these are the realities of this place. You're a valuable person; if you stay here you're going to end up hurting yourself."

There was one girl in Beast Barracks who got the worst hazing of any of us. She was *physically* hazed . . . one time a gang of guys grabbed her. They shut her up inside a metal locker and then started pounding on it. The poor girl was terrified. She was reduced to a trembling nothing; by the end of the summer she quit. When she gave up, one of our female classmates said, "She didn't have what it takes."

Most of us couldn't tolerate weakness. . . .

Admittedly, we weren't highly comforting friends to women who were struggling. Everyone's image was linked somehow. In fact, there were times when we'd cringe at the performance of a less capable female classmate. We'd think, To hell with unity; I'm a member of my platoon. There was constant tension between showing solidarity with female classmates and wanting to be one of the group. As [one] said, "Sometimes, you just wanted to belong. For crying out loud, you just wanted to *belong.*"

We weren't always hostile toward those women who couldn't keep up—but we would snap at them or make caustic comments. We knew we were living according to an intensely competitive system governed by a stopwatch. We'd distance ourselves from any woman who wasn't performing up to par. We'd damn her with silence by refusing to defend her against a male classmate's negative observations. Because, factually, the men's assessments of the women were generally true— yes, the woman did fall out of X number of runs. If the men were saying something slanderous, we might have said something in her behalf, but if it were related to performance, we wouldn't. We didn't want to get into the issue of performance indicators; we just didn't want to open up that wound.

Linda Maloney
(1961–)
U.S. Navy

Linda Maloney served twenty years in the Navy, first as an enlisted air traffic controller, and later as a naval flight officer. She flew both the A6 Intruder and EA6B Prowler. One of the first women in U.S. history to join a combat military flying squadron, she received numerous military awards, including the Distinguished Air Medal for combat, awarded for flights flown over southern Iraq in support of the no-fly zone during her deployment to the Arabian Gulf. She retired in 2004. In 2016 former Army pilot and author Shannon Huffman Polson interviewed Maloney; the excerpts below are transcribed from Polson's blog.

I was flying in the EA-6A for about 6 months when on a warm February day in 1991 I was scheduled to fly an electronic attack aggressor flight with a senior pilot in the squadron. We were flying up Jacksonville, with another EA-6A. The flight would be a training exercise for the USS *Forrestal* and its battle group, about 100 miles off the Florida coast. The pilot of my aircraft was the Mission Commander and he briefed the flight for the two EA-6As and all the emergency procedures. The flight would take all day since we would do a couple of "runs" on the USS *Forrestal* and then fly into an Air Force Base up near Tampa to refuel and then fly back out to conduct an afternoon mission.

We launched from NAS Key West in our vintage EA-6A and headed up the coastline to work with the carrier battle group for an electronic warfare exercise. It was a beautiful sunny February morning. It took about an hour to fly from Key West to the area east of Jacksonville, Florida, where the battle group was stationed. I radioed the ship that we were ready to begin our simulated electronic and missile attacks. After several runs on the ship, about 12:30 pm, we radioed the ship we were complete and would see them later in the afternoon. We told our wingman to rendezvous and then go to a cruise position. Then we headed for Patrick Air Force Base (AFB), approximately 200 miles away. The area controller cleared us on our way at 15,000 feet.

As we started our climb, the plane acted a little sluggish. The pilot adjusted the controls. The aircraft fishtailed as though we had flown through some mild jet wash. Then the master caution light on the front display panel began flashing and the backup hydraulics light illuminated. The flight hydraulic system indicated zero pressure.

I started going through the procedures for a single hydraulic failure, instructing the pilot to secure the automatic flight control system. He pulled back the throttle to slow down from our 300 knots. We called our wingman, and discussed options, deciding that we needed to take an arrested landing over at Naval Air Station (NAS) Cecil Field.

I radioed to the Air Traffic Controller that we were declaring an emergency and needed clearance to Cecil Field for an arrested landing. He cleared us directly to NAS Cecil Field. My pilot and I quickly discussed our game plan, and then began to climb to 15,000 feet and slow to 270 knots. Neither of us expected what happened next.

The master caution light illuminated again and then the rudder-throw light came on. A quick glance showed the combined hydraulic system at zero. No sooner had I noticed the reading, the aircraft began a rapid roll to the left and the nose fell below the horizon. The pilot pulled the stick to the right and aft to no effect. He fed in full right rudder, but the airplane did not respond. The aircraft continued to roll left and descend. As we passed through 60 degrees left bank, and 20 degrees nose down, I heard the pilot say, "I don't have control, Eject!"

I grabbed the upper ejection handle and my seat exploded through the canopy glass. I recall a tremendous explosion, riding the rails of the ejection seat upward amidst the yellow confetti of my kneeboard paper. I lost consciousness and when I came to, I was hanging in my parachute descending towards the ocean. I usually would wear my contacts but that day I'd decided to wear glasses. My helmet visor had ripped off from the force of the ejection and my glasses were gone. All I could see was the ocean below me and the shoreline far in the distance.

[Maloney remembers her post-ejection procedures and is picked up by Navy search and rescue.]

I still have [the rescuer's] nametag in my Navy Scrapbook.

[Maloney's squadron deploys for weeks at a time to conduct training for ships and for combat squadrons. During one detachment to Puerto Rico, an aircraft carrier pulls in and the aviators onboard the carrier host a Foc'sle Follies, a party with skits and jokes for only the squadron members assigned to the carrier. The air wing extends the invitation to Maloney's squadron since they are in the area.]

I remember thinking it was great to be included, but that changed quickly when several of the jokes and skits were directed towards the women in my squadron. The A-6 squadron guys stood up, lifted their shirts and yelled towards several women sitting behind them, "Show us your t * * *!" while the F-14 guys yelled "No c * * * * except in the rack." We were taken aback a bit and not quite sure how to respond. After the party, they invited us to the Officers Club to have drinks but I remember feeling conflicted and uncomfortable knowing we had been insulted but also expected us to take it as a joke.

[In 1993 Secretary of the Navy Les Aspin ordered the military to drop restrictions that prevented women from flying combat missions. By April 1994 more than sixty female naval aviators received orders to combat squadrons deployed on aircraft carriers and other naval combatants.]

A year after the law's repeal, I got my wish. I was assigned to a fleet combat squadron as a naval flight officer in the EA-6B Prowler, a four-seater jammer jet, and deployed on the aircraft carrier USS *Abraham Lincoln* heading to Iraq in April 1995. . . .

I didn't understand the implications of what it was to live under so much scrutiny and attention. It was like living in a fishbowl. In my opinion the naval aviation community didn't handle it well. We all knew the behaviors exhibited at Tailhook were part of naval aviation . . . it was part of the ego and camraderie ingrained in being a naval aviator. But initially, many in the naval aviation community denied there was anything inappropriate going on instead of admitting what we all knew happened at Tailhook and agreeing to change going forward. Tailhook grew into an ugly scandal and along with many careers negatively impacted, the incident pitted many of the guys against the women aviators. The combat exclusion law was officially repealed within a few years of Tailhook, but the whole time period was angst-ridden with strong antagonism by some male aviators toward the women in their ranks.

. . .

During an October 1994 detachment on the *Lincoln*, as the squadron duty officer for the day, I was in the ready room, coordinating the Prowlers' flight schedule, answering the phone, and documenting the squadron pilots' carrier qualifications. I could see all the aircraft conducting their approaches on the ready room television. When my aviator girlfriends approached the carrier in their F/A-18 Hornets and F-14 Tomcats, I paid particular attention; our excitement and pride at being assigned to combat squadrons remained extremely high. As I documented one carrier landing, I saw Kara [Hultgreen] approaching the *Lincoln* in her F-14. Within seconds, I knew something was horribly wrong.

Horrified, I watched her aircraft lose altitude and start rolling to the left. The landing signal officers screamed, "Power, power, power!" and then yelled for the crew to eject. Kara and her back-seater, the radar intercept officer (RIO), ejected.

I waited anxiously for the carrier's loudspeaker to announce that both aviators were safe. The call came that one of the carrier's helicopters had picked up the RIO, but Kara was missing.

I watched in shock, unable to believe what was happening, expecting to see the boat's helicopter land on the deck with Kara aboard. About two hours later, a few women aviators met in one of our staterooms, looking at each other in disbelief, fearing the worst. We kept hoping Kara would be found, until it was obvious she had not survived. Several weeks later, divers discovered her body on the ocean floor, still strapped in her ejection seat. . . .

When we had arrived, the attitude toward us was tentative. But after Kara died, it went downhill.

[Polson asks what advice Maloney would give a new officer today.]

Become the best at every job you have, even if it's the worst in the command. Strive to be a professional in all aspects of your job. Take advantage of every professional and educational opportunity that comes your way. Be a team player, but stand up for your convictions. I'd also say to take time to really contemplate what you want in life. The earlier you take time to really listen to yourself, the better the decisions you'll be able to make along the way. When I initially joined the squadron—VAQ-135, the Black Ravens, the command leadership was very supportive of having women aviators as part of the aircrew. However, when a new squadron commander took charge, bringing along several aviators from his previous squadron, the aviators that followed him to our squadron changed the environment of the command literally overnight to one extremely hostile toward women aviators.

I actually was okay with the men who you knew didn't want you there. At least you knew where they stood. It was the guys who would act like you were part of the team but would turn on you in a group setting that bothered me. The guys who were the most supportive and trustworthy were the other minority aviators in the squadron. I still keep in touch with some of them and am thankful to have served with them.

It was a difficult and challenging time. As I look back on it now, I would have handled it much differently. I was passionate and deter mined but also naïve and immature, and wore my heart on my sleeve too much. Of course I have age and experience now on my side. If I had had a mentor to confide in and with whom to discuss career or professional decisions, and even personal challenges or decisions, it would have made a world of difference. . . .

[Aviation integration is] something I haven't quite come to terms with yet. There is still a painful feeling looking back and contemplating the military aviation integration transition and those professional relationships with many of my male contemporaries. I wonder how many of them are dads now, especially dads of daughters. I wonder what they say to their daughters about achieving their goals and aspirations and if their attitudes have changed over the years towards women in non-traditional jobs such as flying military combat aircraft.

It is interesting for me as a mother of boys now aged nine and twelve years. I feel like part of my job as a mother is train my boys to be encouraging to their friends and schoolmates, whether boys or girls. I tell them every day that I have confidence in them and they can achieve anything if they are determined and work hard. I love that they don't think it is odd or out of the ordinary for girls to want to fly jets or pursue other traditionally male jobs. To them, life has always been that way.

Victoria Hudson
(1959–)
U.S. ARMY

Victoria Hudson, the author of *No Red Pen: Writers, Writing Groups and Critique*, earned her Master of Fine Arts degree from Saint Mary's College of California in 2008. Her poetry and essays have been published in a variety of online and print literary journals, and anthologies, and she sponsors an annual registration scholarship for one writer to attend the San Francisco Writers Conference. She is an urban farmer, voracious reader and photographer. She coaches women's and youth rugby and is a mom and wife. In 2012, she retired after thirty-three years' service. The following is an original essay submitted for inclusion in this collection.

My Army Wife

In a way, 9/11 helped solidify my relationship. When the towers went down, Monika and I had been dating about nine months—and the U-haul hadn't been pulled up to the door yet. I was packing and checking my field gear, getting ready to mobilize right after the attacks when we had a discussion about being gay in the military and what that might mean for us. I pretty much said if you can't do this, break up with me now. And no. We can't be friends if you do.

Three years later, we got married. We had a year engagement and then a wedding at Central Reform Congregation in St. Louis, Missouri, where I'd been stationed on my second recall to active duty after 9/11. Two weeks before our wedding, Mayor Gavin Newsom of San Francisco decided to allow same sex marriages and the night before Valentine's Day in 2004, I asked Monika if she wanted to get married the next day. Surprised is not the word. Given my military status, getting married to someone of the same gender was a specific prohibition in military regulations. Two weeks later, we had our religious ceremony. I wore a civilian suit with my military medals on the lapel, and cut the cake with my officer's sword. We spoke at the reception about how the very act of wedding, both of them, were acts of civil disobedience and grounds for my discharge from the service.

The San Francisco weddings were declared invalid. In 2008, same sex marriages were declared legal, but we decided two weddings, legal or not, were enough. Then Monika became pregnant. Just before election day, with the risk of Proposition Eight passing and once again making marriage not legal, we were married again, locally, at San Leandro Temple Beth Shalom. We registered the marriage license as a protected marriage. It would not show up in any public record search. This was our only means for protection against any action of DADT pursuit or normal security recertification of my Top Secret clearance for the military. The prospect of parenthood and not being legally married, which would have left me without solidified parental rights to our child, was unthinkable. We are a family, and marriage so our child would have two parents was an important value.

When our daughter was born, a new issue with the military came up—how to register her as a dependent without outing myself at the same time. I had to register her before she turned a year old. We spent the year trying to find the best way. If I adopted her, Monika would be required to renounce her parental rights. That certainly defeated the point of our third marriage and first legal one intended to secure parental rights. We tried to do a special adoption where Monika would not have to give up her rights, but no judge would assist with that process. In either course, a new birth certificate would have been issued, without Monika listed as the mother. This would certainly have protected me from the military, but how could I deny our daughter her own biological mother?

In the end, Bridget Wilson, one of the attorneys that is a resource for what was then the Servicemembers Legal Defense Network (now a different organization), noted that the wheels of military justice turn slowly and the military is after all a bureaucracy. With that in mind, I took in her birth certificate, which had both my and Monika's name as parents, and registered our daughter. No one actually looked at the document. Which I'd been counting on. No questions were asked. I was no longer a single soldier with no dependents, I was a single mother with one child dependent.

Single parents are required to maintain a "family care plan" which married service members do not have to maintain. It's a plan with power of attorney and notarized agreements regarding who will care for the child if the "single" parent is deployed. Obviously, Monika was on my plan. As a "friend."

Monika was also listed as "friend" on the DD 93 emergency data form. The DD 93 is the document that provides direction when a service member is killed or wounded in service. Because I declined to list any "related" kin, and had "no" spouse, I was required to receive counseling regarding my "unusual" choice of beneficiary for my death benefits. I found this particularly insulting and offensive given the ten years we'd been together. Monika, like every other military spouse, like every other Army wife, steadfastly supported me while I deployed to war and otherwise served the nation. She took over and cared for all aspects of my life while I was gone. Paid my bills, fed and cared for my pets, took care of our home, raised our child while I was gone on duty, was the support that enabled me to serve without worry about the home front.

And she did it all alone. No family support group, no phone calls to check in and see if she needed anything, no lifeline of unofficial information via the Family Readiness Group grapevine. No one to talk with about her fears and worries when she didn't hear from me for a few days or longer while I was in a war zone. All alone. The DD-93 is the form that tells the service who to notify. I was not allowed to list my spouse on that form as a spouse, which would ensure that she would receive the respect, courtesy, and dignity of a family notification.

I volunteered for the service. She just volunteered to love me.

Postscript

This essay was originally due to appear in the May 2012 issue of *OutServe Magazine*. Barely a few weeks before it was due to print, I received a call from my commanding general to discuss the piece. There were concerns that I would be retroactively charged with potential violations of the UCMJ based upon some of the writing so I revised the essay to clarify those identified portions. Follow up calls then resulted in the CG issuing a direct order to rescind the essay from publication. This came after President Obama on May 9, 2012, made known his support for gay marriage. The CG thought that publishing the essay would have potential negative consequences on my career in the current political climate at the time. She added that now that the president had made his statement, in an election year, the issue of gay marriage was part of the political process and as such, my essay was potential "prohibited speech" since serving members of the military are restricted from any public endorsements or statements that are partisan. The essay was pulled from publication at the last minute.

I was not sure if the CG truly had acted out of concern for my career wellbeing or if there was another agenda in play. Regardless, I had received an order and would comply with 100 percent support to my commander regardless of personal belief or feelings in the matter. It was a legal, moral, and ethical order. I would soldier on and comply.

Months later in August 2012, I attended the change of command for that commanding general, who was about to retire. We had a few moments to speak privately at the farewell dinner. Grasping my hand in both of hers, she told me how personally proud she was for the work I was doing to bring full equality to all military families and the importance of my participation in the suit challenging the constitutionality of the Defense of Marriage Act. That she was very proud of me for these actions and for standing up for GLBT soldiers. She reiterated her concern that publishing the essay when it had been planned would have resulted in significant possibility for negative actions against me. (After my retirement might be better timing.)

I retired in December 2012 after thirty-three years of service. In my last three assignments, I commanded battalions but only in the last one was my family visible and known. During my final change of command, my wife was honored with the traditional roses of farewell from her Army family, the soldiers of the battalion I commanded. She was thanked from the podium by the brigade commander and personally by many of the soldiers I had led. And during my own retirement ceremony, the presiding general officer specifically honored Monika for her devotion, dedication, and service as a military spouse.

After two years of application, the Veterans Administration has recently acknowledged Monika as my spouse. The Army has accepted her inclusion as beneficiary for my Survivor's Benefit Plan. Finally, she carries her own military dependent spouse identification card which she proudly uses every opportunity when an ID is requested. She is a proud Army wife.

Donna Doe
(n.d.–)
U.S. Army

"Donna Doe," a veteran of Operation Iraqi Freedom and Operation Enduring Freedom, survived a violent sexual assault when she was a cadet in an ROTC program. She was offered the opportunity to disenroll from ROTC after the assault, but when she recovered, she chose to complete her bachelor's degree and accept a commission in the Army. She subsequently earned a law degree. She is still on active duty as of 2016, and she publishes nonfiction about her experiences and about military policy on sexual violence and mental health under the pen name "Donna Doe" to maintain her privacy. The following is an original essay submitted for inclusion in this collection.

"If you bury this, it will haunt you," the social worker said the fifth and final time as I threw her out of my hospital room, my tray clanging after her after she shut the door. Truer words were never spoken, and her curse followed me across time zones and continents. But I had no time to talk, no need to itemize the injuries and insults. I only wanted to go home, the same as my first night there, as I begged the orderly not to call my parents. "Please," I sobbed, "please let me go home."

And so it should not have come as a surprise to me, a few years later, law degree in hand, when I completely unraveled. Though I saw it as my destiny to become an avenging spirit, tipping the scales of justice towards the victim, the truth was that their stories rang in my ears like a gong, rattling my brain and wearing away on my psyche. Sitting beside them, holding their hands, promising them it was not their fault but being careful not to promise anything else eroded the brick and mortar between advocate and survivor. I became like an exposed nerve, painful and raw. Unconsciously I tensed my shoulders and stomach as they related the details of their assault, like a person waiting to be struck.

Inevitably I'd have to ask them the questions we both were dreading, the ones the defense attorney would use to carefully shred their credibility and their souls. "And then what happened?" Over and over. "And why did you do that?" Gingerly asking the same questions they'd no doubt asked themselves dozens of times. Why? Why? Why?

This case was like all of the others. A private first class, barely out of her teens, decided to trust the untrustworthy. In this case it was her squad leader. She thought she was among friends, battle buddies and team mates. The ones who are supposed to have your back when the shit hits the fan. The alcohol, the predator, the set-up. It was always the same. Over and over again, these shattered women sat beside me. And over and over again, the system betrayed them.

Though not a great speaker, I was thorough. I wanted to get it right. I memorized dates and details. Practiced cross-examinations and openings. I had a duty to right what had once been wronged. The day before trial I would practice in front of my boss, a kind man who wasn't afraid to give honest feedback.

As I stood at the lectern, inhaling deeply, staring at an imaginary judge, I said these words: "This is a case about a young woman who just wanted to go home." And I could say no more. The grief rent the earth open, and swallowed me whole. I cried for four hours. I cried when my boss asked me if I wanted to go to Landstuhl. I cried when we stopped at my house to pack some clothes. I cried when they had me turn over my dog tags and bootlaces, lest I hang myself.

By the morning of the day after I was horrified at my loss of composure, clamoring to break free of inpatient treatment and return to do the case. The SJA, leaning in and speaking in hushed tones, as if speaking of the dead, assured me the case was in good hands. By that time I was shuffling around in a hospital gown and slipper socks brought by well-intentioned ladies from the Red Cross who were unsure how to talk to us or where to focus their eyes. I was on "Nine Charlie," the euphemism they used when talking about the looney bin.

I wanted, I needed, to be back at work. That was the only way it all made sense: God had let this happen to me because it was my destiny to fight for justice. It imbued me with a sense of purpose. Without my profession, without the dais and the jury and the verdicts, none of it made sense. The hours I'd laid in the rain, crawling my way toward the light. The nagging ache in my hips and back reminding me of where and how I'd been broken. Without my job my assault had no meaning.

So at night when the psychiatric nurse asked me if I needed Valium to help me sleep, I said "Yes." Because on top of potentially losing my career, on top of the pain in my heart, lying in the hospital bed at Landstuhl gave me flashbacks to the last time I was in the hospital: the Indian doctor exclaiming, "It's cut all the way to the bone!" as she stitched up my arm. The nurse who held my hand as evidence was collected. The tears. The pain.

A lot of what happened at Landstuhl is fuzzy. I alternated between doing pushups and situps beside my bed to stay in shape and weeping uncontrollably over what I believed was the loss of my career. The second day a Red Cross therapy dog visited us, tail wagging ferociously as he deposited a saliva-soaked tennis ball in my lap. I remember an Air Force chaplain relating how he'd been hit by a car while bicycling, leading him to question his faith. "And I'm here to tell you," he said, looking directly into my eyes, "it's going to be okay."

I wasn't so sure.

In terms of "okay-ness," it's all relative. There are good and bad days. I didn't get medically retired, mainly because I downplayed my symptoms to get out of treatment and convince my chain of command I was "okay-enough." That is the fundamental problem when you link treatment with employment status.

I wish I were better. I know that I cannot now and probably will never be able to try sexual assault cases, though I'd love to be involved with informing military policy on the treatment of victims. It's just too painful. I've learned the value of tactical patience, learning when to lie in wait for my symptoms to diminish and when it's no-kidding time to talk to someone again. The best I can do is be self-aware, to know when to suck it up and when it's time to take a knee.

I've learned we all are haunted: the missed opportunity, the lost loved one. We must be kind to ourselves and our fellow travelers along this spooky journey. For those of us who hear the howling winds and rattling chains of our past, we must remember to reach out and cling to those who love us. The dawn always comes eventually.

10

Desert Storm

"Women Could Not Be in Combat"

The fourth day of Operation Desert Storm was so cold that Maj. Rhonda Cornum could see her breath when she woke up. That afternoon the Army flight surgeon—the mother of a teenage daughter—and seven of her colleagues went out to a UH-60 Black Hawk for a routine passenger shuttle flight. After they were airborne they received a new mission. Air Force fighter pilot Bill Andrews had been shot down behind enemy lines and was stranded with a broken leg. En route, still several kilometers from Andrews's position, the helo began taking enemy fire.

The helicopter went down rapidly. Cornum thought about her grandfather, a Marine who fought at Iwo Jima, who had told her that living with dishonor was a lot worse than dying. Her last thought was, *At least I'm dying doing something honorable.*

She regained consciousness after dark. She saw the wrecked helicopter and a body. Part of the helicopter pinned her down. She dug some sand out to release her right leg, which was immobile, and then pushed herself out from beneath the wreckage with her left leg. When she tried to stand, her arms didn't respond. *Oh, this is very bad,* she thought. She tried again to turn over, and when she looked up, five Iraqi soldiers had their guns pointed at her head. She was a prisoner of war.

One of the soldiers reached down and stood her up. She knew from the pain that her arms were broken. Her knee was injured and she had been shot in the shoulder. She saw no other survivors, and assumed she was alone. The soldiers took her to a bunker and questioned her.

When they emerged, they dragged her to a group of soldiers and tossed her into the center of the circle with another soldier: Spc. Troy Dunlap, another survivor of the crash. The soldiers put pistols to the backs of the prisoners' heads. Cornum and Dunlap thought they were about to die. The sound of a trigger—*click.* But no bullets.

The Iraqis pulled Cornum and Dunlap to their feet and took them to another bunker. They began removing the prisoners' gear: flak vests, survival vests, and weapons. When they pulled Cornum's helmet off, her long hair spilled down and the excited Iraqis realized she was a woman. Soon they loaded Cornum and Dunlap onto a truck.

Cornum tried to relax. Then the soldier sitting next to her put his hands on her face and kissed her.

Well, how bizarre! Cornum thought in disbelief. *Surely he can do better! How can he possibly want to do this?* She was bloody, dirty, and smelly.

The soldier unzipped her flight suit and began fondling her breasts and genitals. She couldn't fight back because her broken arms were swollen. She thought about biting him, but didn't want to make him angry. She resisted only when he tried to force her head into his lap. The pain in her arms was excruciating, and she screamed. The soldier knew, she thought, that he was not supposed to touch her; if she screamed, he quit. He seemed not to want the men in the front of the truck to know what he was doing.

Around thirty minutes later the soldier stopped groping Cornum and zipped up her flight suit.

The Iraqis took Cornum and Dunlap out of the truck and into an underground prison, where they and the third survivor of the helo crash remained for eight days. Cornum and twenty-three other prisoners were then repatriated in a prisoner exchange.

Asked about the sexual assault after her release, Cornum said simply, "In the hierarchy of things that were going wrong, that was pretty low on my list." She decided that whatever didn't prevent her from getting out of prison, didn't pose a risk of death, wouldn't result in permanent disability or disfigurement, and wasn't excruciating simply wasn't important.

Army policy supposedly prevented women who deployed in Desert Storm from assignment at the battalion level, under the assumption that higher command echelons were sufficiently protected from exposure to combat situations. Low-intensity conflicts in the 1980s and early 1990s had already demonstrated that the assumption was false.

In 1983 military rebels deposed and murdered the prime minister of the Caribbean island of Grenada. On October 25 the United States deployed some 7,000 troops in Operation Urgent Fury to reclaim the government, purportedly at the request of the island's governor general. Around 170 women soldiers filled support billets in intelligence, military police, transportation, and communication roles. One, a captain, was responsible for detonating unexploded ammunition. Four women MPs, upon arriving in Grenada, were ordered back to North Carolina; when they arrived, the commanding general of the Eighty-Second Airborne ordered them to return to Grenada. Coast Guard women crewed vessels patrolling nearby waters; women flew operational missions on OH-58 helicopters over Grenada; women served as flight engineers and loadmasters on other aircraft that took part in the operation. A woman pilot, Lt. Celeste Hayes, delivered troops from the Eighty-Second Airborne to Salinas Airfield when there was fighting in the area. Around two hundred Army women took part in the operation.

In 1987 Defense Advisory Committee on Women in the Services (DACOWITS) members traveled to the Pacific theater and found low morale among women, sexual harassment, job discrimination, and lack of communication between Navy leadership and enlisted women. Their report and the resulting bad press led to creation of the Department of Defense Task Force on Women in the Military that September. The task force found that services applied the combat exclusion rules differently; it had never been clear whether the combat exclusion laws were intended to prevent women from serving in combat roles, or to protect them from harm. The task force, therefore, recommended that the Department of Defense write an unambiguous statute evaluating positions to be closed to women.

This statute was the 1988 DoD Risk Rule: noncombat positions could be closed to women if the risk of exposure to direct combat, hostile fire, or capture equaled or exceeded that experienced by combat units in the same theater of operations. Thirty thousand noncombat positions opened to women. However, the Risk Rule did not fully resolve ambiguities, and the underlying assumption was fundamentally flawed: service in higher echelons and support roles does not guarantee safety from enemy fire, especially in modern warfare.

The following year, U.S. troops deployed again. On December 15, 1989, the Panamanian legislature declared dictator Manuel Noriega president and declared that a state of war existed between the United States and Panama. President George H. W. Bush ordered 25,000 troops to Panama to arrest Noriega and bring him to the United States for trial. More than eight hundred Army and Air Force women participated in the operation. Often under enemy fire, women pilots flew Black Hawk helicopters in with supplies and troops; women in the Air Force flew cargo and refueling missions. Women also served in intelligence, administrative, and communications positions. On December 20, Army Capt. Linda Bray led a company of military police in a firefight against Panamanian Defense Force troops defending a weapons cache.

Afterward, Pentagon and service spokesmen downplayed women's contributions in an attempt to defuse the issue of whether or not implementing the Risk Rule prevented women from participating in combat. Conservatives and many senior military retirees declared that women were weakening the armed forces; some claimed that feminists had exaggerated women's contributions in Grenada and Panama, and that military leaders who knew the truth about women's performance were being silenced in the interest of so-called political correctness.

On August 2, 1990, Iraqi troops invaded Kuwait. The United States responded with a force buildup in Saudi Arabia—Operation

Desert Shield. On the eve of the American invasion five months later, women accounted for about 11 percent of the active duty force and nearly a third of the reserve force. The press initially responded to the deployment of women by running human interest stories that featured military mothers bidding farewell to husbands and children. Many men resented the suggestion that deployment was more emotionally difficult for women; women resented being portrayed as emotional and unprofessional.

Combat began on January 17, 1991, with aerial bombing; the ground war began on February 15. Women served in theater in every military occupational specialty except those considered "direct combat" specialties. They flew on airplanes and helos over the battle area, maintained aircraft and vehicles, loaded ordnance, drove trucks and heavy equipment, manned .50-caliber machine guns, and guarded bases and enemy prisoners of war. Navy women deployed to the Gulf on auxiliary vessels, which often sailed without escort and were vulnerable to Silkworm and Exocet missiles and naval mines—but they were prohibited from serving on aircraft carriers protected by both the air wing and the ships of the battle group. Women in the Coast Guard provided harbor security. Women commanded support brigades, battalions, companies, and platoons. They staffed medical facilities afloat and ashore. They were assigned to Patriot missile batteries, which the Army designated "defensive" rather than "offensive combat" units. Some commanders simply ignored the Risk Rule and assigned women where they were needed. Others transferred women to "noncombat" duties even if they were the best qualified for a "combat" job. By the end of Desert Storm, nearly 41,000 women had served in theater. Thirteen were killed; the Iraqis captured two, Maj. Rhonda Cornum and Spc. Melissa Rathbun-Nealy, and held them as prisoners of war.

Saddam Hussein responded to the invasion of Iraq and liberation of Kuwait with Scud missile attacks that often landed well behind the front lines. The Risk Rule did not protect women from the risks of combat; support units also suffered casualties.

Desert Storm brought home to the military and the American public that the traditional notion of a "front line" no longer applied, and that the United States could no longer deploy its armed forces in a major conflict without the participation of women. Women performed well in a combat environment; they coped with the physical demands of their jobs and austere combat living conditions. They managed the lack of privacy and a shortage of feminine hygiene products. They handled sexual harassment from male colleagues and restrictive Saudi customs that many considered demeaning, such as the requirement to wear the abaya and refrain from driving off base. News of women casualties and prisoners of war did not lead to a public backlash. Seventeen thousand dual-service couples and single parents of both genders deployed; most made adequate family care plans for their children. As a result of women's deployment to and performance in Operation Desert Storm, Congress once again began to consider lifting combat restrictions on women.

A small handful of women who deployed during Operation Desert Storm wrote or cowrote memoirs that received little critical attention. Some described their experiences in articles and professional journals. Others contributed oral histories, letters, and journals to archives years after the end of hostilities. A few are only now beginning work on memoirs of their wartime experiences. The excerpts below were taken from a variety of these sources.

Linda Bray
(1960–)
U.S. ARMY

Linda L. Bray, from Sanford, North Carolina, served in the Army 1982–91. Considered the first woman to lead troops into combat, Bray was commanding the 988th Military Police Company when her company deployed to Panama for Operation Just Cause. When soldiers of the Panamanian Defense Forces (PDF) refused to surrender their positions at a dog kennel where they had concealed a large weapons cache, Bray gave the order to open fire. Her company took control of the weapons cache.

Publicity surrounding Bray's participation in the operation

brought the issue of women in combat to the forefront of public opinion. Bray became the focus of media controversy and scrutiny from Congress and the Department of Defense. When her company returned to the United States in April 1990, she required a second hip surgery for a training injury incurred years earlier. Bray received a medical discharge in 1991.

What follows are excerpts from an oral history recorded through the Betty H. Carter Women Veterans Historical Project (WVHP) at the University of North Carolina at Greensboro.

In 1989 my company got orders to deploy to Panama. We were going to deploy as a peace operation assisting the Panamanian Defense Force, because [Manuel] Noriega and his forces were basically wreaking havoc, and he was in his dictatorship. Some people were getting killed and things like that. So we just—for Panama, Honduras, the MPs always did a rotation just to help maintain the peace. And so I went to the operation center one day and we're getting my company prepared to deploy. We start so many months out. It was like, you know, we had to get shots, we had to do all this other stuff.

[Two months before the deployment] I got a call from the major in the operations center. He said, "Captain Bray, can you come over here now?" And I said, "Yes sir." So I went over to the Emergency Operations Center and I was sitting there. And he was a major and he was looking at me and he says, "Captain Bray, I can't tell you anything." He said, "But if I tell you to keep your head down while you're in Panama, do you understand what I'm trying to tell you?"

And I just looked at him and I said, "Yes sir. I think I understand what you're trying to tell me." And so evidently the look on my face when I walked back into that—into my company and walked in my first sergeant's office and shut the door and looked at him, he said, "Oh god no, no. Oh god, no. No."

I said, "First sergeant, I'm so very sorry." I said, "I know you've been through enough with Vietnam, that you're looking at this and you're saying, 'I'm walking right back into another hot spot or another situation.'" And I said, "I can't tell you that, but I think you get the feeling from what I'm saying."

And he goes, "I do, Captain Bray." He said, "I'll get the guys together."

So we at that time started calling in the operations officer, and Colonel Liebe [the provost marshal who hadn't wanted a woman in command of the 988th; he'd wanted her to take command of a prison company instead] again was mad because I couldn't tell him what was going on. All he knew was I had started training my company with hand-to-hand combat. I took them to the driving range, made them all get re-qualified again. So I blew every budget I had, whether it was bullets budget, training budget, whatever, I blew it getting this company ready to deploy to Panama. My husband was in the Rangers at the time, an airborne ranger master parachutist, so he got the RIS, which are ranger instructors, to come and teach my company. And we did rappelling. We did a whole bunch of things. We did a lot of maneuvers, a lot of training. And this was making him—making Colonel Liebe even more mad at me, because here I was doing this and he couldn't know why. He just was like—he doesn't have any control, and it's like, "You're right, you don't have any control. Sorry. You don't have control of this at this time."

• • •

What the plan was, was we had the kennels [for guard dogs], and from the kennels you could actually go in, crash the gate [of Noriega's Panamanian Defense Forces (PDF) headquarters], and attack it right into the front door, straight on. Well, my goal was to have—in the Humvee [High Mobility Multipurpose Wheeled Vehicle] was going to be a Spanish-speaking soldier and a .50 cal[iber] gunner and another soldier. And what they were supposed to do—meanwhile, the rest of that platoon is waiting back down the road. You know, they're waiting for the go. . . . And another platoon had come in, and so what we were going to do is kind of attack it from the side and from the front, because we didn't know what kind of resistance we were going to get. And so my idea was to have two Humvees, and the colonel said, "No." He said, "You're only going to go with one."

I was like, "Those guys are going out there—those guys are being put out there by themselves." It's like, "Oh no!" You know, it was like I knew—I was like, "Oh my god. They could easily be overtaken." Oh, it was a .60 gunner too. And what else had happened was I was up at the command post up by the school talking on the radio, and what had happened is the two platoons that went OPCON to the infantry battalion, they were still on my radio frequency. So they're calling me and they're telling me what's going on, and they're running into an ambush. So I'm trying to talk to them and at the same time talk to the other two platoons that's getting ready to attack the kennels. And my first sergeant jumps in a Humvee and he gets a driver and he grabs a gun and weapon and everything and he takes off flying down [to the kennels].

And finally I got the two platoons to understand that they were on the wrong frequency and they needed to get onto the infantry frequency so that that commander could help direct them. I wasn't trying to abandon them, but I just needed them to get off my frequency so I could handle what's going on. By that time I just looked at my driver and I . . . said, "Get in, let's go." He got his gun, got his weapon, got his ammo, and we jumped in [the Humvee].

We took off and we got down to the very first stop, and so we left the Humvee there because nobody had put up a roadblock. I was like, "Oh my god! There's supposed to be a roadblock right here." I said, "Here, put the Humvee here." And some of the guys that were sitting there waiting, they said, "What do you want us to do?" I said, "Follow me."

We hit this ditch and we were running in this ditch down to the front gate where the specialist [announced that] gunfire had already started, so he had already announced for them to put down their guns and surrender. Gunfire was starting. Well, the .60 gunner is right here on my right, and so he starts just firing away. And I lay down and I pulled out my gun. . . . I said, "Oh wait a minute. Wait a minute, wait a minute."

And about that time first sergeant said, "Cease fire! Cease fire!" And everybody started yelling, "Cease fire! Cease fire!"

So I . . . said, "Listen, don't start hitting everything out there, because right now I'm telling you, what's over there is a housing area and there are people that are actually out there. And there's a horse riding stables on the other side, so don't just start firing."

So I worked my way up to another soldier crawling on top of him, and then I crawled on top of my first sergeant, and he's like, "What are you doing?"

I said, "Somebody's got to talk to headquarters and let them know what's going on." About that time I get into the Humvee. I'm laying on my stomach, I'm talking on the radio because they're still calling me. I'm talking on the radio telling them exactly what we're doing. We're getting ready to charge the gate with the Humvee. I've got the .50 cal gunner standing on my back. The .50 cal mis-operated, so that .50 cal gunner is having to fire one round at a time, okay. And he's standing on my back. So we crash the gate.

And [my driver] says "What next?"

So I'm like okay, now we have to do this, we have to set up a road-block over here, we have to maintain communications, we have got to stop their communications to getting to their headquarters. So I ran inside, and I had that Swiss Army knife that Jamie [a family friend and former Marine] had given me when I got my commission. I had that Swiss Army knife, and one of the platoon sergeants was standing beside me and the phone started ringing. I said, "Oh no! We've got to stop that."

I pulled the phone line off the wall, took that Swiss Army knife, cut that stuff in half, sparks flew everywhere—matter of fact, one of them hit one of the sergeants on the neck. I said, "Well, that's the end of that line of communication. We don't have to worry about that anymore." So I said, "Let's clear the building."

So now we've got people coming in to clear the building. One of my NCOs [noncommissioned officers] had gone into this room to the right and he goes, "Captain Bray, you need to come here."

And I walked in and I like—I'm like, "Oh, my gosh." There was a cache of weapons by the hundreds, by the hundreds. AK-47s and bay-onets, and it was ... the biggest cache of weapons I'd ever seen. Well, come to find out, when everything was kind of calmed down, said and done, come to find out that kennel was also the home of the Pan-amanian Special [Defense] Forces. So as we go through and we're con-tinuing to clear, then I get some of the guys to go into the sleeping quarters, and so we're going through lockers and we're doing this.

There was a lot . . . of gas mask protection and different things like that, and there was a lot of Cuban money in there. So the assumption from operations is that Cuba was probably helping Noriega out.

Anyway, we finished and then I took one platoon and had them figure out a rotating schedule to secure the area. Because we had to secure the area before we could call in another company to replace us so that then we could go and do other missions.

[The Panamanians] had mostly scattered, because we hit the side [of the kennel] with a [M]203, a grenade launcher.

[Three weeks later, in January, the reporters start arriving.]

We're on Quarry Heights and the reporters are coming in, and I had a female as an M60 gunner. And this reporter, his name was Peter Copeland, walked in and they were checking him in at the gate. [The M60 gunner] was behind the M60 guarding the gate and they were letting these reporters come in. And this reporter walked over to her and he said, "You're a female."

She said, "Yeah?" She's kind of a real sassy, you know. And she said, "Yeah, I'm Specialist So-and-so."

And so he asked her, he said, "Have you been doing missions out here?"

She says, "Heck yeah!" And she's like, "We did this, this. We did this and this," and this guy's mind is about to blow right now.

And he's like, "I didn't even think they let females in combat."

And she goes, "Well heck, that's nothing. My company commander's a female." And then he comes to see me.

And I was like. "Yeah, yeah, yeah, yeah," you know.

And then the story hit the . . . wire [that] said, "Oh my God, first female to lead troops in combat." [Colorado Congresswoman] Patricia Schroeder, [New York] Senator [Al] D'Amato—I got a call from the White House [Press Secretary Marlin Fitzwater]. I had to go talk to all these people, and I had to go talk to my four star commanding general in Panama. I got called in. I had to go see the four-star general commander of the [U.S. Army] Pacific Command. . . .

And of course . . . the army had a military policy that women couldn't be in combat arms units. Patricia Schroeder took that to say women could not be in combat. And "what has the military done?" You know, it was almost an attack, and that got the reporters confused, which then in turn confused the public. It's like they're talking about the combat patch. . . . We weren't going to get the CIB, which is the Combat Infantryman's Badge, even though we were OPCON to an infantry battalion. . . . A lot of civilians [didn't understand] that CIB was designated specifically for the infantry. . . .

They have a new medal now for units that are not infantry, but they get their own combat pin now because of this. Because everybody was arguing about the infantry badge versus the patch. And there's a difference, and that got confusing to public and everybody. . . . The politicians weren't paying attention to the actual verbiage that was coming out. So there would be different stories, and there would be conflicting stories of what was going on and what was going on around in Panama. . . .

And then [there were different versions of her height and weight reported in the press]. What they didn't understand was I was losing weight. So yes, I started out at 5'1.5" at a hundred and five pounds, but . . . I kept losing weight. Now, it gets to the White House and some people are thinking about retracting stories, and then it turned around and it was like they were trying to kill the story. And when I had to go see this four-star general, they were prepping me to get ready for interviews with ABC, CB[S], NBC, and CNN. So I went to see this four-star general, and he sat down beside me and he put his hand on my leg like this, and he said, "Captain Bray, do you know the military's opinion of what's happened here?"

And I looked at him I said, "Yes sir. I do believe I do. I think I have a good understanding of the military's feelings on women in combat."

He said, "Okay," he said "I just wanted to know. I just wanted to make sure that you're okay."

So he turned me over to a colonel in public affairs, and we went downtown Panama to this hotel and got up there, and the colonel looked at me and he said, "Do you know what you're going to say?"

And I said, "No, I have no idea what I'm going to say, but, you know, if you see that I'm going to say something wrong, you know, just hold up your hand and I'll change my train of thought."

And he said, "Okay."

So I got up there and I got on that balcony, and of course here's this big camera, black, facing me. . . . I know my first interview did not go as well as every other interview afterwards, because they asked me the question "What is your stance on women in the military?"

And I sat there and I thought and thought and I said, "I'll tell you what, in 1983 I raised my right hand and I said, 'I, Linda Bray, do solemnly swear to defend,'"—you know, I . . . gave the swearing in oath. I said, "All I've done is exactly what I swore I would do."

And I could see the colonel . . . was waiting to hear what I had to say. And then by the time I was getting to the end of what I had to say, he sits back, he smiles, and he says, "Yes, yes."

So I learned very quickly how to answer questions [from reporters]. I learned it by—what is it, trial by fire or something like that? So my subsequent interviews went a lot better. . . . I stayed with this same concept, you know. I took an oath to defend the country, and I have done what I . . . was told to do, and that's it.

•••

And so during this time, an investigation started. Time went on and that MP colonel in Panama called me in. And he said, "I need for you to tell me about the night at the kennels."

I . . . told him blow by blow. I told him that there were some dogs that we had to kill because . . . we could not even get in the front door because they had guard dogs trained to attack. . . .

He said, "About how many?"

I said, "I will say a total of about four or five, something like that."

And he said, "Are you sure? Will you swear to it?"

I said, "Most definitely. You can talk to people in my company. You can talk to the NCOs that shot them."

He said, "No, no problem, but you need to quit talking to the press. You need to just quit talking to anybody at this point."

And I was like, "Okay." I still didn't know what was going on.

[A] reporter from a magazine . . . took [a] picture of me and my soldiers around a Humvee. And the battalion commander MP in Panama saw it and he came up to me and he said, "Captain Bray, am I going to have to file charges against you for failure to obey an order?"

I said, "No sir. I said I did not talk to that reporter. She just took my picture. She talked to the soldiers, not me."

So he was . . . being a very big butt hole is what I'll say. So I was having a hard time either way I went. It didn't matter.

[She explains that the media attention continued. Reporters showed up at her home and her parents' home and took photos. She also received a letter bomb at the Fort Benning Military Police Station.

In April 1990 Bray returns home. Her weight loss shocks her family and commander, and she is suffering severe hip pain from her earlier training injury. Three weeks after her return, she is summoned to Colonel Liebe's office.]

He told me that the Panamanian government had pressed charges against me for damage to private property, damage to government property, animal cruelty, just a whole array of charges with fines in the millions of dollars. . . .

And I was like, "What are you talking about?"

He said, "You need to go get representation. . . . You need to go get a lawyer."

I said, "What's going to happen?"

He said, "Well, you've launched the largest CID [Criminal Investigation Division] investigation in the whole southeast region."

So I went flying back to my company. I told my first sergeant what was going on, then I had a swarm of CID agents coming in to investigate different people, me . . . I made sure that my soldiers got representation and myself, and so . . . everybody told their side of the story. Everybody was interviewed differently about the attack on the kennels.

[Bray explains that the outcome of the investigation finally revealed that the female commander attached to Fort Meade who replaced her in Panama had given the order to kill the remaining dogs at the kennels.]

[The other female commander] sent a team of soldiers in there and she told them, she said—what was it that was used?—"Take care of the dogs." Well, what happened is those soldiers went in there and shot every dog in the place—shot them in the head.

And afterwards, the Panamanians were pulling all of their dogs out and throwing them in a huge big fire. And when I was told that I was like, "Oh my God. No way would it be me. I guarantee you. No way it would be me, and no way anybody in my company would've done that."

Well this CID investigator kept going and kept digging and kept digging until he found out exactly who it was.... Now, that has really upset the lieutenant colonel of the battalion, because it was his own company that did it. So now I've got him mad at me too, politically.

And then that battalion commander at Fort Meade had to do an OER [officer evaluation report] on my performance down in Panama.... I got that, and I finally got my award, but it didn't come until I was about to get out of the Army. In August I'd gone back to the hospital. The doctor said that they needed to remove the pins [in her hip]. So I told Colonel Liebe to go ahead and get Captain Freeman, that we would go ahead and change command early . . . so that I could go and have my surgery to get these pins out. Because I literally had meat-to-screw, and it was tearing and I was . . . bleeding on the inside. So we did change of command, which made him very happy. And [Liebe] did my OER, and he marked me as a three. For every other man in that command, he marked them as a one. So essentially he just killed my career at that point.

[After her surgery, Bray is reassigned to a medical company and begins working toward a medical discharge. A major disobeys Colonel Liebe's orders about her OER and writes a favorable evaluation.]

By this time I was . . . fed up with everything, and I accepted the medical discharge.

And I . . . was at home and I got a call from the commanding general of Fort Benning, Georgia. And he said, "Captain Bray," he said, "I have an OER on my desk right now that I'm not very happy with."

I said, "I'm sure you're not. I had to sign it. The only thing I can tell you is that I would believe what the major said over what the colonel said."

He said, "Captain Bray, I think there's been a great injustice done here and I want you to know you have a right to appeal this OER and you can get your commission back in the military."

I said, "Sir, you know I hate to say this, but I know I can appeal that OER and I know I could get my commission back . . . but at this point in my life I'm just very tired." It had hit me at this point of what all had transpired over the year or more. And I just said, "No, I think I'll just stay out."

He said, "I don't agree with it, but if that's your wishes then I'll go along with it."

So that was it. I got medically discharged.

Now today looking back, I would've accepted the commander's advice and I would've appealed that OER and I would've stayed in the military. And I could've retired in 2003. But at the time I was in a different situation.

Darlene Iskra
(1952–)
U.S. NAVY

Darlene Iskra, the first woman to command a commissioned naval vessel, assumed command of USS *Opportune* (ARS 41) in December 1990 in Naples, Italy. She took *Opportune* to war during Desert Storm in January 1991. She was also one of the first female line officers to graduate from the Naval School of Diving and Salvage in Washington DC. Iskra retired after twenty-one years of service; her awards include the Defense Meritorious Service Medal. As a Congressional Fellow for Senator Maria Cantwell, Iskra helped to staff and pass an amendment to the 2003 Defense Authorization Bill prohibiting the Department of Defense to require U.S. servicewomen to wear the abaya while stationed in Saudi Arabia. Iskra is the author of *Women in the United States Armed Forces: A Guide to the Issues*. The following is an original essay submitted for inclusion in this collection.

When I first joined the Navy in 1979, the opportunity for command at sea was just not available for women. The only ships that were open to women were a few training ships, like the training carrier USS *Lexington* and about fourteen active duty repair ships (AR, AD, AS). All of the women who were assigned to these ships were junior officers, ensigns to lieutenants. I was assigned to USS *Hector* (AR-7), homeported in the San Francisco Bay Area, as the diving officer and the R-5 (Optical and Others) and R-7 (Divers) division officer. While there I qualified as a surface warfare officer. After my two-year stint, I would have liked to go back to sea to keep up with my male counterparts, but there were few sea billets for follow-on tours for women.

I wound up in San Diego at the Nuclear Weapons Training Group, Pacific. I was assigned as a radiation control instructor and also taught shipboard nuclear weapons safety and nuclear weapons security. Of course that was the time we could neither confirm nor deny the presence of nuclear weapons on any particular platform, but obviously they were somewhere! This was not a career-enhancing job.

I was supposed to be there three years, but after about a year and a half, I learned of a new rescue and salvage ship that was being built and would accommodate women. So, I contacted my assignment officer (detailer in Navy parlance), and asked to terminate shore duty to go back to sea as operations officer on USS *Grasp* (ARS-51). The request was approved. As I was saying goodbye to colleagues at NWTGP, one man suggested that I might become the first woman commanding officer of a ship. This was 1984. I thought not.

I wound up in Norfolk, Virginia (Little Creek Naval Amphibious Base), on USS *Grasp* as operations officer. After two years I was selected, and served as, executive officer on USS *Preserver* (ARS-8) for about two years, and then transferred to USS *Hoist* (ARS-40) as executive officer for another seven months. I needed my engineering duty officer of the watch qualification before I could be selected for command, and I qualified as such while on *Hoist*. Soon thereafter I was selected for command at sea. WOW!

It was not a given that I would be assigned to command right away ... In fact there was a little bit of a controversy between the surface warfare community, which had selected its first women for command in 1989, and the special operations community, of which I was a member, which had selected me in early 1990. The decision of which woman was to get command first went to the chief of Naval Personnel, who at the time was Admiral Jeremy Boorda. Since I actually had more sea time than the other woman, I was selected as the first.

I attended several pre-commanding officer training courses from June 1990 to November 1990, and then was awaiting orders to my ship,

USS *Opportune* (ARS-41), when on December 24, 1990, I was called upon to travel to Naples, Italy, on December 26 to take command. I was supposed to relieve command in January of 1991, but the commanding officer took ill with stomach cancer and had to be evacuated. I took an emergency change of command on December 27, 1990.

Since there was no formal ceremony, I was not prepared for the hoopla that accompanied the event. I had arrived in Naples early in the morning of December 27; the ceremony consisted of me getting on the 1MC (the ship's public address system) and announcing to the crew that I had assumed command. I held a Captain's Call (a meeting with the crew) on the fantail of the ship later that day after I had a chance to get my bearings ... briefings with the executive officer and the department heads, as well as the senior enlisted advisor of the ship. Since I was the only woman on the ship at the time, I remember the most pressing question was, "Our bathing area is down the hall from our berthing (sleeping) area ... how do we get from here to there?" I was confused. I asked, well how do you get there now? They indicated that they went naked or in their underwear ... so I said, well, just wear a towel or a robe and that will not be a problem! For me it wasn't, as I rarely spent the mornings in that part of the ship. *My* concern was what to wear when I was called upon in the middle of the night to go to the bridge ... I usually wore sweat pants and a T-shirt and sweatshirt to bed so I could get up in the middle of the night without having to worry about being properly clothed.

The day after I took command, I was asked by the Sixth Fleet public affairs officer to hold a press conference. You have to realize that Desert Shield had started in August 1990 ... the preparations for war against Suddam Hussein in Iraq. So, in early January 1991, my picture and story were on the front page of most international newspapers throughout the world. I did not realize it at the time, but my husband, a Navy SEAL, was concerned for my safety ... I had no idea.

When I reported aboard, I also found on my desk many letters from strangers congratulating me on my achievement. Some of these letters were from people I had known pre-Navy or in the early part of my Navy career ... It was awesome. I decided that I needed to answer each of my well-wishers with a personal letter. .... Out of that came friendships with two very special senior citizens, who I continued to communicate with until they passed on, many years later.

We left Naples in early January, heading towards Taranto, Italy, in the very center of the arch of the heel of the Italian peninsula. *Opportune* was escorting USS *South Carolina*, a nuclear-powered cruiser, to the port in case she needed emergency towing assistance. During that port visit, Operation Desert Storm started and both ships were ordered to their respective stations.

Opportune was ordered to a station about fifty miles from the entrance to the Suez Canal, in case we needed to either defuse mines or help clear the canal of obstacles. We had embarked an explosive ordnance team to help us in this mission.

The lack of information about the progress of the war in the Middle East, the lack of knowledge about the SCUD missiles that the Iraqis had launched against Israel, and other military maneuvers made us sitting ducks and very nervous. *Opportune* had very little in the way of defensive weapons (dual .50-caliber machines guns on the port and starboard bow and fantail, which could, in a pinch, deter a small craft; and two 20-mm antiaircraft guns on the port and starboard bridge wings). We were not prepared for war and not trained to deter small craft, let alone a torpedo or air-launched missile. We also had no communication with the civil air patrol craft that, daily, came at us at a very hostile (low-flying) profile. We were on our own.

Luckily, the worst that happened occurred during a resupply trip in Port Said, at the entrance to the Suez Canal in the Mediterranean. We were ordered to anchor there to get food, mail, and supplies needed for about thirty days of underway steaming. We got into port okay and embarked the husbanding agent, when suddenly all of these small boats started toward the ship and were trying to tie up and come aboard to sell their wares. I was frantic and asked the husbanding agent to keep the boats away, but he was not able to do so. We negotiated that they could tie up alongside so they could sell their goods, but they were not allowed on board. I called this "fantail liberty," and the crew really enjoyed it. A few of the husbanding agent's friends were allowed to set up shop on the fantail, but were not allowed on any other part of the ship. Even with this compromise I did not feel comfortable. Luckily, after we received our needed fuel, food, and supplies, we left the harbor without incident. Ten years later USS *Cole* (DDG-67) in Aden harbor, Yemen, was not so lucky.

We spent the war outside of the entrance to Suez Canal, our mission being to salvage any ship that happened to hit a mine or was otherwise injured in the Suez Canal, or to defuse any mines that were laid in the canal. We did not have to exercise any of those mission profiles. When the war ended three weeks later, in early February 1991, *Opportune* continued its Mediterranean deployment and returned to Little Creek, Virginia, to a hero's welcome in April 1991.

My command tour would continue for another two years. In March 1993, I was relieved of command prior to *Opportune*'s decommissioning in June of that year.

Command is something that most naval officers aspire to. It can be a blessing and a curse depending on your superior officers and your crew. I was blessed with an awesome and supportive crew, especially during Operation Desert Storm. We worked together to try to overcome the disadvantages of being a noncombatant vessel in hostile waters. But the most trying for the commanding officer was to overcome the hostile attitudes of my superiors toward my personal achievement of command. Yes, I was the first woman to command a ship. Yes, I had worked just as hard or harder for this achievement as my male peers. But what I did not get was the mentoring and advice from my seniors that my male peers received. I was left to fend for myself when I made a mistake or a misjudgment.

Over the years since my command tour I have reconciled my issues. I realize that as a first there are not only roadblocks, but hazards that must be met with honorable intentions, assertiveness, and a willingness to push boundaries that have not been breached. I was not aware of those boundaries, and it caused conflict in my professional and personal life. But in hindsight, I am pleased with my accomplishments and my legacy. I am proud to say I was the first woman to command a ship in the Navy, and I welcome many more women to the fold.

Mary V. "Ginger" Jacocks
(1950–)
U.S. MARINE CORPS

Mary "Ginger" Jacocks, from Zachary, Louisiana, joined the Marine Corps in 1974 as an intelligence officer. During her career, she accomplished several "firsts." She was the first female officer assigned to a combat support operational billet at the regimental level. She was the first female to command a Marine Security Guard battalion, responsible for Marine Security Guards throughout Russia, former Warsaw Pact, Yugoslavia (as it disintegrated), Greece, Turkey, Austria, Germany, and Finland. Jacocks was the first female student to attend and graduate from the Marine Corps War College and the first female faculty adviser at the Marine Corps Command and Staff College. During Operations Desert Shield/Desert Storm, she served as the regimental intelligence officer and provided direct combat service support for the First and Second Marine Divisions. She retired as a lieutenant colonel in 1997. The following excerpt is from an interview published by the Marine Corps History Division.

> From the beginning, we knew that somebody would be going [to deploy]. My first task, because 4th MEB was the first element that went from II MEF, was to decide who to send out of the G-2 to be the S-2 element for the combat service support element of the MEB. . . . We kept the maps every day. It would not be uncommon for [Brigadier] General Krulak to be over in our section two [or] three days out of the week, stopping by to look at the situation map even though I was giving briefs at the staff meetings. But he would come over and look at the situation. "Okay, what do you think is happening? Why is this happening? Why are they doing this?" And so on. So we pretty much kept up with the running situation and developing our own estimate from day one, whether we were going to go or not, just to keep the general informed.

> • • •

> As the situation progressed, it became a little bit clearer . . . that 2d FSSG was going as a command. Now at that point it was still the policy of

the Marine Corps that the women [did] not deploy; however, General Krulak felt very strongly, and I'm sure there were other general officers that felt strongly also, but I know General Krulak felt very strongly that his command had women in critical billets, and in order for the command to be able to carry out its mission, it would need to take its women. And I know that he sent a message to the Commandant relating that feeling in some manner, and shortly after that, it came back and we were told that women filling billets that were required would be deploying. Besides my being the G-2, we had a female as G-1, and the staff [secretary] was a female. There were several women as company commanders in critical billets that needed to go, and there were just too many women [in the unit] to have been able to carry out the mission the way we had trained without us.

[The interviewer asks about other women in her unit.]

I had a female gunnery sergeant and a female, I think she was a corporal, when we went over there. She may have been a lance corporal. [Jacocks notes that there were fourteen Marines in her section.]

[The interviewer asks about the duties of the G-2 in Saudi Arabia with the Direct Support Command.]

Well, the intelligence function is always to keep the commander informed regarding enemy activity—also responsible for the effects of weather and terrain on operations. With a combat service support element, of course, you also focus on the logistical intelligence that's required, things like where are the piers, where are our wells, building supplies, MSRs [main supply routes], structures, and things like that.

[The interviewer asks if she felt pressure as the G-2 (staff intelligence officer) with the DSC deployed forward.]

You know, I wouldn't say that I felt any pressure. I knew that the general was depending on me to get information and to provide him intelligence, and General Krulak made sure that I knew what information he expected. . . . Once we were deployed, he spent a lot of time in the G-2 section sitting in front of the map talking to [me and] the Marines that worked for me, because he wanted to make sure that if he had a question or he wanted a response from them, that there was a rapport between him and the corporals and the sergeants that were there—that they would be able to talk to each other, that the sergeants wouldn't be so intimidated that they wouldn't be able to think. So he would come over and actually work with all of us and kind of set up the situation. So I wouldn't say there was pressure.

We knew what we were supposed to do. We worked hard at doing it. We had a tremendous team. Even though it was a small intelligence section, we had worked at forming a good coherent team, and everybody worked effectively together. We did some really good analysis. We sent out collection requests for things that we needed. We went back to a lot of the good old-fashion[ed] ways of analyzing things and coming up with information and putting it down, and thank goodness we were in a command that didn't care about dog and pony show type things. We could stick a map on the wall, use a pencil as a pointer, and point out what we were talking about as long as we got the information across, which I think invariably we always did.

[The interviewer asks about her role in the actual liberation of Kuwait.]

Well, I guess you'd just describe it as keeping my commander and his staff and subordinate commanders apprised of the situation so that they could better perform their duties. We worked very closely with the commanders for the engineering battalions that were going to work the breaches you know as far as diagrams of the breach sites, the width of the minefield, the types of mines that were there. All that information turned out to be very accurate so that they could plan and rehearse.

We also, through map studies, tried to work with the resupply plan. There was emergency re-supply set up that had already been determined by the units being supported, what type of emergency resupply units would like at different points in the battle, and a lot of that was prestaged so that it could be delivered either by land or air. So if it was air, the intel section had picked out some spots that could have been used as LZs [landing zones] to go in and put some of those down. Of course, all of that had to be fluid based on the situation of what was going on. But other than that, basically the G-2 role in the actual invasion was keeping people apprised of what was there and what was going on in front of them.

Probably the hardest part of being the G-2 is doing all the analysis and the estimates beforehand. So when things are actually happening and moving ahead, of course, you're trying to see further ahead, but things moved so swiftly in Desert Storm and the Iraqis started fleeing so soon that there really wasn't a whole lot of intel to do. As the red disappeared off the map, so to speak, then our job became more one of looking at various area security-type functions and the exploitation of documents and things like that, what to do with enemy weapons, and things of that nature.

[The interviewer asks if there were any issues with deploying male and female Marines together.]

You know, I don't think so, and I think one of the things that I learned and I think many of the men in the command element [CE] learned was that it really didn't matter if you were male or female. When we had the first NBC [nuclear, biological, and chemical] alarm and had to go into full MOPP [mission-oriented protective posture] gear, when you looked around there and you saw everybody trying to open up those suits for the first time and getting into everything, everybody had the same big eyes and everybody reacted the same and everybody helped each other, and I don't think it made any difference. We had women out manning the machine-gun positions on the perimeter along with the males. Everybody filled their own sandbags and worked. Of course, General Krulak filled sandbags and worked too. So we had good leadership and everybody was inspired to work side by side.

I think one of the things that we found was that we were all Marines, and we were all one family, not necessarily brothers—you know the Marine Corps brother thing kind of went out the window—but I think we were all brothers and sisters. As far as living in the desert, there weren't that many differences, at least when we were out there. We didn't mark the heads for male and female. You kind of waited, and a couple [of] women would go in together, so you wouldn't fill up one whole area and keep the men from being able to use the head or anything. [She chuckles.] But you know, I think everybody kind of looked at it as there wasn't really time to worry about that stuff, and I think it worked really well.

The only thing I would say is at that point, you know the Marine Corps had been training women to go to the field for a little while. When I came in, they didn't, however. You know, we did a few things out in the field with the men at Basic School but that was it. But as things changed, the Marine Corps never went back and trained the women who were already in higher positions. You just were expected to already know how to go out to the field and do all the stuff. And while we were over there, I know a reporter asked me if I felt the Marine Corps had trained me adequately to be able to live in the field, and I told him, no, I didn't think they had. However, the Girl Scouts had.

11

Operation Enduring Freedom and Operation Iraqi Freedom

"This Is My War Story"

The RQ-2 Pioneer unmanned aerial vehicle, or UAV, waited for the takeoff command. The two-stroke, two-cylinder engine started with an abrupt buzz. Moments later, the UAV shot upward like an arrow fired from a taut bow. It flew north over Iraq's Highway Seven from Qalat Sikur toward Kut, its onboard camera capturing the terrain below and linking the footage back to a tent manned by Marines.

A number of white vehicles appeared on the screen. Men dressed in black moved among them. One had a motorcycle.

Lt. Jane Blair ordered the payload operator to keep the UAV in the area. The men on the ground, she told him, were forward observers for Iraqi artillery. One of the sergeants suggested they might find Iraqi mortars a few kilometers out; artillery could be twenty to forty kilometers farther away. She directed the UAV to search to the northwest.

Exactly where they'd expected: Iraqi infantry on the side of the road near a canal, and twenty kilometers away—two batteries of Soviet-designed 122-mm anti-tank howitzers. Soldiers walked around the guns and prepared to load them. To the south, U.S. Marines advanced on the city of Kut and would soon be in range of the Iraqi artillery.

Blair ordered a Marine to wake up the commanding officer to authorize a fire mission. Another notified the Fire Direction Center, where other Marines would choose the best way to put rounds on target. An artillery unit directed Blair to keep the UAV in orbit over the target.

The screen filled with plumes of smoke when the first U.S. rounds landed on the battery. The Marine artillerymen made one range correction. Fired for effect. Rounds rained down on the Iraqi position.

When the smoke cleared, Blair reported the battle damage assessment. Dozens of dead soldiers lay among the destroyed artillery pieces. The Marines around Blair cheered, but she felt numb. "In one instant," she recalled in her 2011 memoir, "I had become their executioner. There was blood on my hands now.... Once you kill, you can't take it back."

Beginning in the mid-1980s, women aviators from the Navy, Air Force, and Army came to Capitol Hill under the auspices of two women's advocacy groups, the Women's Research and Education Institute (WREI) and the National Women's Law Center (NWLC). Using their personal leave time for meetings, and in civilian clothes to avoid creating a perception that they were engaging in political activity in uniform, the women educated members of Congress on their training, their duties, and the adverse effects of the combat aviation exclusion law on their careers. They found allies among congresswomen and congressmen, in both political parties, and in the House and Senate. One was Rep. Patricia Schroeder (D-Colorado), an outspoken advocate for military reform.

When Desert Storm ended in February 1991, Schroeder recognized that public approval of women's performance in the conflict presented an ideal opportunity to try again to repeal the combat exclusion laws prohibiting women from serving on naval combatants and in combat aircraft. On the morning of May 8, during the House Armed Services Committee markup of the 1992–93 defense authorization bill, in a surprise move Schroeder introduced an amendment repealing 10 USC 8549 and authorizing Air Force women to fly in combat aircraft. Rep. Beverly Byron (D-Maryland) added language extending the amendment to women aviators in the Navy. The measure passed the House on a voice vote, which surprised even Schroeder. When the appropriations bill went to the Senate in July, Senators Edward Kennedy (D-Massachusetts) and William Roth (R-Delaware) cosponsored a similar amendment in the Senate Armed Forces Committee (SASC).

The Senate Armed Services Committee held an acrimonious and emotional hearing on the proposed amendment on June 18. All four service chiefs opposed the amendment, and the assistant secretary of defense offered that while SecDef also opposed the repeal, he welcomed flexibility and the authority to make policy. Six servicemembers testified; the four Army and Marine Corps personnel—including one woman—opposed the repeal, while Navy and Air Force representatives testified that women should have the opportunity to fly in combat. The chair of DACOWITS and the director of the National Women's Law Center also spoke in support of repeal, while DACOWITS member and executive director of the conservative think tank Center for Military Readiness Elaine Donnelly and former Marine Corps Commandant General Robert Barrow opposed it.

Four senators—John Glenn (D-Ohio), John McCain (R-Arizona), Sam Nunn (D-Georgia), and John Warner (R-Virginia)—countered the Kennedy-Roth Amendment with a separate amendment offering a temporary repeal of combat exclusion while a presidential commission studied the assignment of military women. Both amendments passed, and the bill went to conference committee for resolution. Compromise legislation fully repealed the combat exclusion law for women aviators, but established the Presidential Commission on the Assignment of Women in the Armed Forces to study the issue. The Department of Defense refrained from assigning women to combat aviation units while the commission conducted its review.

The George H. W. Bush administration included five vocal critics of women in combat among the fifteen commission members. Eight of the fifteen had served in the military, but only one had aviation experience. Nine were men and six women. The members could not come to consensus. Five (including a senior Air Force enlisted woman) who opposed women in combat walked out of the meeting and refused to participate again until the other members allowed them to publish dissenting views as part of the commission's report. In 1992 the commission recommended that military readiness should be the primary concern when developing assignment policies. While the final report recommended repeal of the law preventing women from assignment to naval combatants, it also recommended continued exclusion of women from direct land combat units and positions and retention of the Risk Rule.

President Bush passed the report to Congress without endorsement, and Congress took no action on it. After President Clinton took office in 1993, Congress repealed the law prohibiting women from serving on naval combatants. Secretary of Defense Les Aspin rescinded the Risk Rule. He approved a new Direct Ground Combat and Assignment Rule excluding women from assignment to units below the brigade level whose primary mission was engaging the enemy in direct ground combat (defined as engaging the enemy with individual or crew served weapons while being exposed to hostile fire and a high probability of direct physical contact with enemy personnel). Women could also be restricted from assignments to units and positions physically collocated with ground combat units closed to women.

Following the September 11, 2001, terrorist attacks on U.S. territory, President George W. Bush ordered troops into Afghanistan for Operation Enduring Freedom. The Taliban, which had been harboring 9/11 mastermind Osama bin Laden, declined to extradite him to the United States. American and allied troops backed the "Northern Alliance," a primarily ethnic Tajik military faction, in its overthrow of the Taliban government. The Taliban responded with an increasingly lethal insurgency campaign. Planning for a concurrent invasion of Iraq, intended to remove the Ba'athist government of Saddam Hussein and cripple its weapons of mass destruction program, began almost immediately after 9/11; forces were deployed to the region late in 2002, and on March 20, 2003, U.S. and allied forces invaded. Not long after a multinational Coalition Provisional Authority assumed responsibility as a transitional government of Iraq, insurgent groups began targeting U.S. troops and the new Iraqi Security Force.

Counterinsurgency operations blurred the lines between forward and rear operating areas, and support units frequently ended up in close proximity to active engagements or defending themselves from insurgent attacks. Public debate over the assignment of women resurfaced when three women assigned to the Army's 507th Maintenance Company—Pvts. First Class Jessica Lynch and Lori Piestewa and Spc. Shoshana Johnson—were injured and captured in an ambush (Piestewa, a Native American, died of her injuries in an Iraqi hospital).

To support the rotation and training required by fighting wars in two countries, the Army began reorganizing into "modular units." The Brigade Combat Team (BCT) became the basic large tactical combat unit. BCTs were supported by collocated Multi-Functional Support Brigades, which included "noncombat" personnel. Many were women. The Army, however, had not updated its assignment policy for women to match the less restrictive DoD policy implemented in 1994: women could not be assigned to units smaller than a battalion whose mission was "direct combat"—"closing the enemy by fire, maneuver, and shock effect in order to destroy or capture the enemy, or while repelling the enemy's assault by fire, close combat or counterattack." However, the fluidity of the "front line" in Iraq and Afghanistan meant that women in Multi-Functional Support Brigades did repel enemy assault.

In May 2005, Rep. John McHugh (R-New York), chairman of the Military Personnel Subcommittee of the House Armed Services Committee, introduced at the request of HASC Chairman Duncan Hunter (R-California) an amendment to the FY 2006 National Defense Authorization bill to ban women from service in "forward support companies," which would have closed almost 22,000 jobs to women. Twenty-seven Democrats and one Republican in the HASC wrote to oppose the amendment. They pointed out that Army leaders also opposed the amendment, feeling that it tied their hands in a time of war. Army officials also argued that the amendment would impose "unwarranted" obstacles on servicewomen's career advancement opportunities, adversely affect recruiting, and undermine cohesiveness and morale by drawing "unsupported gender distinctions on deployment of trained personnel."

Representative McHugh responded with a substitute amendment barring women from Army forward support companies, codifying into law the four categories of exclusion previously permitted at service discretion, and prohibiting the opening of military occupational specialties to women without changes in the law. The final bill passed without these measures, requiring only that DoD notify Congress of planned changes in assignment of women while Congress would be in session for a minimum of thirty days, with a description of and justification for the change—and an analysis of the change's legal implications for constitutionality of the Military Selective Service Act.

In the meantime, the undersecretary of Defense for Personnel and Readiness had commissioned the RAND National Defense Research Institute to study the 1994 DoD assignment policy. Their 2007 report "Assessing the Assignment Policy for Army Women" found differences in the Army and DoD assignment policies and a lack of clarity in both. They noted that strict compliance with the restrictive 1992 Army policy would prohibit women from participating in Army operations in Iraq and would prevent the Army from completing its mission. The study recommended redrafting assignment policies to conform clearly to the nature of modern and future warfare, but stopped short of recommending that the Army open more assignments to women. That July, Secretary of Defense Robert Gates informed congressional defense committees that the services' assignment policies were in compliance with the 1994 DoD policy, and that the Army's reorganization into modular units did not conflict with DoD assignment policy for women.

Beginning in 2005, the Marine Corps formally implemented its Lioness program, in which women Marines and some Army female soldiers were tasked to conduct physical searches of Iraqi women at checkpoints for concealed weapons and explosive devices and to conduct outreach with Iraqi women. Volunteers for the Lioness program were given one week of training in weapons systems, language and cultural norms, Marine Corps Martial Arts Program tactics, and combat lifesaving techniques. Although the women in the Lioness program performed the same missions at the checkpoints as men in infantry and combat arms military occupational specialties, the Marine Corps managed to avoid violating the Direct Ground Combat and Assignment Rule by forming the Lioness teams as a brigade-sized element. Over time the mission evolved to include women in civil affairs and outreach operations. Five years later the Marine Corps deployed its first trained Female Engagement Teams—women Marines who volunteered to form relationships with Afghan women and to conduct civil affairs and outreach missions in Afghanistan's Helmand Province in support of counterinsurgency goals. In the summer of 2010, a congressional inquiry over whether the women were violating combat exclusion co-location rules led to a policy of deploying the female engagement teams to the field for a maximum of forty-five days ("reset"), then returning them to a major base for a short time before they returned to the field. In that same time frame, Adm. William McRaven, commander of the Joint Special Operations Command, created the Army's Cultural Support Teams. Volunteers screened in a physically and mentally demanding program to be selected for the program, and then trained for six weeks prior to deployment with civil affairs teams and the Army's Seventy-Fifth Ranger Regiment in Afghanistan.

More than 280,000 women served in Iraq and Afghanistan during the "Long Wars." As of October 2015, 161 women have died and 1,016 were wounded in action. More than 9,000 received Army Combat Action Badges for "actively engaging or being engaged by the enemy." Two—Army Spc. Monica Lin Brown, a medic, and Kentucky Army National Guard Sgt. Leigh Ann Hester, a military policeman—were awarded the Silver Star for gallantry in action against an enemy. Three women earned the Distinguished Flying Cross, thirty-one earned the Air Medal, and sixteen earned the Bronze Star.

Not only were military women engaged in combat operations in the most recent wars; when they returned, they began telling their stories in print. In 2006 former Arabic linguist Kayla Williams published *Love My Rifle More Than You: Young and Female in the U.S. Army*, a memoir of her experiences in Iraq. Navy psychologist Heidi Squier Kraft published her Iraq memoir in 2007, and former Marine Jane Blair published hers in 2011. A number of women veterans took advantage of GI Bill funds to attend master of fine arts programs and sought to elevate accounts of their wartime experiences to the level of literary art. Unlike women of earlier generations, who often spend parts of their narratives apologizing for their effrontery in violating social norms for women's behavior and taking on traditionally masculine roles, women veterans of recent wars assertively claim their wartime experiences, demand to be heard, and insist on being taken as seriously in print as they were in uniform.

Miyoko Hikiji
(1976–)
U.S. ARMY

In 2003 author and writing instructor Miyoko Hikiji published a memoir of her 2003–2004 Iraq deployment with the 2133rd Transportation Company. Hikiji holds BS degrees in journalism, mass communication, and psychology from Iowa State University. Her interviews and book reviews have been broadcast nationwide on NPR's "Tell Me More" and published in USA *Today*, *Marie Claire*, and *Stars and Stripes*. She is a member of the National Women Veterans Speakers Bureau and the military sexual trauma project director for the Iowa nonprofit group Veterans National Recovery Center. The following are excerpts from her memoir, *All I Could Be: My Story as a Woman Warrior in Iraq.*

> This is my war story. It's part military history, part personal revelation, part therapy. . . . Though it maintains a high degree of factual integrity, my story is partly a creative endeavor and solely my own truth. In war, like in life, truth is a reflection, a perspective on past events. My memories of these events were shaped by years of examination.
>
> I began this book during the deployment. . . . In reading the ini-

tial drafts, I realized that some incidents simply did not make sense because war does not occur in a logical sequence and people often act "out of character." While I was deployed, my struggle to piece together "life as I knew it" with "life as it was" led to moments of sheer craziness. When I came home, these times persisted. My initial hope was to heal myself through writing my story. Through this cathartic undertaking, reliving the painful events of my deployment. . . . produced further traumatic stress.

There are days my deployment seems so long ago and so far removed that I can hardly believe it happened at all. Then one morning at the kitchen table, I finish my breakfast and instinctively reach under my chair for my rifle and panic when I come up empty-handed before realizing that there are no insurgents in my backyard and I no longer carry a weapon. In effect, all of my experiences, real and imagined, are part of my real life. I now believe there is no cure, per se, or route back to who I was. The only path is forward and by telling my story I can apply a comforting salve to wounds that will never heal.

• • •

Iraq was a beautiful hell. I roasted atop a stone retaining wall listening to music through my head phones. I watched the Euphrates dance of water bugs and emerald birds with triangular wings. Behind me stretched a green grass courtyard that, despite the desert environment, was able to flourish through a river-fed sprinkler system. At the tip of my platoon's pie slice of land was one of the former palaces of Saddam Hussein, who was currently hiding. Its dome, now toppled and upside-down, had been blown off by a missile whose partial casing (now festooned with a Ron Jon Surf Shop sticker) lay at the center of the ruins. The front of the palace had a gaping, jagged hole through which we could see a crumbling marble staircase. The thought occurred to me that maybe only a few months before Saddam had climbed that staircase to peer through the window in the rotunda as if he were, and always would be, king of his world.

I was on a week-long mission in the provincial capital of Ar Ramadi supporting a Florida National Guard infantry unit that was in charge of the city's security. The outpost was about the size of three city blocks. The infantry lived in a partially destroyed building that had also been part of the palace grounds. My co-driver Nick [whose name, like others in the book, has been changed] and I shared one of the four frame tents with another truck team. The second and third tents held four other truck teams including Di, the only other woman on the mission, and the last tent housed the platoon sergeant and his driver. That tent doubled as an office. A cleverly crafted patio area had been constructed using scavenged pallets covered with scrap wood for a floor. Camouflage bits stretched and tied between and the open spaces of low tree branches provided relief from the relentless sun. Waving atop a few extra tent poles in the center of our compound was the Iowa state flag.

It was July 2003 and we had just moved to this forward operating base in preparation for our fourth mission since arriving in Iraq. With nothing to do beside clean my M16 and kick the tires on my truck, I moved languidly about trying to find the least miserable spot in which to endure the day's heat. I circled from my bunk to the patio to the retaining wall and back like one of the emerald birds.

A small rusty pick-up truck pulled alongside the tents. It was a local Iraqi merchant selling blocks of ice as long and thick as railroad ties. Three soldiers would share the cost of an eight-dollar block and then use their bayonet knives to chip it into sections that fit in their small coolers. I grabbed my cooler, put in my ice chips, then, packed two Fanta sodas, a tuna kit, three energy bars and a handful of jerky around it. The ice would be melted by evening, then thrown out on the grass. But in the meantime, I could enjoy cold food and drinks.

• • •

The cooks worked miracles with powdered eggs and canned meats, and often incorporated locally grown produce into the menu, except on days like today, when the delivery truck got blown up by an improvised explosive device (IED), scattering our salads all across the street. Lunch was an MRE (meal ready-to-eat). . . . Hot, hungry, and forever needing energy, I was careful never to miss chow. I needed all the strength I could get—we all did.

I ate alone while the other male soldiers strutted around like peacocks. They were okay Joes for the most part, but they were hopelessly hormonally charged. This made it difficult for me to participate in their discussions of whores, strip clubs, and no-boundaries masturbation. The privates gathered around the platoon sergeant asking, "When was your first combat jerk?" like kids gather around grandpa to hear "'Twas the Night before Christmas." Whenever they spotted me walking toward the patio, they tried to change their topic of discussion to something less offensive, like music or movies, but it rapidly fizzled into an uncomfortable stretch of silence, as it wasn't nearly as interesting as what they just been razzing about. I ate alone while the other male soldiers strutted around like peacocks.

My team leader, Lowman, jumped up and suggested a swim to cool off. The others agreed and bolted off toward the water's edge with shirts and boots flying. As Lowman caught up with me, he slowed to talk.

"You comin' with?"

"Not this time," I said in a sad tone.

"Live a little," he said with disgust. "You should be diving in head first every chance you get a chance. Don't know how many more of those chances you'll have, you know."

Then, he turned to run off and join the lot.

I headed for my bunk to sulk over the fact that the thick pad soaking up a heavy period made a dip in the river impossible. Maintaining my dignity required privacy, so I kept my feminine products out of sight and my reasons for not swimming to myself. Live a little reverberated in my head. I'm living it like everybody else—full color, 3-D, surround sound—except that this shitty movie has been playing for 137 days now without a single barrel of extra-butter popcorn or quart-sized Coke.

I looked out over the palace lawn at my buddies, jumping off a makeshift diving platform, splashing the others in the water below. Near the platform was our open-air latrine—a 55-gallon metal drum topped with a sheet of plywood with a hole cut in its center. In front of the drum was a heavy door from Saddam's bombed out palace that was positioned on its side to conceal me, or any other soldier using the latrine, for some privacy. But, it did not allow for complete privacy, only from one angle and waist high. Yesterday, when sitting upon this throne, a river patrol boat roared up from behind, allowing them a full view of me partially naked sitting there doing my business. I turned to see a soldier standing up in the boat with binoculars, drawing nearer. There was nowhere to hide, so sheepishly I waved. He returned a quick wave back. As the boat continued down river, I shimmied my cargo pants up and hustled back to my tent.

. . .

We pulled rear security for the patrol convoy. Over my rifle sights, I tried to draw a mental map of streets and landmarks, especially alleys that were too narrow for turning around a vehicle. The city was full of trapdoors—dark windows and rooftops perfect for snipers, narrow streets ideal for an ambush, and sidewalks piled high with rubble and trash that made it hard to distinguish IEDs. Along the street curbs sat stagnant ponds of human waste, the result of an unmaintained sewer system.

A volley of small arms fire and heavy return fire reverberated from the city's center throughout the night. Radio transmissions scripted a dismal scene. Fortunately, all was quiet on our street just a few blocks away. The locals remained inside their darkened homes.

[The convoy encounters a group of men in the middle of a card game, and after careful investigation, the convoy moves on. This type of scenario will play out several times while her unit is on its security patrol.]

The pop, whir and whiz of small arms fire brought my mind back to focus. A glowing red tracer round ricocheted off the road ahead of our vehicle. We made a sharp turn, then slowed to a crawl as the infantrymen leapt out of the truck, fanned out across the street and disappeared in the dense palms and vegetation. I pulled my night vision goggles down from my helmet, clicked the safety switch to auto and scanned my sector, waiting for movement or another shot to reveal my target. The infantrymen called this quarter-mile stretch of road near the river's edge "Sniper Alley."

"It's nothin'," one of them finally called out, breaking the silence.

"Yeah, just some bastard that thinks it's the 4th of July or something," said another as they began re-emerging from the foliage.

"You've got our attention now," our driver mumbled. "One more shot and we'll light you up like a Christmas tree."

Iraqi women, outside past curfew to wash the human waste from the gates to their homes, hurry back inside when they spot the Americans.

My finger relaxed from against the trigger. I looked back to get a thumbs up from Nick and saw that he was dripping wet—doused in slushy feces. . . . "Oh shit," I said.

"That's right, I'm covered in human poop," he said, wiping his face with the back of one hand.

"Fucked up sewer!" I shouted over the wind as we picked up speed.

"Fucked up country!" he shouted back.

• • •

As we approached summer's end, fights ignited across the entire platoon. When we were on a mission, we complained; when we were on base, we complained. Our list of things to hate exploded from heat and danger to food, rooms, duty roster, waiting at the phone center, waiting at the washing machines, waiting at the PX, items at the PX, no hot water, broken generators, busted trucks, inept squad leaders, lazy platoon leaders and fat platoon sergeants. Hate spread like wildfire. Had we been the 4077 M*A*S*H, psychiatrist Sidney Freedman would have recommended the whole platoon get together to torch the place for therapy and start over again.

As our camaraderie slowly dissolved, it seemed only a commitment to real soldiering could get us back together, which required true leadership. We needed inspiration, vision, a renewal of pride, and an example of discipline and self-control before we tore each other to pieces.

The lieutenant's leadership plan to raise morale is to have the entire unit watch the film "Gettysburg" and write a self-reflective essay about it. No one is happy about this assignment, and everyone tries to find excuses out of it.

I don't recall much from the movie. I may have been sleeping with my eyes open or I may have been lost in the mental construction of my essay, which would be less about Gettysburg and more about Al Asad. The movie was just a launching pad for a rant that I had to let loose.

I didn't want to cash out in Iraq, but the odds didn't seem to be on my side—or rather, the randomness of death didn't give me much faith in them. Truck drivers had the most dangerous job in Iraq. The roadways were filled with IEDs and our convoys were a large and slow moving target. There was always KIA ("Killed-In-Action") announced during the morning intel briefing. About 50 from the 3d ACR had already died here. Yesterday it was a guy from Florida. Today it would be a guy from Colorado. Tomorrow it could be a gal from Iowa.

Lauren Kay Halloran
(1983–)
U.S. AIR FORCE

A former Air Force public affairs officer, Lauren Kay Halloran served in the West African Republic of Mali and deployed to Afghanistan as part of a Provincial Reconstruction Team working to build governance and development in southeastern Paktia Province. After her discharge, she earned her MFA in creative writing from Emerson College in Boston. Her work has been widely published and has been used in the creation of dance and theater productions. She lives in Boston with her husband, a fellow veteran-writer; two cats; and hundreds of books. The following is from her memoir-in-progress, *The Fine Art of Camouflage*. It first appeared in the December 2016 issue of *Drunken Boat*.

Inheritance of War

I don't remember much from the time Mom was at war. I was seven years old; the memories blur into a fuzzy background, punctuated by snapshot images of clarity. I know my world expanded that winter. I learned new words like "Desert Storm," "Saddam Hussein," and "Hate." Dad pointed out Saudi Arabia on our office globe. Mom was there, inside the little star that represented the capital of Riyadh. It didn't look very far away.

I remember cheese quesadillas—"cheese pies," I called them—cooked in the microwave. A mom from school served them to us while we waited at her house for Dad to pick us up after work.

I remember crying in bed every night after Mom's tape-recorded voice finished reading a bedtime story, and my sister—a more silent griever—shushing me from across our shared bedroom. I saw the school counselor for a few weeks. I don't recall her name or what she looked like, or even what we talked about, but I remember staring out her window at the snow-crusted ground. My classmates were at recess, throwing snowballs, having fun.

Despite our proximity to multiple military bases outside Seattle, we were the only local kids who had a parent deployed. Our neighbors took turns babysitting and delivering meals. A yellow ribbon hugged the big maple tree in front of our elementary school. When she returned, Mom would cut the ribbon off to a whooping chorus of cheers from our classmates. But while she was gone it hung there, through rain and wind and snow. I saw the ribbon every day, and I hated it.

I didn't learn until years later that the deployment orders had been for an undetermined length of up to two years. I didn't know that because of the threat of chemical weapons and the size of Mom's medical unit—which made them an appealing target—it was thought to be a suicide mission. In her phone calls and letters home, Mom didn't discuss her terror at the nightly air raids, or her aching loneliness, or her doubts about her ability to handle combat. I didn't know she carried trauma with her every day, even after she returned home. All I ever saw was her strength.

• • •

The elementary school, my Girl Scout troop, and Mom's college roommate showed up at McChord Air Force Base on the morning of March 12, the date my mother returned.

The Tacoma, Washington, military base, near the Army hospital where Mom's unit worked, was overrun with hundreds of family members, local residents, community leaders, and media. We stood behind a chain link fence, watching the empty runway. My sister and I held homemade signs. My brother, just two years old, didn't understand where Mommy had been or why; he just knew today was the day she was coming home. He coiled his tiny hands around the fence and rocked back and forth, back and forth, eyes glued to the tarmac.

His expectant face, framed by a puffy black and red jacket, became a popular clip on local news segments.

I don't know how long we waited before we heard the drone of an approaching aircraft. The crowd hushed, twisted heads frantically and shielded eyes from the sun, pointed at a dark speck on the horizon, then erupted into a cacophony of cheers. The dark speck got bigger and turned into a plane that drifted slowly across the landscape. As it inched closer, the crowd grew wild. We screamed and shook the fence. My dad scooped up my brother. Someone, a grandparent maybe, grabbed my hand. Reporters yelled into their microphones. We were supposed to stay behind the fence, but when the plane landed and the first camouflaged figure emerged, we stampeded onto the runway. All I could see was legs. Jeans and khakis and sweats, then a trickle of camouflage moving upstream, then a pair of legs that stopped and dropped a bag and bent and hugged and cried, then I was in her arms and nuzzling my face into her permed curls and the world was whole again.

• • •

By the time I joined the Air Force in 2006, deployments were predictable. So were homecomings. At Hurlburt Field, an Air Force Special Operations base on the Florida panhandle and one of the main suppliers of pilots and Special Forces to Iraq and Afghanistan, the cycle had clockwork regularity. Once a month, a contracted aircraft took hundreds of troops away. Once a month, an aircraft brought hundreds back. Because of the consistency, or perhaps in spite of it, the base turned each homecoming into a fanfare event.

The public affairs office where I worked played a prominent role in the planning of "Operation Homecoming." We invited local and regional media and always had takers. This was a military town, and everyone loved a feel-good story, especially when the date fell near a holiday. (Of course, for every planeload that came home in time for Christmas another left just before, but we focused on the positive.) Local civic leaders were invited, too. Mayors, school administrators, presidents of chambers of commerce, and business owners formed a receiving line with base leadership to shake hands with each returning hero.

The events were always the same. The sun was up or down, or somewhere in between. We gathered in the east hangar or the west. Patriotic music played on a loop. A female reporter wore too much makeup, but drew approving looks from the men in the audience. There were American flags and yellow ribbons and a huge crowd of family and friends. Everyone looked anxious. Children held hand-painted signs: "WELCOME HOME DADDY!" "WE MISSED YOU MOMMY!" Some sat on cement barricades that flanked the walkway to the flightline. Others ran giggling through the throng. A few slept in parents' arms.

There were babies who'd never met their fathers, always a media hit. One of my public affairs colleagues or I would approach the new mother and ask her permission to be photographed, videotaped or interviewed. If she agreed, we gave her the security guidelines: keep locations and timelines general (Southwest Asia, six months); it's okay to talk about deployments being difficult, but don't dwell on the negative—we're here to celebrate.

Some wives and girlfriends dressed up. They wore short skirts, even in December, when temperatures dipped into the 20s and wind rattled through the gaping hangar. Once, a woman wore a trench coat which appeared to have nothing beneath. Others wore pajamas, no hairspray or makeup; they had done this many times before. Eventually, routine trumps excitement. But you never get used to the waiting.

It was always too hot or too cold. After 24 hours of transit from the Middle East, layovers and customs proceedings, often a Gulf Coast storm, the flight was never on time. Inside the hangar, the patriotic loop started over. The pretty reporter's lipstick smudged. A baby cried. A girlfriend chewed nervously on her fingernails. Her boyfriend would propose when he got off the plane—we would feature a photo on the front page of the base newspaper—but she didn't know that yet. Flags twitched. Signs drooped under tired arms. Then an announcement: "The plane is five minutes out!" and the crowd was rejuvenated. Signs snapped to attention. City and base leaders took their places along the center aisle. The media angled their cameras at the empty runway. Parents woke sleeping children and joined the growing mob straining at the barricades.

I liked to stand near the back. From there, I could see the media, make sure their cameras didn't pan to the other end of the flightline where our covert Special Operations aircraft were parked. I could pick out familiar faces in the crowd of returning airmen and dart in for a quick, tired hug. I could watch clusters of families and friends point and squeal and jump up and down and cry, and kids run into a pair of open, camouflaged arms.

I attended almost every homecoming at Hurlburt Field. Initially, I went because it was my job. Since the events were often outside normal duty hours, we rotated assigned personnel, but I quickly started volunteering to help on my days off. I genuinely enjoyed the ceremonies. In contrast to the stress and frustration of my daily job and the constant mass media flow of bad news from the war zone, these little happy endings were refreshing. For a few hours, no one had to worry about what happened yesterday or last week, or what could happen tomorrow or the next day. It didn't matter if the sun was up or down, if it was hot or cold. The world zoomed in on the east hangar or the west, and that hangar was full of joy.

Mostly I went because every homecoming reminded me of my mom.

• • •

I knew my turn would come eventually. Deployments were the reality of military service in the post-9/11 era. I wanted to go; I wouldn't feel like I was fulfilling my duty otherwise. I didn't think about the possibility of not coming home—the idea was too vague, too surreal, too terrifying—but I dreamed about my homecoming. I had been in the crowd and on the fringes, and someday I would be on the plane. I would hear people cheering as the front door creaked open and the Florida sunlight or moonlight spilled into the cabin. It would take forever to unload. My family would grow impatient, like thousands of families before: Where is she? Everyone looks the same! What if she's not there? Then I would make my way out the door, down the stairs, and onto the tarmac to be funneled through the outstretched hands of the base commanders and city leadership. The scene would probably be overwhelming, a sea of arms like the legs in my memory. But it would be heartwarming to get such a reception. Commanders I'd worked with would pat me on the back, maybe even offer a hug or a high five. *Welcome back, L-T,* they'd say. *We missed you!* Working my way down the line, I would see my colleagues hovering by the media, and they would grin and wave. The reporters might recognize me from past media escorts and wave, too. Flags and posters would dance past as I reached the main crowd. The shouting, the colors and the patriotic music would build into a bubble of emotions. Then I would see my family at the same time they saw me. It would be just like all the homecomings I'd witnessed. It would be perfect.

• • •

When I flew back from Afghanistan in March 2010—almost exactly nineteen years after my mom came home—I was the only military passenger on my commercial airliner. I had traveled by helicopter from a small Forward Operating Base near the Pakistan border, then left some of my deployed unit at Bagram Air Base, the military's main hub in Afghanistan, where their home units required additional paperwork prior to departure. Others had flown with me to Baltimore-Washington International Airport, where we were herded through a small crowd of USO volunteers whose cheers and unfamiliar faces were as genuine as they were jarring; then through customs, then to separate terminals for separate flights back to wherever home—or home base—might be, barely registering that after nearly a year of living, eating and working together, depending on each other for survival, those jetlagged, bewildered moments might be the last we ever shared.

Most of us made the final leg of the journey alone. When mine ended at the Tampa International Airport, there was no celebration waiting for me. No screaming spectators or clicking flashbulbs, no important hands to shake. The air wasn't filled with patriotic music or glitter blowing off homemade signs. I didn't need to elbow through throngs of camouflage to find who I was looking for.

In the last year, I had seen my family for four days—a brief foray to my hometown outside Seattle after three months at an isolated training base and before my nine-month deployment. We emailed frequently and talked by phone when my work schedule, the twelve-and-a-half-hour time difference, and third world technology allowed. I'd shielded them from much. I didn't talk about the creeping fear that even fifty pounds of body armor couldn't keep away; the local attacks that sent ripples of paranoia through our tiny, vulnerable compound. I didn't mention the frustration and hopelessness that clouded daily operations, each small victory overshadowed by corruption, violence, or bureaucratic red tape. I didn't admit my isolation—even on a base crowded with soldiers, contractors and local Afghan workers. Once, in a phone call, Mom told me it was harder for her having me deployed than when she'd been gone herself. It was the closest I got to crying to my parents.

Six months later I emerged at the Tampa airport. I had been in transit for eight days, including nearly twenty-four hours of straight flight time from Afghanistan to Turkey to Germany to Baltimore, where I had sleepwalked through a few hours' layover. My internal clock was stuck halfway around the world. My head was straining through a thick fog to make sense of the sleek terminal and bright windows, people in civilian clothes, neon restaurant signs, the discordant symphony of music and newscasts and flight updates, the missing weight against my thigh where my pistol should be holstered. I felt like I was on another planet.

Then I saw my family. My six-foot-two brother was easy to spot at the end of the terminal ramp. Next to him was his girlfriend, holding a small American flag, and my parents, straining against the security rope. All my senses zeroed in on them. My mom yelled, "There she is! There's Lauren!" Then I was seven years old and running into her arms, crying into her hair.

And for a moment, the world was perfect.

Tiffany Wilson
(1985–)
U.S. Marine Corps

Tiffany Wilson of Adrian, Michigan, joined the Marine Corps Reserve in 2004. During her time in the Reserve, she earned a bachelor's degree in secondary education from Eastern Michigan University. Upon graduation she volunteered for a deployment to Afghanistan as team leader of a Female Engagement Team (FET).

After her discharge from the Marine Corps in May 2012, she earned a master's degree in professional counseling from Liberty University. Below are excerpts of letters she shared with a blog hosted by the Women Marines Association.

From "Life as a FET 2," posted October 28, 2011

We have had some interesting experiences since I last wrote. We had to go console the family of a village elder that was killed hours prior. It was extremely sad.

I was really nervous. This was the same house [in which] I made bread, so we had been there before and started to establish a relationship with them. We knew the boys really well because we have been to the school many times. But I was afraid they blamed us for his death. It's hard enough to comfort someone after a loss when you're close to them, so trying to say the right thing to someone who is of a different culture, different language, and you only barely know. . . . I thought it was going to be tough. The 11-year-old daughter was the only witness and as soon as she saw us she started spilling the story. It's like she needed to tell it.

• • •

In Afghanistan, this area anyway, they don't have funeral homes, so they have to bury the body right away. And they don't bury them under the ground. We have walked through one of their graveyards and there are people-shaped mounds of rocks and dirt everywhere. They decorate the graves with long sticks with different color pieces of cloth. I know it's hard to picture. The women do not get to go to the burial. So when we arrived at the house to console the family it was just the women there. We went in the house and there were 20 women all dressed in black gathered together sitting on the floor. I have never seen so many women here in the same place. We sat down in front of them and they all crowded around and we did our best to offer condolences. I told them I was sorry for their loss and if there was anything they needed to let us know. My linguist said a prayer from the Koran. The eldest daughter who is in her 20s had tears rolling down her face. I barely knew the guy but seeing the women in so much pain, I had trouble trying not to cry, too. I know, very un-Marine of me. They asked if we would come back, though, so I took that as a good sign.

• • •

Besides that we have been doing a lot of the same. Going out on patrols, going into the homes of the locals, and trying to talk to the women. No matter how much I try to reason with myself it still gets to me that the women, usually the older women more so, don't think their opinion has any value. We asked them if they want to send their daughters to school and they said, "I'm just a woman, it doesn't matter what I think, you should ask my husband." I try to tell them that I care what they think and that it does matter. Just to maybe plant a tiny seed of change in their minds. I'm not expecting to change their culture and really we're not here to do that. We're here to give them a voice, learn their concerns, and do what we can to improve their lives. But it still gets to me.

Today we went back to the home of the man who was killed. I think we had the best conversation we have had so far. It was more real and honest than the women normally get. You see, although they talk to us, you can tell they're always holding back. Today there was no holding back. They said one of their sons was told, "If you go to school we will cut your head off" after we were at the school that very day handing out supplies. How brave is that kid to still go to school! But hearing things like this affects me so much. I can't help it. Is there such a thing as caring too much? The women also said today, "Do you think I want to marry off my 10-year-old daughter, no I do not, but we know we cannot provide for her and feel we have no other choice."

There were fun moments, too. They wanted to know if in America the men have to pay money to the bride's family like they do here to get married. So we tried to explain that in America you meet someone and you fall in love, and then you eventually get married. They were amused at this. They asked if it is the man or woman who falls in love. When we told them both, it was a surprise to them. They asked if I had met someone who I loved yet. I said not yet, hopefully someday. The one woman said, "Don't get married, men are a hassle." They had a lot of questions for us today, which makes it interesting. They asked if it would offend us if they call us "Americans." We told them no, but I'm still trying to figure out why they would think it would be offensive. One of the women tried to give me her baby. No joke. She said *Take him, he will make you happy.*

From "Hello from Afghanistan," posted November 26, 2011

We went out to the front gate of the base and started blowing up balloons and blowing bubbles. And soon enough the kids started coming. At first it was three or four, and then they just started trickling over and we ended up with about twenty. They loved the balloons. We had those really long balloons, so we made them hats. Again, it strikes me that these simple little toys that American kids take for [granted are] something they have never seen before. Kids here aren't really kids in some instances. They work hard, and help take care of the younger kids.

We went yesterday . . . finally . . . and did a VCP (Vehicle Check Point). Which is basically where the Marines and the ANA (Afghan National Army) and the ANP (Afghan National Police) search all the vehicles/donkeys/bicycles/people walking that come through. You're probably thinking, *Donkeys?* But it is very common here to have kids riding around on donkeys. They also use them to carry crops they are harvesting. Sometimes the donkey will be carrying so much stuff you can't even see the donkey, and then there will be a kid sitting on top of it. They don't have horses here that I have seen. Motorbikes are also a HUGE thing here. Most of them don't own a car but they usually have a motorbike. You would be amazed how many people they fit on those things, too. A family of four, three men. . . . It's not unusual.

[At] the checkpoint, the ANP and the ANA do most of the searching, except for the women . . . that's why the FET are there. The ANA and ANP do not have women, or at least it's extremely rare. Out of the seventy-five people that came. . . . There were eight women. Sometimes the insurgents will put things on the women because more times than not there is no woman to search the women. A lot of times if they see a woman in the car or on the bike [the guards] won't even search the men. So you can imagine how useful this can be to insurgents.

The women if they are out are always escorted by a male relative.

And they are usually wearing a burqa or some other sheet-like cloth that covers their entire body. It's not like this in all of Afghanistan. In the cities women walk around by themselves and don't cover everything up. But Helmand Province is the most conservative . . . it has a lot to do with their tribes. Afghan is a tribal society. The Pashtuns that are mostly in Helmand are more conservative. . . .

Yesterday, when the women realized that we're women they lifted up the burqa (they wear clothes under[neath]) and let us see their face and search them. The older women usually don't wear a burqa; they just cover up with a huge scarf that wraps around the entire body, and hide their faces. Many of the women as soon as they realized we were women started talking to us, telling us their medical problems. How do I know, you ask? They say the word doctor a bunch of times. One woman even took my hand and put it on the places on her body that hurt; her head, her chest, and her knee. We didn't have our linguist so there wasn't much we could do. We couldn't tell them anything. I gave one woman my water because she said she had a headache. They don't drink water so a lot of times that is the cause of headaches. I don't know why they assume that we are doctors or can help them medically. They always do, though.

During the vCPs I always try to give the kids something, candy or snacks when they come through. I want to make it seem less intimidating. It has to feel that way, I imagine. Just think if it were you and you were stopped by a bunch of people in uniform with big guns [who said that] you and your belongings have to be searched. It's for their own safety and our safety and they are probably used to it by now, but there's no reason not to make it a little bit better of an experience.

When we are doing these types of things we always get a few different reactions from the men and children. There is the look of shock and the stare without saying anything. It happens often. You can see the surprise on their face when they realize there are women out with the men in uniform. They stare as they are walking. Don't say anything . . . just stare. I'm surprised sometimes they don't hurt their necks. Then there is the man giggling. That's what I like to call it. I'll say "Salaam aleikum" and they will say it back but giggle as they do, because they can't believe I'm a female. Or they will turn to whoever they are with and say something like "It's a girl" and giggle and stare. The ANA and ANP are the same way. The Afghan men seem to be fascinated by us! The women, on the other hand, are very hard to read. They rarely show emotion or let their face show any expressions. You can never really tell what an Afghan woman is thinking.

• • •

"Happy Thanksgiving from Afghanistan," posted November 26, 2011
I'm just getting back from what we call "reset." Female Marines cannot be with an infantry unit for longer than forty-five days at a time. So the FET comes together and does additional training and classes every forty-five days or so. Each of the two women FET teams gave a brief on their projects, activities, and lessons learned from the past forty-five days. It was really good to hear all the different stories and experiences we are all having. Some of the FET Marines are in a more kinetic area, meaning there is more fighting and it's more dangerous.

Others, like myself, aren't.

It seemed like those of us in the less kinetic area are able to interact more with the children and the women. We are building relationships and hopefully "winning hearts and minds." In the other areas it is harder to accomplish those things, so they are finding other ways to contribute. I guess one of the main things we learned this reset was that success is measured not by comparing one team to another but by the improvements we make in our own areas. I think we probably learned more at breakfast, lunch, and dinner sharing stories than during the classes, but it was overall a good experience.

We had our first visit to the base by Afghan women yesterday. It probably doesn't seem that amazing, but this has never happened before. We met them on patrol a few days earlier. One of the women had a big cut over her eye and her mother (probably in her late fifties) came and asked us to help. So we cleaned it up and gave her some [Band-Aids]. Then they show up at the base because it wasn't getting any better. We gave them hygiene classes on brushing teeth, washing hair, and other things along these lines. They were so thankful and sociable. It was so much fun. The older woman told us "May your dust turn into gold," and said we were like daughters. AND ... she let me take a picture with her, which again was a first. She touched the top of our heads as she was leaving ... which doesn't seem like much, but it was definitely a sign of affection. It's little victories like this that make all of it worthwhile. Or walking down the street and hearing kids call out my name, "Aziza, Aziza" (that's my Afghan name). I feel blessed to be here with the opportunity to make a difference.

The school we always visit is suffering from a lack of attendance. Last time we visited, four children were present out of eighty. . . . We have been tasked with finding ways to promote attendance at the schools in our area of operation. No small task considering all these kids are up against. Most of the kids we talk to say they are scared to go to school. Others say it's because of the harvest . . . they have to help their families work in the fields. So it's my mission to get the kids back to school and to show everyone the importance of education. Wish me luck!! We are going to the school soon and handing out new supplies, maybe motivate them to show up at least one day so we can convince them to keep showing up. We had a meeting with the principal and he is a great ally in this fight.

We have a new unit [of Marines] here now and we're trying to win them over. The commanding officer has given us many new tasks. Who would have thought I would come to Afghanistan and be put in charge of assessing and identifying all the schools in the area we're located [in]? It's a good thing education happens to be one of my passions (thank you Madison School teachers for instilling in me the importance of education). They have never had a FET before or worked with females. It's been a challenge to show them our worth, especially in the lower ranks. . . .

I just want to say thank you to all those who read my e-mails and have spread the word. We have already begun receiving hygiene gear to hand out to the women. I got nine packages yesterday . . . six from people I've never even spoken to. One woman told me about her grand-daughter who sold pictures she drew for 25 cents, house to house, to buy toys for the Afghan kids. She raised four dollars . . . amazing. My linguist cried at the generosity of you all.

De Khodai Pu Amman (May you be in the safety of God).

Lori Imsdahl

(1982–)

U.S. ARMY

Lori Imsdahl, born and raised in Minnesota, attended West Point and spent five years in the United States Army. In 2012 she was runner-up for the Melanie Hook Rice Award in Creative Nonfiction at Hollins University, where she completed her MFA in 2013. Her work has appeared in *Emerge Literary Journal*, *Green Briar Review*, and *Slow Trains Literary Journal*. The following is excerpted from her essay "Freak Accidents," originally published in the winter 2015 issue of *O-Dark-Thirty*, the literary journal of the Veterans Writing Project.

Sergeant First Class Rocky Herrera, Sergeant Cory Clark, and Sergeant Bryce Howard died in Jaji Province, Afghanistan, on the morning of August 28, 2007, beside a bridge that they were constructing over a dry streambed.

I was sitting in my Humvee, one hundred meters away from them, when it happened.

Moments later, I saw Sergeant First Class Herrera on the ground. Our medic, Specialist Gary Olund, knelt beside him and felt for a pulse. "He's dead," the medic announced. Then I helped heave Sergeant Clark from a ditch. There was a hole in Clark's head and his body was still warm. And then I watched Corporal Howard gasp for breath and bleed out in the arms of Specialist Olund.

I felt nothing.

I woke up the next morning, expecting to feel something, but again I felt nothing. I felt nothing at the memorial service, either.

They died in Jaji Province, Afghanistan, a farming district on the Pakistani border.

In May 1987, Jaji Province was a place where Osama Bin Laden came to prominence by leading Afghani forces against the Soviet Army. Twenty years later, in August 2007, it was a place with no borders, a place where people trafficked opium and passed across the Pakistani border unimpeded.

I was Third Platoon Leader for 585th Engineer Company, 555th Engineer Brigade from Joint Base Lewis-McChord. In the summer of 2007, my company's mission was to build a Forward Operating Base (FOB) on high ground near the Pakistani border. The Army believed that the soldiers who lived at that FOB could assert control and bring stability to Jaji Province.

In July 2007, we convoyed to the area from Logar Province where we had begun construction of FOB Shank in April. We drove over miles of rutted roads. The landscape of undulating woods and farmland was strangely idyllic. Our convoy passed streams, fields of flowers, mud buildings, and plots of wheat and corn. We observed forlorn goats tied to trees and wild dogs panting in the summer heat.

A few kilometers from the area where we would establish the base, we came over a hill and entered a field of marijuana. The field was larger than a football stadium and the plants were six feet tall. The musky smell of cannabis seeped into my vehicle through the gunner's hatch. After the marijuana plot, we crossed a barren field, a dry streambed, and a local village. Then we crested another hill and arrived at the place we'd call home for the next four months.

The area was on the edge of a cliff, and Pakistan was the land-mass on the other side of it. The topography changed at that cliff, going from undulating woods and farmland to miles of mountains, desert, and desolation.

After we parked our vehicles, I stood in the dirt and stared out at Pakistan. One of my soldiers operated a grader, leveling the place where we'd live while constructing the outpost. The Army had attached an infantry platoon to 585th Engineer Company and the infantry had come just ahead of us and erected a perimeter. They were still living out of their vehicles.

I saw their platoon leader talking to First Sergeant Meyer and I walked over to introduce myself. I can't recall this lieutenant's name but I'll never forget the look of anguish on his face, later, when the helicopters were landing to pick up the injured and the dead. His job was to provide security, but three soldiers had died on his watch.

After the lieutenant and I exchanged hellos, I continued to look at Pakistan.

This is the edge of the world, I thought. This is the furthest I can get from home. It was a feeling both profoundly thrilling and profoundly sad. Now that I've traveled more, I'm aware of how little I've seen. But I still wonder if I'll ever stand at the edge of the world and feel that far from home again.

On the morning of August 28, 2007, I woke up at around six a.m. and coaxed myself out of my sleeping bag. That morning, I was running a logistical convoy to FOB Shank to drop off soldiers and supplies. Including myself, there would be nineteen soldiers in the convoy.

First I changed into a tan T-shirt and the top and bottom of an Army Combat Uniform. Then I sat on my cot and put on wool socks and combat boots. I wound the laces around the backside of the boot and tucked the ends inside the shoe as my squad leader had taught me to do six years ago, during Basic Training.

Then I put on a patrol cap. Afterwards, I gathered my Kevlar helmet, gloves, sunglasses, and flak vest. I stopped to ensure that my neck, groin, and shoulder protectors were attached to the vest. I also gathered my M16 rifle and an assault pack with a notebook, toothbrush, and a change of clothing. Then I walked outside.

A line of vehicles was staged in front of my tent in marching order: senior squad leader's vehicle, platoon sergeant's vehicle, my vehicle, and heavy vehicles interspersed with Humvees. The sun was starting to rise and I could see pink smears across the sky. I put my gear into the passenger seat of my Humvee, then walked to the mess hall for a cup of coffee. On the way inside, Sergeant Howard intercepted me. "Ma'am, this is for Staff Sergeant Jimenez," he said, handing me a white, three-ring binder to give to my platoon sergeant. Sergeant Howard was a surveyor in Support Platoon and the binder was full of measurements he'd taken of the hill on which we were going to build the FOB.

"Thanks," I said and took the binder. I gave Sergeant Howard a passing glance. He was young and there was a rugged attractiveness to his face. There were bags beneath his eyes. He looks tired, I thought. And four hours later, he was dead.

On the morning of August 28, 2007, our convoy was scheduled to leave at around seven or eight a.m. However, at the last minute, the company commander instructed me to bring along additional supplies to FOB Shank—several light sets and a generator. The light sets and generator were too heavy to be lifted manually, so a forklift operator would need to load them on the back of an M870 trailer. At first it seemed like a quick task, but then everything went wrong.

First, our supply sergeant couldn't locate one of the light sets.

Then it was determined that our forklift had mechanical problems. A functional forklift was located, but before the operator could get to work, soldiers needed to shift around the equipment on the back of the M870 trailer to make room for the light sets and generator.

As a result, we departed for FOB Shank later than expected. I think about that a lot. About chance, luck, and fate. About freak accidents. About how we wouldn't have been near the bridge if we'd left earlier. About how we were the first responders to the scene because we departed late.

Around nine or ten a.m. on August 28, 2007, our convoy drove out of the COP, past two soldiers with M240Bs manning the entry control point.

We wound around barriers that were arranged in a serpentine formation to slow incoming traffic. Then we headed downhill, the roads rutted and edged with weeds. We drove through the village, the streets lined with mud buildings. Barefoot men wearing salwar kameezes sat cross-legged outside of storefronts besides boxes of produce, bottles of soda, and trinkets. A few children frolicked in the streets.

Women were absent, as they usually were, in every village and encounter.

Through the village, we drove into the barren field and across the dry streambed that was prone to flooding in the winter. That was where we saw Support Platoon building the bridge. They'd erected a perimeter of up-armored vehicles around their job site and soldiers with automatic weapons were standing in turrets and pulling security. Other soldiers were building the bridge. Everyone was wearing a flak vest.

Sergeant First Class Herrera, Support Platoon Sergeant, was standing near the road, supervising soldiers. He was a stocky fellow with white hair and a rosy complexion. In the final moments of his life, Herrera turned to watch our convoy and raised his arm to wave. Some of the soldiers in my convoy waved back. But we kept driving.

I was looking straight ahead at the rutted road when I heard the explosion. It rocked the ground. The lead vehicle in our convoy came to a halt and the other vehicles followed suit. And then it was silent.

In the moment after the explosion, I thought, *I don't know what the hell that was*. And then, *I don't want to deal with this right now*. But I knew I had to deal with it, whatever it was, and I had to deal with it now. Seconds after this realization, my driver, Sergeant Adriel Moreno—who was on the bridge side of our vehicle—swiveled toward me. Wide-eyed, he picked up the hand microphone and said into the radio, "I see casualties."

A moment later, we saw the medic running out of his vehicle and toward the bridge.

I took the hand microphone from Sergeant Moreno. "Gunners, stay with your vehicles," I said. Then Sergeant Moreno and I got out of our vehicle and started running, too.

The first thing I saw when I stepped out of my Humvee was a foot. It was not one of my soldiers? This foot was brown, dusty, calloused, and wedged inside a gray sandal.

The style of sandal was familiar. I'd seen other Afghan men wear it. The foot was severed at the ankle. As I ran toward the bridge, I noticed hundreds of shards of skin scattered across the ground like confetti. The entire job site was permeated with the smell of blood. It reminded me of tampons, but different. This smell was more than blood. It was damp, fishy, fecal.

The next thing I saw was Sergeant First Class Herrera. When I'd seen him a few seconds earlier from inside my Humvee he'd been supervising soldiers. The blast had thrown him twenty feet away, and he was lying on his back in the dirt.

Herrera, forty-three, was a gentle, soft-spoken leader from Salt Lake City. After he died, a soldier from Support Platoon characterized him as "that rare individual you meet and trust five minutes later." Herrera had a wife named Traci, four children, and two grandchildren. Traci's name was tattooed across his chest.

The medic was kneeling beside Herrera. First, he checked for responsiveness. "Can you hear me?" he yelled, shaking Herrera's shoulder. Herrera was unresponsive. Next, the medic pushed on the back of Herrera's neck, raising his chin and opening his airway. He checked for airflow by placing his ear close to Herrera's nose and mouth. He couldn't detect any breathing. He traced the contours of Herrera's body, sliding his fingers beneath the man's back and legs. There was no pulse and he felt dampness. He discovered that shrapnel had penetrated Herrera's body. Brain matter was dripping into the dirt. The medic got to his feet and faced me. There were more pressing matters to attend to. "He's dead," he said. And he took off running, again.

Instinctively, I headed to the hub of activity: a ditch near the bridge. That's when I encountered Staff Sergeant Jimenez. Jimenez was staring into the ditch and moaning. Another soldier, Sergeant Bubba Pickren, was doing the same. I stood next to them and peered down. The ditch was five feet deep, and Sergeant Clark was lying at the bottom of it.

For weeks before the incident, Sergeant Clark told members of Support Platoon about a recurring nightmare: he would be blown up by the enemy and die from a head wound. Sadly, on August 28, 2007, sometime after nine a.m., this is exactly what would happen. Twenty-five-year-old Clark had a wife named Monica and four children younger than six. He came from Plant City, Florida, where he'd joined the Army a few months before September 11th to escape his job in the freezer warehouse of a Food Lion. After his death, Clark's mother, Wrenita Codrington, told the *Military Times* that Clark had told her he'd "rather get a little dirty than a lot cold all the time." Clark's dream was to go to culinary school and open a restaurant with Monica. He had last tried to contact her on August 26, 2007, but she had not been at home, and he had left a voice mail telling her that he loved her.

After I saw Clark's body, I lowered myself into the ditch and knelt beside him. There was no need for me to run through the steps of evaluating a casualty as the medic had done with Sergeant First Class Herrera. There was a large hole in Clark's temple and his brain was visible. It was clear he'd died on impact. "We need to get him out of here," I yelled to Jimenez and Pickren. "Help me lift him."

Jimenez slid into the ditch. I grabbed Clark's legs and Jimenez grabbed his torso. Pickren reached down and took hold of Clark's head and shoulders. "Lift," I commanded. We lifted. Because of their strength, Jimenez and Pickren did the majority of the work. I may have lifted thirty pounds of Clark's weight. I'd never touched a dead body before, and Clark's legs were still soft and limp and warm.

We got him out of the ditch. Then I scrambled out of it, heard yelling, and turned to my left. The medic was kneeling next to Sergeant Howard.

Howard, twenty-four, was a snowboard and motorcycle enthusiast from Washington State. He'd joined the Army in 2002 and had served another tour in Iraq. He had a wife named Amber and two sons named Caleb and Ryan. He was mathematically gifted and hoped to become a mechanical engineer after the Army.

Later, I was informed that Howard died of a sucking chest wound. Jimenez told me that after he exited the ditch, he knelt next to Howard and the medic and tried to ask Howard a question. Howard tried to respond to Jimenez, but no words came out of his mouth, only blood.

The medic managed to open Howard's flak vest and unzip the blouse of his Army Combat Uniform. The only thing standing between the medic and Howard's skin was a tan T-shirt. "I need a scissors. I need a scissors. I need a scissors," the medic said.

I was acting, still, a player in a video game. "Who has a scissors?" I yelled to everyone in earshot. Specialist Tanya Vitacolonna, our only female gunner, was standing in the turret of her Humvee. She swiveled to face me.

"I have scissors, ma'am," she said, reaching down to unclip them from her flak vest. She threw them to the medic and he started cutting off Howard's T-shirt.

That's when I thought: *What the fuck are you doing? You're the fucking convoy commander. Your job is to be on the radio.* I ran back to my vehicle. Along the way, I surveyed the perimeter. I noted that there were holes in it. I ran up to one of my convoy's Humvees. The gunner was still inside as ordered. "Move your vehicle over there and man the area between those two trees," I said, pointing. I ran up to a second vehicle and a third vehicle and told the gunners inside where to move and what their field of fire should be.

Again, I'm not sure how much time had elapsed since the explosion. Looking back, I'm sure that it was no more than five to ten minutes, but at the time that was difficult to gauge. I thought that maybe someone had remotely detonated an improvised explosive device or that a soldier from Support Platoon had stepped on a pressure-triggered mine. I still hadn't figured out that the foot I'd encountered was the foot of a suicide bomber.

I don't know personal details about the man who killed our soldiers: his name, how old he was, where he lived, who his parents were, or what he did for a living. All I know is that he strapped on a suicide bomb vest and convinced two local girls to accompany him to the bridge site. He walked behind them, hunched over, trying to conceal himself.

In their sworn statements, several members of Support Platoon noted that they saw the girls standing beneath some trees. The soldiers didn't think that was unusual; many children came to observe construction, bringing along animals and infant siblings. But that day, the area was noticeably devoid of children. Besides the two girls, no one had come to watch, and the soldiers did not see the man behind them.

But the girls suspected something, or maybe the suicide bomber gave them a warning. Either way, they suddenly ran, shrieking, into a scrubby field that, moments later, we would use as a landing zone for a medical evacuation helicopter.

In his sworn statement, Sergeant Chris Taylor wrote that he saw the two girls running into the field, and a man behind them, that he hadn't noticed before, clearing the trees and entering the job site. It happened quickly. Sergeant Taylor raised his weapon, but before he could shoot he was knocked over by the blast.

After ensuring that the perimeter was secure, I threw open the door of my Humvee and grabbed the hand microphone. "Roughneck TOC, Roughneck TOC, this is Roughneck 3–6, over." The company communications guy, Specialist James Bartron, responded.

"Roughneck 3–6, Roughneck 3–6, this is Roughneck TOC, over."

"Roughneck TOC, we have two casualties at the bridge site."

I could hear rustling in the background. I expected to hear the commander's voice, but it was the voice of Lieutenant Grayson Pranin. I told Pranin the names of the two dead soldiers, one of whom was his platoon sergeant. I told him that Howard was possibly dead, too.

"What is the status of the rest of the platoon?" Pranin wanted to know.

I couldn't tell him. I'd only encountered the bodies of Herrera, Clark, and Howard. I hadn't seen anyone else. "I'll find out," I said.

I grabbed the notebook from my assault pack and ran back to the bridge. Staff Sergeant Jimenez was establishing a casualty collection point in an open field near the bridge. Soldiers from my convoy were transporting injured members of Support Platoon to the casualty collection point on stretchers or by fireman's carry. Some of the injured were able to walk on their own. "Sergeant Howard just died," someone informed me.

Every time I encountered an injured soldier, I wrote his name in my notebook and jotted notes next to it. After collecting data, I returned to the radio. "There are twelve injured," I told Pranin. I told him their names and type of injury. I told him everything I knew.

"We've called in a helicopter," Pranin said. He told me the estimated time of arrival. Then he asked me to switch to the helicopter's radio frequency and give the soldiers on board a better description of what I was seeing.

After I spoke to the soldiers on the helicopter, I stepped away from the radio. One of my soldiers approached and handed me a purple smoke grenade. I carried it to Staff Sergeant Jimenez at the casualty collection point.

On the way to Jimenez, I passed the lieutenant from Arkansas. He was sitting cross-legged in the dirt, talking with someone on a radio. I'm not sure when he'd arrived. I also noticed that First Sergeant Meyer had shown up. First Sergeant Meyer stood solemnly over Sergeant First Class Herrera's body, mouthing the words to a prayer and rendering a salute. The men had grown up together in the Army and had met one another as young privates.

Someone in the Tactical Operations Center told me that after I radioed in about the two casualties, the commander had dropped to his knees and began moaning. First Sergeant Meyer had run past the commander and outside, grabbed the nearest soldier and told him, "Take me to the bridge."

The soldier and First Sergeant Meyer threw on their flak vests, jumped into the nearest Humvee, and raced downhill without the commander. They wound their way through the village, sped across the barren field, roared over the dry streambed, and reached the bridge site. This makes me believe that only a few minutes elapsed between the explosion and the time the helicopter arrived. However, it still felt like hours.

I reached Staff Sergeant Jimenez. He was standing at the casualty collection point surrounded by the injured. The bodies of Herrera, Clark, and Howard were nearby. Jimenez's combat boots were covered in blood. I handed him the purple smoke grenade. "The helicopter will be here in a few minutes," I told him. "They told me there are going to be two: one for the injured and one for the dead."

"OK," Jimenez said. He took the smoke grenade from my hands. I watched him pull the pin. Purple smoke swirled up and over the tree line, alerting the helicopter of our location.

Seven or eight minutes after Staff Sergeant Jimenez pulled the pin on the purple smoke grenade, the first helicopter arrived, picked up the injured soldiers, and took them to a hospital at Kandahar Airfield. Two or three minutes later, the second helicopter picked up Howard, Herrera, and Clark.

The helicopters lifted off with a roar of their blades, creating a cloud of dust. And then it was just members of my convoy, First Sergeant Meyer, the lieutenant from Arkansas, and the soldiers from Support Platoon who weren't dead or injured.

First Sergeant Meyer gathered the soldiers who were not manning the perimeter around him. He was a grizzled man who harkened from a generation where women were a rarity in the armed forces and noncommissioned officers could physically abuse a private for not complying with orders. Some soldiers in 585th Engineer Company found him intimidating, unflinching, and archaic, but none of that seemed to matter now, in an open field by a bridge in eastern Afghanistan.

"You all did the best you could," First Sergeant Meyer told us. "Now it's time to go back to the COP. Everyone get inside your vehicles. I'll bring up the rear."

We got back into our vehicles. I got on the radio and told the gunners to stay low in their turrets. We'd barely crossed the dry streambed when someone I didn't recognize came on the radio. "Roughneck 3–6, Roughneck 3–6, this is Crazyhorse 18, over."

"Crazyhorse 18, Crazyhorse 18, this is Roughneck 3–6, over."

"Roughneck 3–6, would you like us to shadow your convoy, over?"

I turned to my driver for help. Sergeant Moreno was in his early thirties and had deployed multiple times.

"Who's Crazyhorse 18?" I asked him. "And why are they shadowing us?"

"It's an Apache helicopter," Sergeant Moreno said. "They want to know if we want them to pull security for us while we convoy up the hill."

The AH-64 Apache is an attack helicopter with a nose-mounted sensor for target acquisition and night vision systems. It's armed with an M230 chain gun carried beneath the aircraft's forward fuselage. It has four weapons systems, typically a mixture of AGM-114 Hellfire missiles and Hydra 70 rocket pods. I got back on the radio.

"Crazyhorse 18, this is Roughneck 3–6. That's an affirmative. Please shadow us until we reach our COP."

We headed uphill slowly, dismally, while the Apache helicopter hovered overhead, silhouetted against the mid-morning sun.

After their memorial ceremony, I kept on waiting to feel something, some validation that I was not a sociopath. It's been seven years, and I still haven't felt anything. And, in the first five years after the incident, I only told their story four times.

The first time I told their story was in a sworn statement on the day it happened.

The second time was in an e-mail to my father. It was a few days after the incident. I wasn't sure if he'd already heard the news through the Family Readiness Group, but I wanted him to hear it from me, also. In the future, when I was depressed, my father would sometimes mention their story and ask me if I was suffering from post-traumatic stress disorder, and I would tell him "No" or "Nothing's changed."

The third time was to Michael Oktavec in Bagram, Afghanistan.

It was October 2007 and Michael was a man I'd loved a little at West Point. I hadn't seen Michael since our graduation, and while I told Michael their story, I floated outside of myself, remembering a time at West Point when I'd sprained my ankle. Michael had told me to stay put that day, and he'd returned with ice cubes wrapped in paper napkins from the mess hall. And I recalled the feel of those napkins when they were applied to the place where it hurt.

The fourth time I told their story was to my sister in Old Town, San Diego. It was March 2008 and we were drinking tequila at El Agave on San Diego Avenue, and I only told her because I was drunk. I was so drunk I barely remember her reaction. After El Agave, the two of us walked to our car, rolled open the windows, and sprawled across the seats. And we slept until we were sober.

Sometimes, I tell myself that my feelings are simply dormant. They'll surface when I'm thirty-seven or fifty-two or eighty-six. They'll surface, and they'll debilitate me, but it will be okay, because then at least I'll know I'm not defective.

Other times, I resign myself to the idea that they don't exist. Because I remember moments before I went to Afghanistan when I felt no emotion, or was unable to express the emotion I felt.

Maybe it's genetic; even from a young age, I was less emotionally expressive than my sisters. The human narrative inherent in playing house and dolls bored me. I preferred riding my bike and climbing trees.

Maybe it's environmental. I come from a family of seven. It was imperative to differentiate myself, to have an identity. My identity was the Tough One and I demonstrated it repeatedly, like the time in elementary school when my younger sister and I crashed our bikes. My abrasion was large and littered with gravel. Hers was only a scratch. I still recall her sitting in the bathtub, screaming, as my mother ran the faucet. My leg hurt, but I told myself I wouldn't cry. I had to be the Tough One. So I didn't.

And I won't.

Emotions aside, the incident did leave me with a strong conviction. Afterward, I told my dad that I didn't believe in freak accidents anymore. "When it's your time to go, it's your time to go," I told him.

I came to this conviction after analyzing every moment between the explosion and when the helicopter arrived.

Even though there was chaos at the job site, I had also detected a strange calm. I had the distinct impression that the dead were looking down at us, calmly surveying the scene, and that they were enlightened.

They were not like us anymore, who, at the time, were caught up in the moment and seeing everything in tunnel vision. They could see the big picture about everything—about racism, sexism, classism, war, and all the other issues affecting society. Everything they had been ignorant about was clear. Death did not equate to hell and punishment. Rather, it was an experience of love, forgiveness, and enlightenment.

After detecting this strange calm at the job site, I realized I wasn't scared to die anymore, because nothing about the experience seemed terrible to me. Though I wasn't scared to die, I wanted to believe that death was not in my near future, for I felt that I still had things to accomplish: words to write, issues to be an activist about, and children to raise. But I understood that Herrera, Howard, and Clark must have felt that they still had things left to accomplish, too. For this reason, I came to believe that whether or not I lived was not my prerogative, but the prerogative of something bigger than me. My time to die would come when my purpose had been served, whether or not I knew it had been served.

Thus my conviction: there are no freak accidents.

I'm sure that most would argue that this conviction was the stress response of a young lieutenant. A young lieutenant trying to make sense of the horror she saw in Afghanistan and not wanting to comprehend that this horror could just as easily have befallen her. I've analyzed the merits of my conviction and I understand that my reasons for believing it are based on my feelings, intuition, and personal experience rather than scientific evidence.

Scientific evidence notwithstanding, I still hold the conviction today.

Teresa Fazio
(1980–)
U.S. MARINE CORPS

Teresa Fazio, a Marine Corps lieutenant from 2002 to 2006, deployed once to Iraq. Her writing has been published in the *New York Times*,

Task and Purpose, Vassar Quarterly, Penthouse, and *Consequence Magazine.* Her awards include *Consequence Magazine*'s 2015 Fiction Prize and Words After War's 2015 Submission Contest, and her manuscript *Unbecoming* was a finalist in the 2015 Autumn House Press Nonfiction Contest. She was in residency at Yaddo in spring 2015 and is a current MFA student in the Bennington Writing Seminars. She works in technology commercialization and splits her time between Boston and New York. The following is an original essay submitted for inclusion in this collection.

Brothers

CAMP TAQADDUM, IRAQ, 2004

July Fourth weekend, after the Iraqis assumed their own government, everything went to shit. The heat topped 130. Mortars sliced sky, and explosions dug out buried cable. Then our giant switchboard went tits-up. Half my responsibility was that giant switchboard; the other half was repairing the fiber optic network that kept getting cut. Forget any holiday fireworks; I wanted to go home.

We were soft, according to Marine standards. We had flush toilets in trailers on this base; there were even showers. Fourth of July, we could even take two near-beers from the chow hall, though they were no replacement for a real buzz, which I wanted badly. While Marines fought and died outside the wire, my platoon only had to get the connectivity situation straightened out—and even that, as their platoon commander, I was fucking up.

My staff sergeant wanted the cables run one way. My operations officer, who supervised us both, wanted something different. Both were older than me, and opinionated. Instead of brokering real peace between them, I told them both yes to please them. Until my lack of decisiveness, my eagerness to please, squeezed me out of decision making altogether. They wound up arguing with each other; nothing I said pacified them.

I was not particularly assertive, a twenty-three-year-old devil pup nine years before *Lean In.* I stepped out of network-planning conflicts and accommodated the wishes of other officers around me, "going along to get along." They'd been at this war thing longer than I had. The approval I enjoyed for "being a good listener," plus the ease of not having to think too hard, was addictive. I consciously traded what little power I had in order to seem more likable. Of this I felt ashamed, but it made my life easier.

I masked my shame with furious overwork. Workaholism was part of my armor; the reaction came up with a metallic *shink*, like my brothers' comic-book superheroes, or the football helmets we'd donned at the Basic School before battering each other with pugil sticks. The tactic won me increased approval. When something exploded, we kept our heads down, counted each other quick. If nothing exploded, we just worked harder 'til something did. My little legs churned as I trotted across our gravel compound, giving the company commander our reports. I could be a cartoon scampering across a lunchbox; I looked like Harry Potter in camo.

Fixing our broken gear took two full days that early July. Hashimoto, my sole switchboard tech, tried not to drip sweat into the fragile electronic cards he soldered together. In the maintenance bay, more Marines spliced fiber optic cable cut by mortars. The staff sergeant and I swigged near-beers on the steps of a trailer, waiting for a borrowed forklift that arrived at two in the morning. We jury-rigged everything: the switchboard, the sand-clogged generators, the broken air conditioners. Eventually the Marines got the telephone and data networks back up.

We all needed a break from the stress of decisions and electrons and photons that refused to go through. So, in true Marine fashion, we held classes in beating the crap out of each other. Martial arts helped the troops' scores for promotion. And stuck on a base, unable to shoot back against mortars, we needed to do something warlike in order to feel like real Marines.

When I taught martial arts classes, I did speak up. And our Marines listened, spreading out across an eighth-acre sand pit. We warmed up to earsplitting whistle blasts. While I demonstrated ground-fighting moves, I felt sand work its way down my shorts, and thought of nothing but the class. I needed to tire them—and myself—out.

So we grunted and punched and kicked as the Predators droned overhead. We did bull-in-the-ring drills, where one person took turns fighting everybody, because—if ever we needed this—the enemy wouldn't pair up according to size.

During the monotone of knife strikes and punches and timing bouts of wrestling, I sometimes looked up at the star-pricked sky. Our Land of the Free was eight thousand miles away. I wanted to teleport up and away. Instead, I taught men to throw each other's solid weight. I only came up to their shoulders, but my low center of gravity worked to my advantage. They orbited me, watching, learning.

And in the moments that weren't bogged in the slow-time of attacks or repairs, they could afford to be kids again. The Marines continued their wrestling carnival after we shut off the floodlight. They clowned in their tents, wrapped legs around necks, body-slammed each other on cots. One busted a cauliflower ear on the wooden deck. Marines hung off Dyjak, our maintenance platoon's Polish giant. He laughed, still able to move. He could carry refrigerator-sized air conditioners a hundred yards across our compound. In a slight Polish accent he called me ma'am. Someone snaps a picture of the two of us flexing our biceps. I'm a foot shorter, a hundred pounds lighter: the dwarf.

My Marines reminded me of my brothers and their friends, of the roving packs of kids at the lightly supervised day camps and after-school programs of my suburban childhood. I could play and rest with them.

A buddy sent me a skateboard, and I spent evenings trying to ollie on a piece of plywood. Two of our Marines rode unicycles. We recited scenes from *Homestar Runner*, the data platoon's favorite web comic, and acted in the radio sergeant's video parodies of Budweiser commercials. Hashimoto danced, raving with Twizzlers up his nose. Was my youth or my rank or my gender the key to my entrée, or the fact that I didn't have a need to prove my brass balls like some males felt they did?

I may have indulged them too much. I pretended not to notice the porn rife on flash drives, instead focusing on the spreadsheets also saved there. When the maintenance Marines taped up Playboy and Maxim girls, I joked about getting my own corner for David Duchovny and Heath Ledger. I have three younger brothers in real life; in Iraq, it felt like I had over thirty.

One of the lance corporals had a birthday that summer, after we got the switchboard back up. Our wire platoon finagled a chocolate fudge cake from the chow hall. They smeared icing on the birthday boy's cheeks: streaks of war paint. In the dark, they knifed open green chemlights, and sprayed each other with neon, laughing.

Until the next round of fireworks, we were safe.

Sylvia Bowersox
(1965–)
U.S. Army

Sylvia Bowersox first deployed to Iraq in 2003–2004 as a broadcast journalist with the 101st Airborne Division in Mosul. Her assignments took her around the country, but much of her time was spent in Baghdad, at Coalition Provisional Authority headquarters. She deployed twice more to Iraq as a press officer assigned to the U.S. Embassy Baghdad public affairs office, and later to the Special Investigator General for Iraq (SIGIR). She holds a BA in English Literature from San Francisco State University and a master's degree in creative writing from California State University, Chico, where she lives with her veteran husband and her black Labrador service dog, Timothy. The essay below was originally published in *O-Dark-Thirty*, the literary journal of the Veterans Writing Project.

This War Can't Be All Bad

This war can't be all bad. We sing karaoke on Mondays and Wednesdays and sit by the pool behind Saddam's Presidential Palace after work and smoke cigarettes. By midnight we are watching others smoke cigarettes and drink and jump off the high dive naked. Jokes that any teenage boy would roll his eyes at explain the meter-wide butt-shaped flattening of the sand bags behind your buddy's trailer. It's another episode of "Operation Green Card Get Me Out of Here Sex," and today the happy contestant was the Kurdish woman who works in his office. By dawn KBR, that American multinational corporation providing support services to our war, is doing our laundry and by day we go to meetings where the Iraqi employees cry with fear over the sentence of death imposed on them by the insurgents for the crime of working for us here at the Embassy.

This war can't be all bad. We get visited by senators, representatives, and university professors who arrive by night to write books, collect hazard pay, and earn their sand cred. We acknowledge their positions and provide thank you notes for the well-meaning people in their districts who send us collections of the worst books and magazines ever published. We get mail from the trailer behind the palace and buy paintings from the PX whose creators rarely sign their work. We buy rugs made by children imported from somewhere else and purchase Saddam Hussein watches at the Hajji Mart from the smiling man in the washed out dishdasha until the whole thing was blown up by that suicide bomber on the same day that other suicide bomber blew up the Green Zone Café and all the people in it. We always get our hair done in the palace by three liberated Iraqi women in tight jeans and a KBR employee from San Diego. We play piano and guitar for parties and eat Chinese food at the "Bad Chinese Food" restaurant until it was closed because of the chickens hanging in the toilets and that guy who got hepatitis. Nobody notices the massage place above the kitchen but everybody knows that there are no happy endings there. And yesterday afternoon the general's translator told us over lunch that the young female translator who helped us in Mosul was shot dead outside the gate on her way home from work.

This war can't be all bad. We get good food, except for that week when the delivery trucks were delayed by too much death, that week we ate MREs and multi-use potato dishes. Now we get yummy food; we get mint chip ice cream and avocado salads and made to order omelets and lattes by our Pakistani cooks, and catered parties with martinis at noon and beer and wine and music under the awning and pizza in the parking lot and steak and crab on Thursdays. We only have to hide under our tables and desks when rockets land in the courtyard.

We get to hang out of windows celebrating football and soccer and gossip about who is doing what to whom and how. We go on dates at the Blue Star Café and talk to friends a million miles away on our cell phones and have screaming debates about fixing the country. We watch the Academy Awards and the Grammys and the Daily Show and we get up early to watch the election and stay up late to watch the game and I got cake on my birthday and flowers when I sang, and I always haggled over prices with the black clad ladies minding the bathrooms and everyone always politely listens when an old Iraqi man tells us he is afraid for his life. Two weeks later someone asks me if I have seen him.

This war can't be all bad. I got here by showing up at my Army Reserve center in California in time to jump aboard the Baghdad bus with my unit and here I am, a thirty something Army broadcast journalist with an M16 on my back and a Sony Video camera in my hands doing television stories for the American Forces Network and the Pentagon Channel. I live in a trailer behind the palace, take a Blackhawk to work and get to hang out with reporters from the western and Iraqi media. Members of our group operate cameras at press conferences with Coalition Provisional Authority spokesman Dan Senor and military spokesman for the Coalition Forces General Mark Kimmet, and when we were under a credible kidnapping threat we got to walk around the office with our M16s loaded.

This war can't be all bad. We watch DVDs on huge TVs and roll over and go back to sleep during alerts. We get to eat at the outpost restaurants in the Green Zone and laugh at that guy in the gorilla suit and buy toys and jewelry from the locals and feel good about ourselves for spreading shoes and pencils and candy and democracy and by sending emails and keeping blogs and taking pictures. Sometimes, one of us, in a fervor of hopeful, democratic consumerism, jumps the fortified fence to go shopping in the Monsour district. And sometimes the shopper even comes back and sometimes that shopper even shows me pictures of their field trip and feeds me sweets from the shops. And the music at the Embassy memorial services is always beautiful and the deceased always looks so happy in their memorial pamphlet picture.

This war can't be all bad. Because of it, all of our resumés look great and will find us high-paying jobs back home and everyone here thanks me personally for giving them their freedom and everyone at home thanks me for my service and I get to mourn in silence. We get to drive cars and pick up journalists at Checkpoint Three and every

American wants a pet Iraqi and every Iraqi wants a pet American and it is not even strange anymore when you know someone who has been killed, kidnapped, or kidnapped and killed.

This war can't be all bad. The pundits should know that God is taken care of here. We have church on Sunday, synagogue on Friday, prayer groups on Tuesday, witness services on Wednesday, a Muslim prayer rug lives behind a screen in the chapel under the ninety-nine names of Allah. Buddhists meditate alone and the Wiccan stays indoors on Saturdays with her boyfriend. Someone said to someone in the bomb shelter next to the parking lot during an attack that Mormons do their best work in war zones, and I believe it. The fun of it all is that we all get to boss the Iraqis around and feel important by telling them what we are going to do for them and what is good for them and we never have to take no for an answer and we always assure our diplomats that we have Iraqi buy-in and our diplomats always assure their secretaries that they have Iraqi buy-in and their secretaries always assure the President that they have Iraqi buy-in and the President always assures the American People that we have Iraqi buy-in and the American People don't care. And the Iraqi who works in your office and thanks you personally for granting him his freedom from Saddam Hussein plants IEDs on the roadways by moonlight while the movie theater downstairs plays *Oceans Eleven* six time a week and *Breaker Morant* twice and later in the Big Office someone important takes notes for the eventual PowerPoint presentation as a man pleads for us to do something about the Christian genocide and mentions in passing that there are only eighty-five Jews left in the country.

This war can't be all bad. Big men growing weapons from their armpits give us protection when we go on missions in the Red Zone and we get to feel like celebrities in large white SUVs as these hunks and their guns open our doors and scan sectors while we gather phrases for government documents from obsequious Iraqi officials who become glorious resistance fighters after we go home. On our days off we play volleyball and horseshoes and Marco Polo and on the 4th of July we eat too much and feel good about ourselves, sing in the chorus and tape together empty water bottles for the "Empty Water Bottles Taped Together" raft race. We also hide in the basement or under our beds or not at all during rockets attacks on those days. We can't be the ones to die, not on those days.

This war can't be all bad. The President's plan for success in Iraq is working and we don't even need to know what that plan is this week and Zal once stopped me in the hallway to tell me he saw me perform last night in the Baghdad Idol semi-finals and what a talented singer he thought I was and I shook hands with Colin Powell, Condi Rice, John McCain, Senator Barry Obama, Senator John Kerry, Governor Jeb Bush, a beauty queen, Geraldo Rivera, an actor who used to play Superman on TV and some folks with earnest smiles that I had never heard of. I also exercised in the same gym and ran on the same dusty track behind the palace with Dave Petraeus and waited in line to see President Bush when he came to Baghdad and the soldiers assigned to AFN, who had to clean the blood off of Kimberly Dozier's cameras, didn't know who she was.

We all had cameras and took pictures of people around the palace and Iraqis around the rubble and ordered clothes from Gap.com and condoms from Drugstore.com and DVDs and yoga mats from Amazon.com and partied at the British Embassy, enjoyed Pizza Night at the Italian Embassy, danced with the Ukrainian ambassador and laughed at the Iraqi women who wore all the makeup ever made all at the same time all the time, and men who thought we were in Washington and wore dark grey and black wool suits and went to redundant meetings and car bombs went off in the middle of Iraqis waiting in crowds to get in to see us and the pictures of dead Americans hanging from a bridge frightened little children alone at night watching television.

This war can't be all bad. Once you've been there you'll be back again, and again, and again, and again, and again, and then Iraq will live in your dreams and be the most exciting horrible thing to ever take over your life and then you will have the right to declare with a clear conscience and a steady mind and the moral sense born out of 9/11, and YouTube video clips, and statements from the Dixie Chicks, and Sean Penn and Ted Nugent's guitar and Cindy Sheehan's campground and the Occupy Movement's rants, and Obama's mother and my mother and your mother and all mothers, whether or not, all and all, with all things considered, in the conflict between good and evil, lock, stock and barrel, under the eyes of the Global War on Terror, the mind of God, Osama Bin Laden's ghost and the sinking economy, this war can't be all bad.

Brooke King
(1985–)
U.S. ARMY

Brooke King, from Tampa, Florida, deployed to Iraq in 2006 and served as a wheeled vehicle mechanic, machine gunner, and recovery specialist. Wife of a fellow veteran and mother to twin boys who were conceived in Iraq, King began writing about her unique experiences as a way to cope with PTSD. She has a bachelor's degree from Saint Leo University and an MFA from Sierra Nevada University. Her work has been published in the *Sandhill Review*; *O-Dark-Thirty*; *Prairie Schooner*; and *War, Literature, and the Arts* and has been anthologized in *Red, White, and True: Stories from Veterans and Families*; in *WWII to Present*; *Home of the Brave: Somewhere in the Sand*; and in the Hudson Whitman Excelsior Press Anthology *Retire the Colors*. King has also been a featured veteran on the KPBS radio literary series *Incoming*, on which she shared this essay.

Redeployment Packing Checklist

Pack your Army Combat Uniforms first. Military roll. Cram the black Under Armour sports bras, the tan undershirts, and the lucky convoy socks around the bottom inside edges of your green Army issued duffle bag. Tuck the laminated photo into the bag, but don't look at it. You don't want to look at it. It's the picture that you held after your first recovery mission in the sandbox, where you bagged and tagged three soldiers who had burned alive after their Stryker rolled over a pressure plate IED.

Your brother's smirk and your father's wide grin, your look of disenchantment, the picture taken when you were on R&R, all three of you standing in front of the house, each one of you pretending that nothing had changed since you left for Iraq. It helped you fall asleep that night. You can't help yourself. You unpack the photo to look at it once more. The corner edges are falling apart. The girl in the photo used to be you, but that's not the face you see in the mirror anymore.

Pack your camo-covered Army Bible. The pages have to be rubberbanded shut, otherwise it opens to Psalm 23. Pack your tan "Rite in the Rain" combat notebook, another sort of bible: the name and rank of every soldier you ever placed into a black body bag written on its pages. Poems. Letters to your father that you never mailed.

Pack the maroon prayer rug you stole while raiding a house in Sadr City. Unpack the prayer rug. Kneel on it while you pack the empty M4 magazines, the pistol holster, ammo pouches, and desert combat boots. Pick up your aviator gloves, the feel of manning the .50-cal machine gun.

Pick up the shell casing from your first confirmed kill. One of six 7.62-caliber bullets that you fired into a fifteen-year-old boy's chest. He was shooting an AK-47 at you. You shouldn't have the shell casings. You shouldn't have the gloves. Women weren't supposed to see combat. Pack it all into the duffle.

Pack the hours spent in a cement bunker waiting for mortar rounds to stop whistling into base. Pack the hate and the anger. Pack the fear. Pack the shame and disenchantment for a job done too well. Pack the back to back months spent going out on convoy without a day off. Pack your combat lifesaver bag, your hajji killing license, and the rest of your dignity. Pack them all next to the Army Core Values and the bulls—t promise your government made to protect innocent civilians. Pack your worn copy of Hemingway's *The Sun Also Rises*. Pack the tattered American flag you picked up off the ground outside Abu Ghraib. Fold over the top flaps. Shut it up tight. Lock it. Heave it onto your back. Carry it all home.

Epilogue

The last U.S. troops withdrew from Iraq in December 2011, leaving behind some twenty thousand American security advisers. On January 1, 2015, U.S. forces turned over responsibility to Afghan security forces and most U.S. troops withdrew. The battle over women's military status continued back home, however, played out on the battlefields of congressional subcommittees, amendments to the defense budget, the pages of studies conducted by think tanks and commissions, and on the ground in Marine Corps exercises and the Army's elite Ranger School.

In 2010 both the Military Leadership Diversity Commission chartered by Congress and the Defense Advisory Committee on Women in the Services (DACOWITS) recommended elimination of combat exclusion policies and an end to gender-based restrictions on military assignments.

The Department of Defense (DoD) understood that incremental increases in numbers of women recruited into support units over the years meant that an all-volunteer military could no longer go to war without women. And women's service in Iraq and Afghanistan—especially in combat engagements in which, at least on paper, they were not supposed to participate—proved that at least some women could handle the rigors of combat.

The Department of the Navy notified Congress of their intent to phase in assignment of women to submarines beginning in 2011, and that the Marine Corps would open counterintelligence and human source intelligence operations officer occupational specialties to women. Congress did not object. The following year, DoD officials advised Congress that they intended to eliminate the co-location exclusion, permitting assignment of women at the battalion level. They added that the services supported establishment of gender-neutral occupational standards, but they needed time to study job-related physical requirements and their impact on assignment. And they asserted that existing assignment policies did not deny women less than equitable opportunities to compete and excel.

Some servicewomen disagreed. Two groups of military women filed lawsuits in federal court alleging that they had been denied ground combat assignments and therefore equal access to promotion opportunities because of their gender. The possibility that the lawsuits would be adjudicated in favor of the plaintiffs increased pressure on the DoD to rescind ground combat exclusion regulations before the courts forced them to do so.

On January 24, 2013, outgoing Secretary of Defense Leon Panetta and Chairman of the Joint Chiefs of Staff Martin Dempsey rescinded the 1994 DoD assignment policy with the caveat that the services would establish "validated, gender-neutral occupational standards" and would notify Congress of changes as required. They directed that integration of women be completed no later than January 1, 2016. They also established standards for implementation. The first priority would be to preserve unit readiness, cohesion, and morale. The second would be to ensure equal opportunity for women to succeed with viable career paths. The third was to retain public trust by promoting policies to ensure the quality of the military and its personnel. Services finding that assignment of women conflicted with these principles could request specific exceptions to the assignment of women. These changes opened nearly 37,000 more positions to women.

Only the Marine Corps requested an exception. In September 2015, the Marine Corps released an executive summary of the results of the 2014–15 Ground Combat Element Integrated Task Force study. It claimed that women participants sustained significantly higher injury rates than men, were less accurate with infantry weapons, and had more difficulty moving "wounded" troops off the battlefield. Secretary of the Navy Ray Mabus rejected the report as flawed from the outset, writing in a *New York Times* op-ed that the study failed to evaluate the performance of individual women Marines and used only irrelevant performance averages. Others questioned the screening process for the women who participated, and noted that the study did not establish occupation-relevant standards for combat positions prior to evaluating women's performance in them. Not mentioned in the executive summary was the study's finding that "gender integration, in and of itself, will not have a significant impact on unit morale." Mabus directed the Marines to integrate combat units. To date, more than two hundred enlisted women have graduated from the Infantry Training Battalion; none of the twenty-nine women who attempted the Infantry Officer Course have yet succeeded.

Lifting the restrictions remains controversial. Proponents argue that "attaching" but not "assigning" women to combat units—as was the case with Female Engagement Teams and Cultural Support Teams—allows the military to use servicewomen in combat without having to recognize their service. They point out that women attached to combat units do not get the same level of combat training as the men they serve alongside, and as a result are at increased safety risk when in the field. They suggest that gender-based assignment restrictions create a divisive culture in which women are seen as second-class servicemembers—an attitude that may increase the incidence of sexual assault and rape. They insist that no one is advocating for lowering standards for the armed forces' most physically demanding jobs, only that the standards be based on individual performance rather than gender. Finally, they argue that women veterans who served in combat are frequently perceived not to have been in combat; therefore, they have more difficulty producing documentation for combat-connected medical conditions that would entitle them to additional benefits and the level of post-service health care automatically given to men who served in combat.

Opponents continue to express concern over lowering of physical standards, the potential impact of pregnancy on deployment, and the impact of integrating women on unit cohesion and morale. They continue to insist that integration is a liberal feminist social experiment that will degrade military readiness. And they suggest that greater exposure of women to men in combat units increases the potential for sexual assault and rape.

In an effort to derail the integration effort, in 2016 Iraq War veteran Rep. Duncan Hunter (R-California) introduced legislation requiring women to register with the Selective Service. The move backfired. The American public raised no significant outcry of protest; several House Republicans supported the bill, which passed the House Armed Services Committee without Hunter's support. The measure remains undecided at this time. If passed, it is unlikely to reverse the course of women's full integration into direct combat units.

Capt. Kristen Griest and 1st Lt. Shaye Haver, both West Point alumni, became the first women to graduate from the Army's elite Ranger School on August 21, 2015. Less than a month later, Congressman Steve Russell (R-Oklahoma)—a former Ranger-qualified infantry officer—wrote to Secretary of the Army John McHugh:

"In order to ensure that the Army retrains its ability to defend the nation, we must ensure that our readiness is not sacrificed. This letter serves to request the following information and documents ... regarding the female graduates and those female candidates that entered Ranger School beginning 1 May 2015." For every phase of training including "recycle" phases (in which Ranger candidates must repeat part of the course due to a prior failure), Representative Russell requested the women's patrol grade sheets with instructors' comments; spot reports; critical test evaluation sheets; phase evaluation reports; peer evaluation reports; sick call reports and evaluations "to indicate injury without compromising confidentiality of medical records"; a complete breakdown of each female candidate's recycle history; and a complete pre-training history of each female candidate.

A spokesman for Russell told the Columbus (Georgia) *Ledger-*

Enquirer that the congressman had received "information from some people with the Ranger school who alleged [the women candidates] were not held to the same standards. We asked for the records to make sure that all of the people who passed the course deserved to pass it." In his letter, Russell did not request the records of the men.

A group of women alumni of West Point, led by Class of 1980 graduate Sue Fulton, responded with a request under the Freedom of Information Act for the Ranger School records of Representative Russell. Fulton wrote, "If Cong[ressman] Russell claims that Rangers lie, and can be influenced to ignore standards, perhaps he experienced that when he went through Ranger School. We would like to see definitive proof that he is entitled to his [Ranger] tab." She tweeted: "Let's see YOUR #RangerSchool records, Congressman."

On April 28, 2016, Ranger School graduate Capt. Kristen Griest became the first woman assigned to a job in the infantry.

Conclusion

When history is written by and for elites—nearly all men, in the case of military history—much is lost. The picture is incomplete. The rest of the story can be found in the voices of the lower ranks and in those of the women who served briefly, moved on, and reintegrated; those whose service was denigrated, overlooked, or forgotten. As women join the military elite—as they make rank, pursue careers, and continue into congressional, cabinet, and senior policymaking jobs—they will do well to acknowledge and remember the contributions of earlier generations of American women, whose struggle and sacrifice earned them the opportunities they now enjoy.

From the earliest days of nationhood, America's fighting women have been telling their stories and writing them down for posterity. It is past time for America to listen. From the earliest days of American independence, women have wanted to contribute to the common defense to the fullest extent of their abilities. They have defied social conventions and found ways to join the armed forces even when women's service was prohibited by law and custom. They have served despite criticism from society and their families, and despite disdain, harassment, and outright abuse from many of the men with whom they served. They have served voluntarily—without equal pay, equal rank, equal benefits, equal rights and protection under the law, equal opportunity to contribute and to advance in rank, and equal recognition of their service. They have been wounded and have died in defense of the Constitution.

Women who wanted to serve in the armed forces have needed not just to perform their duties but to excel in them, simply to be allowed to serve alongside men. They have taken great pride in their service and their contributions, though they often dismiss them as insignificant. They have struggled to balance military duties and family life, often advocating for family policy changes that benefited men as well as themselves. They have shared with men the trauma of combat service and the difficulty of reintegration into civilian society following a war.

Tension between women's conventional roles and society's expectations of them, on the one hand, and their abilities and desires on the other, has remained constant in some form for nearly two and a half centuries. Progress toward integration has often been met with hostility until, over time, changes become the new normal. Those changes have been incremental; changes appearing radical have often been, in reality, laws passed to codify actual conditions of women's service and to ensure that women received equal pay, benefits, and recognition for work they had already been doing.

Perhaps most important, the story of women in America's armed forces has been one of women's agency. American women have seen a need for their participation in the national defense, especially in times of crisis. They stepped forward without hesitation regardless of the risk. They have initiated necessary changes and ignored the "brass ceiling" to serve to the utmost of their ability. They have not been pawns of radical feminists determined to impose change at the expense of military readiness, or victims of men in power who used their talents and discarded them on a whim. Since they first heard the call to arms against an oppressive colonial power an ocean away, America's fighting women have been—and remain—patriots and warriors.

SOURCE ACKNOWLEDGMENTS

Excerpts have been taken from the following sources with permission. Full publication details for printed works are available in the bibliography.

Excerpts from Mary Edwards Walker's "Incidents Connected with the Army" are reprinted with permission of the Special Collections Research Center, Syracuse University Libraries.

Excerpts from Kittie (Whiting) Eastman Doxsee's "Memoirs of a Spanish-American War Nurse" are reprinted with permission of the Women in Military Service for America Memorial Foundation.

Excerpts from Beatrice MacDonald's "Experiences in a British Casualty Clearing Station and an American Evacuation Hospital during 1917 and 1918" are reprinted with permission of the Radcliffe Institute, Harvard University.

Excerpts from Joy Bright Hancock's *Lady in the Navy: A Personal Reminiscence* are reprinted with permission of the Naval Institute Press.

Lela Leibrand's "The Girl Marines" originally appeared in Linda L. Hewitt's *Women Marines in World War I* and is reprinted with permission of the U.S. Marine Corps, History and Museums Division.

Excerpts from Merle Egan Anderson's unpublished memoir, "The Army's Forgotten Women," are reprinted with permission of the Women in Military Service for America Memorial Foundation.

Excerpts from Charity Adams Earley's *One Woman's Army: A Black*

Officer Remembers the WAC are reprinted with permission of Texas A&M University Press. Copyright Texas A&M University Press.

Excerpts from Josette Dermody Wingo's *"Mother Was a Gunner's Mate": World War II in the* WAVES are reprinted with permission of the Naval Institute Press.

Excerpts from Cornelia Fort's article were originally published in *Woman's Home Companion* and are reprinted courtesy of Special Collections, Blagg-Huey Library, Texas Woman's University.

Excerpts from Mary C. Lyne's *Three Years behind the Mast: The Story of the United States Coast Guard* SPARS are reprinted with permission of the U.S. Coast Guard.

Excerpts from Stephanie Czech Rader's interview are reprinted with permission of the Women in Military Service for America Memorial Foundation.

Excerpts from Ruth M. Anderson's *Barbed Wire for Sale* are reprinted with permission of the author.

Excerpts from Margaret Chase Smith's letter to James Forrestal are reprinted with permission of the Margaret Chase Smith Library in Skowhegan, Maine.

Jean Kirnak's "Kunuri" is reprinted with permission of the Women in Military Service for America Foundation.

Excerpts from Sarah Griffin Chapman's interview are reprinted with permission of the BUMED Oral History Collection.

Excerpts from Mildred Stumpe Kennedy's interview are reprinted with permission of the Women in Military Service for America Foundation.

Excerpts from Lynda Van Devanter's *Home before Morning: The Story of an Army Nurse in Vietnam* are reprinted with permission of her daughter, Molly Stillman.

Excerpts from Angel Pilato's *Angel's Truck Stop: A Woman's Love, Laughter, and Loss during the Vietnam War* are reprinted with permission of the author.

Excerpts from LouAnne Johnson's *Making Waves: A Woman in This Man's Navy* are reprinted with permission of the author.

Lee Wilson's oral history appears with permission of the Betty H. Carter Women Veterans Historical Project, University of North Carolina at Greensboro.

Excerpts from Barbara J. Dulinsky's unpublished memoir are reprinted with permission of the Library of the Marine Corps.

Linda Maloney's interview previously appeared as "She's Got Grit: A Conversation with Pioneer Navy Navigator Linda Maloney" on Shannon Huffman Polson's blog, aborderlife.com. Excerpts are reprinted with permission of the author and the interviewer.

Excerpts from Linda Bray's oral history appear with permission of the Betty H. Carter Women Veterans Historical Project, University of North Carolina at Greensboro.

Mary V. "Ginger" Jacocks's interview originally appeared in *Desert Voices: An Oral History Anthology of Marines in the Gulf War, 1990–1991*. Excerpts are reprinted with permission of the author.

Excerpts from Miyoko Hikiji's *All I Could Be: My Story as a Woman Warrior in Iraq* are reprinted with permission of the History Publishing Company.

Lauren K. Halloran's "The Inheritance of War" originally appeared as "Folio: Leaving Home, Coming Home, and Finding Home in Between" in *Drunken Boat* and is reprinted by permission of the author.

Tiffany Wilson's letters originally appeared as "Hello from Afghanistan" on the blog of the Women Marines Association, women-marines.wordpress.com. Excerpts are reprinted with permission of the Women Marines Association.

Lori Imsdahl's contribution originally appeared as "Freak Accidents" in *O-Dark-Thirty* and is reprinted by permission of the author.

Sylvia Bowersox's "This War Can't Be All Bad" originally appeared in *O-Dark-Thirty* and is reprinted by permission of the author.

Brooke King's "Redeployment Packing Checklist" was originally broadcast by KBPS and So Say We All in San Diego on May 5, 2015, and is reprinted by permission of the author.

BIBLIOGRAPHY

Anderson, Merle Egan. "Women in Military Service for America." Unpublished memoir. Women in Military Service for America Foundation, Arlington VA.

Anderson, Ruth M., and J. M. Anderson. *Barbed Wire for Sale*. N.p.: Ruth M. Anderson, 1999.

Barkalow, Carol, with Andrea Raab. *In the Men's House*. New York: Poseidon Press, 1990.

Bowersox, Sylvia. "This War Can't Be All Bad." *O-Dark-Thirty* 2, no. 4 (Summer 2014): 11–16.

Boyd, Belle. *Belle Boyd: In Camp and Prison*. 1865. Reprinted with a new foreword by Drew Gilpin Faust and a new introduction by Sharon Kennedy-Nolle. Baton Rouge: Louisiana State University Press, 1998.

Bray, Linda L. "Oral History Interview with Linda L. Bray." 2008. Linda L. Bray Papers (WV0432.5.001). Betty H. Carter Women Veterans Historical Project, Martha Blakeney Hodges Special Collections and University Archives, University of North Carolina, Greensboro.

Chapman, Sarah Griffin. "U.S. Navy Medical Department Oral History Program Oral History with LT (Ret.) Sara Griffin Chapman, NC, USN." Interview by Jan K. Herman. March 18, 2002. Navy Medicine. Accessed June 7, 2016. http://www.med.navy.mil/bumed/nmhistory/Oral%20histories2/chapman,%20sara.pdf.

Coleman, Eunice. Letter, November 15, 1950. U.S. Medical Department AMEDD Records 1947–1961, RG No. 112, 390, Row 17, Compartment 34, Shelf 5–, Boxes 22–24. National Archives and Records Administration, College Park MD.

———. Letter, January 1, 1951. U.S. Medical Department AMEDD Records 1947–1961, RG No. 112, 390, Row 17, Compartment 34, Shelf 5–, Boxes 22–24. National Archives and Records Administration, College Park MD.

Doxsee, Kittie (Whiting) Eastman. "Memoirs of a Spanish-American War Nurse." Women in Military Service for America Memorial Foundation, Arlington VA.

Dulinsky, Barbara Jean. Unpublished memoir. Archives and Special Collections, Library of the Marine Corps, Quantico VA.

Earley, Charity Adams. *One Woman's Army: A Black Officer Remembers the WAC*.

Texas A&M University Military History Series 12. College Station: Texas
A&M University, 1989.

Edmonds, Sarah Emma. *Memoirs of a Soldier, Nurse and Spy: A Woman's Adventures in the Union Army*. DeKalb: Northern Illinois University Press, 1999.

Fort, Cornelia. "At the Twilight's Last Gleaming." *Woman's Home Companion*, June 1943. http://www.pbs.org/wgbh/amex/flygirls/filmmore/reference/primary/lettersarticles01.html.

Gannett, Deborah Sampson. "An Address, Delivered with Applause, at the Federal-Street Theatre, Boston, Four Successive Nights of the Different Plays, Beginning March 22, 1802; And After, at Other Principal Towns, a Number of Nights Successively at Each Place." Speech, March 22, 1802. In *Extra Number*, vol. 124 of *Magazine of History with Notes and Queries*. Sharon MA: Sharon Historical Society, 1905.

Graydon, Mary Ellen (Liz). *Love & War (One WAC Remembers World War II)*. N.p.: printed by author, 1998.

Halloran, Lauren Kay. "Inheritance of War." *Drunken Boat* 24 (December 15, 2016). http://www.drunkenboat.com/db24/home/lauren-kay-halloran.

Hancock, Cornelia. *Letters of a Civil War Nurse: Cornelia Hancock, 1863–1865*. Edited by Henrietta Stratton Jaquette. Lincoln: University of Nebraska Press, 1998.

Hancock, Joy Bright. *Lady in the Navy: A Personal Reminiscence*. Annapolis MD: Naval Institute Press, 2013.

Hasson, Esther Voorhees. "The Navy Nurse Corps." *American Journal of Nursing* 9, no. 4 (March 1909): 267–68.

Herron, Berneice A. *Dearest Folks: Sister Leatherneck's Letter Excerpts and World War II Experiences*. N.p.: iUniverse, 2006.

Hikiji, Miyoko. *All I Could Be: The Story of a Woman Warrior in Iraq*. Palisades NY: Chronology Books, 2013.

Holm, Jeanne M. "Interview with Jeanne M. Holm (1/23/2003)." Experiencing War: Stories from the Veterans History Project. Accessed August 7, 2015. https://memory.loc.gov/diglib/vhp-stories/loc.natlib.afc2001001.04293/transcript?id=mv0001.

Imsdahl, Lori. "Freak Accidents." *O-Dark-Thirty* 3, no. 2 (Winter 2015): 11–26.

Johnson, LouAnne. *Making Waves: A Woman in This Man's Navy*. New York: St. Martin's Press, 1986.

Kennedy, Mildred Stumpe. "Oral History Interview with Mildred Stumpe Kennedy." 2001. Women in Military Service for America Memorial Foundation, Arlington VA.

Kirnak, Jean. "Kunuri." #4460 Folder 1. Ina Bowen Kirnak Collection. Women in Military Service for America Memorial Foundation, Arlington VA.

Leibrand, Lela. "The Girl Marines." In *Women Marines in World War I*, by Linda L. Hewitt, 75–77. Washington DC: History and Museums Division, Headquarters, U.S. Marine Corps, 1974.

Lyne, Mary C., and Kay Arthur. *Three Years behind the Mast: The Story of the United States Coast Guard* SPARS. N.p., 1946. http://www.uscg.mil/history /WomenIndex.asp.

MacDonald, Beatrice. "Experiences in a British Casualty Clearing Station and an American Evacuation Hospital during 1917 and 1918." *Quarterly Magazine*, 15–22. In Beatrice MacDonald Scrapbook, Ann Fraser Brewer Papers, Radcliffe Institute for Advanced Study, Harvard University. Accessed June 7, 2016. http://nrs.harvard.edu/urn-3:rad.schl:10354150.

"Major Mary V. 'Ginger' Jacocks." In *Desert Voices: An Oral History Anthology of Marines in the Gulf War, 1990–1991*, edited by Paul W. Westermeyer and Alexander N. Hinman, 83–92. Quantico VA: United States Marine Corps History Division, 2016.

Maloney, Linda. "She's Got Grit: A Conversation with Pioneer Navy Navigator Linda Maloney." Interview by Shannon Huffman Polson. The Grit Project. Last modified November 10, 2015. Accessed June 7, 2016. http://aborderlife .com/grit-project-blog/grit-flygirl-linda.

McGee, Anita Newcomb. "Report to the Daughters of the American Revolution." Address, June 28, 1898. U.S. Army Medical Department, Office of Medical History. Quoted in "Dr. Anita Newcomb McGee and What She Has Done for the Nursing Profession," by Dita H. Kinney, originally published in *Trained Nurse and Hospital Review*, March 1901. Accessed June 7, 2016. http://history.amedd.army.mil/ancwebsite/McGeewhmspecial/McGee _Extract.html.

———. "Report to the Daughters of the American Revolution." Address, September 1898. U.S. Army Medical Department, Office of Medical History. Quoted in "Dr. Anita Newcomb McGee and What She Has Done for the Nursing Profession" by Dita H. Kinney, originally published in *Trained Nurse and Hospital Review*, March 1901. Accessed June 7, 2016. http://history.amedd.army .mil/ancwebsite/McGeewhmspecial/McGee_Extract.html.

New York Times. "Kept House Nineteen Years on Robbin's Reef." March 5, 1905. Article on Kate Walker, USLHS.

"Oral History Interview with Lee Wilson." Lee Wilson Papers (WV0449). Betty H. Carter Women Veterans Historical Project, Martha Blakeney Hodges Special Collections and University Archives. University of North Carolina, Greensboro.

Osborn, Sarah. Pension Deposition of Sarah Osborn. Last modified November 20, 1837. NARA M804, Revolutionary War Pension and Bounty-Land Warrant Application Files; Case Files of Pension and Bounty-Land Warrant Applications Based on Revolutionary War Service, compiled ca. 1800–ca. 1912, documenting the period ca. 1775–ca. 1900; Record Group 15; Roll 1849; New York; Pension Number W. 4558. Digital file. National Archives and Records Administration, Washington DC.

Pilato, Angel. *Angel's Truck Stop: A Woman's Love, Laughter, and Loss during the Vietnam War*. N.p.: CreateSpace, 2010.

Rader, Stephanie Czech. Interview by Jane Maliszewski. September 2006, Arlington VA. Oral History #074520, two tapes, collection of the Women in Military Service for America Memorial Foundation.

Reynolds, Mary. Mary Reynolds to John J. Pettus, November 26, 1861. In *Women Who Kept the Lights: An Illustrated History of Female Lighthouse Keepers*, by Mary Louise Clifford and J. Candace Clifford, 34–35. Williamsburg VA: Cypress Communications, 1993.

Schorer, Avis D. *A Half Acre of Hell: A Combat Nurse in WWII*. Lakeville MN: Galde Press, 2000.

Smith, Margaret Chase. Margaret Chase Smith to James V. Forrestal, April 22, 1948. In *Declaration of Conscience*, by Margaret Chase Smith, 96–97. Edited by William C. Lewis Jr. Garden City NY: Doubleday, 1972.

———. "Women in the Armed Forces—Regular versus Reserve: Extension of Remarks of Hon. Margaret Chase Smith of Maine in the House of Representatives, Tuesday, April 6, 1948," 80th Cong., 2d Sess.

St. Louis Daily Times. "Cathy Williams' Story." January 2, 1876.

Taylor, Susie King. *A Black Woman's Civil War Memoirs: Reminiscences of My Life in Camp with the 33rd U.S. Colored Troops, Late 1st South Carolina Volunteers*. Edited by Patricia W. Romero. New York: Markus Seiner, 1988.

Telford, Emma P. "Harriet: The Modern Moses of Heroism and Visions." 1905. The Telford Manuscript. Cayuga Museum of History and Art, Auburn NY.

Van Devanter, Lynda. *Home before Morning: The Story of an Army Nurse in Vietnam*. 1983. Reprinted, Amherst: University of Massachusetts Press, 2001.

Van Lew, Elizabeth L. *A Yankee Spy in Richmond: The Civil War Diary of "Crazy Bet" Van Lew*. Edited by David D. Ryan. Mechanicsburg PA: Stackpole Books, 1996.

Velazquez, Loreta Janeta. *The Woman in Battle: A Narrative of the Exploits, Adventures, and Travels of Madame Loreta Janeta Velazquez, Otherwise Known as Lieutenant Harry T. Buford, Confederate States Army*. Edited by C. J. Worthington. Wisconsin Studies in Autobiography. Madison: University of Wisconsin Press, 2003. First published 1876 by Dustin, Gilman, with introduction by Jesse Alemán.

Walker, Mary Edwards. "Incidents Connected with the Army." Mary Edwards Walker Papers. Special Collections Research Center, Syracuse University Libraries, Syracuse NY.

Williams, Denny. *To the Angels*. N.p.: Denson Press, 1985.

Wilson, Tiffany. "Hello from Afghanistan." *Women Marines Association* (blog). Entry posted November 26, 2011. https://womenmarines.wordpress.com/2011/11/26/hello-from-afghanistan.

———. "Life as a FET 2." *Women Marines Association* (blog). Entry posted October 28, 2011. https://womenmarines.wordpress.com/?s=life+as+a+FET&submit=Search.

———. "Happy Thanksgiving." *Women Marines Association* (blog). Entry posted November 26, 2011. https://womenmarines.wordpress.com/?s=happy +thanksgiving&submit=Search.

Wingo, Josette Dermoody. *"Mother Was a Gunner's Mate": World War II in the WAVES*. Annapolis MD: Naval Institute Press, 1994.

FURTHER READING

To write this book, we consulted hundreds of print and online sources. Three of the most important were Brig. Gen. Jeanne Holm's history *Women in the Military: An Unfinished Revolution* (Novato: Presidio, 1987); Evelyn Monahan and Rosemary Neidel-Greenlee's history *A Few Good Women: America's Military Women from World War I to the Wars in Iraq and Afghanistan* (New York: Anchor, 2010); and Judith Bellafaire's *Women in the United States Military: An Annotated Bibliography* (Abingdon UK: Routledge, 2011). Below is a short list of other histories, biographies, and memoirs we found especially useful during our research.

Binkei, Mary Jo. *Her Story: An Oral History Handbook for Collecting Military Women's Stories*. Washington DC: Military Women's Press, 2002.

Blair, Jane. *Hesitation Kills: A Female Marine Officer's Combat Experience in Iraq*. Lanham MD: Rowman & Littlefield, 2011.

Blanton, DeAnne, and Lauren Cook Wise. *They Fought Like Demons: Women Soldiers in the American Civil War*. Baton Rouge: Louisiana State University Press, 2002.

DePauw, Linda Grant. *Battle Cries and Lullabies: Women in War from PreHistory to the Present*. Norman: University of Oklahoma, 1998.

———. "Women in Combat: The Revolutionary War Experience." *Armed Forces and Society* 7 (1981): 209–26. http://afs.sagepub.com.

Ebbert, Jean, and Marie-Beth Hall. *The First, the Few, the Forgotten: Navy and Marine Corps Women in World War I*. Annapolis MD: Naval Institute, 2002.

Frank, Lisa Tendrich, ed. *An Encyclopedia of American Women at War from the Home Front to the Battlefields*. 2 vols. Santa Barbara: ABC-CLIO, 2013.

Goodman, Robin Truth. *Gender for the Warfare State: Literature of Women in Combat*. New York: Routledge, 2016.

Graf, Mercedes H. "Women Nurses in the Spanish-American War." *Minerva: Quarterly Report on Women in the Military* 19, no. 1 (Spring 2001): 3–38.

Harris, Sharon M. *Dr. Mary Walker: An American Radical, 1832–1919.* New Brunswick NJ: Rutgers University Press, 2009.

Kraft, Heidi Squier. *Rule Number Two: Lessons I Learned in a Combat Hospital.* New York: Little, Brown, 2007.

Lemmon, Gayle Tzemach. *Ashley's War: The Untold Story of a Team of Women Soldiers on the Special Ops Battlefield.* New York: Harper Collins, 2015.

Lowery, Donna. *Women Vietnam Veterans: Our Untold Stories.* N.p.: AuthorHouse, 2015.

Maloney, Linda, ed. *Military Fly Moms: Sharing Memories, Building Legacies, Inspiring Hope.* Dowell MD: Tannenbaum, 2012.

Mangerich, Agnes Jensen. *Albanian Escape: The True Story of U.S. Army Nurses behind Enemy Lines.* Lexington: University Press of Kentucky, 1999.

McIntosh, Elizabeth P. *Sisterhood of Spies: Women of the OSS.* Annapolis MD: Naval Institute, 1998.

Miles, Rosalind, and Robin Cross. *Hell Hath No Fury: True Stories of Women at War from Antiquity to Iraq.* New York: Three Rivers, 2008.

North, Louise V., Janet M. Wedge, and Landa M. Freeman. *In the Words of Women: The Revolutionary War and the Birth of the Nation, 1765–1799.* Plymouth, UK: Lexington Books, 2011.

Ritchie, Elspeth Cameron, and Anne L. Naclerio. *Women at War.* New York: Oxford University Press, 2015.

Sarnecky, Mary T. *A History of the U.S. Army Nurse Corps.* Philadelphia: University of Pennsylvania Press, 1999.

Sherman, Janann. *No Place for a Woman: A Life of Senator Margaret Chase Smith.* New Brunswick NJ: Rutgers University Press, 2000.

Smith, Winnie. *American Daughter Gone to War: On the Front Lines with an Army Nurse in Vietnam.* New York: Simon & Schuster, 1992.

Stremlow, Mary V. *A History of the Women Marines, 1946–1977.* Washington DC: History and Museums Division, Headquarters, U.S. Marine Corps, 1986. http://www.marines.mil/Portals/59/Publications/A%20history%20of%20the%20women%20marines%201946–1977%20pcn%2019000309400_1.pdf.

Williams, Kayla. *Love My Rifle More Than You: Young and Female in the U.S. Army.* New York: W. W. Norton, 2006.

———. *Plenty of Time When We Get Home: Love and Recovery in the Aftermath of War.* New York: W. W. Norton, 2014.

Witt, Linda, Judith Bellafaire, Britta Granrud, and Mary Jo Binker. *"A Defense Weapon Known to Be of Value": Servicewomen of the Korean War Era.* Hanover NH: University Press of New England, 2005.

Young, Alfred F. *Masquerade: The Life and Times of Deborah Sampson, Continental Soldier.* New York: Random House, 2004.